The United States Cavalry, 1792–1863

CAVALRY COLUMN ON THE MARCH.

The United States Cavalry, 1792-1863

Campaigns During the Indian Wars, the Mexican War and Civil War

ILLUSTRATED

History of the United States Cavalry

Albert G. Brackett

Captain May's Charge at Resaca de la Palma

J. Frost

LEONAUR

The United States Cavalry, 1792-1863
Campaigns During the Indian Wars, the Mexican War and Civil War
History of the United States Cavalry
by Albert G. Brackett
Captain May's Charge at Resaca de la Palma
by J. Frost

ILLUSTRATED

FIRST EDITION IN THIS FORM

First published in the titles
History of the United States Cavalry
and
The Mexican War and its Warriors (Extract)

Leonaur is an imprint of Oakpast Ltd
Copyright in this form © 2025 Oakpast Ltd

ISBN: 978-1-917666-20-6 (hardcover)
ISBN: 978-1-917666-21-3 (softcover)

http://www.leonaur.com

Contents

THIS BOOK

IS

RESPECTFULLY DEDICATED

TO

SURGEON JOSEPH B. BROWN,

UNITED STATES ARMY,

AND TO

MAJOR CHAUNCEY P. E. JOHNSON,

PAYMASTER UNITED STATES ARMY.

BY

THE AUTHOR.

United States Army Cavalry sergeant, 1866

Preface

The Cavalry Service in the United States of America has never been properly appreciated, and that is my reason for writing this book. I have served several years in the cavalry, and know that our mounted men have not half as many friends as they ought to have, nor as many as they would have if they exerted themselves a little more in recounting their many good deeds. We have had among us some noble men and excellent soldiers; and while our countrymen point with pride to the names of Covington, Johnson, Coffee, Harney, Sumner, Kearney, McClellan, Thomas, Sedgwick, and Hunter, we can feel that it was in our corps they received much of their best training.

Our mounted force during the rebellion is far larger than any which has ever belonged to any nation on earth; and as time moves on, and our men become more experienced, their deeds will become brighter and their fame more extended. Our cavalry soldiers are becoming better every year, and it is safe to say that the finishing blows to the rebellion will be dealt by them.

For a long time, I have thought that a *History of the United States Cavalry Service* ought to be written. I thought that such a work would not only be interesting to the public, but would be doing justice to the officers and soldiers who belonged to it. Thinking thus, and seeing that no person had undertaken the task, I took it upon myself to do it. So far as I know, no history of our cavalry service has ever been written up to this time. I know my work has many imperfections, as, while writing it, I have been in active campaign against the rebels at Atlanta and elsewhere, and have not been able to procure the necessary books and papers to make as thorough and complete a work of it as I could have desired; still, it contains many truths which have been hidden from the public, and does justice to our horsemen, who, in too many cases, have been entirely overlooked.

My descriptions of fights and skirmishes, in many instances, may appear too brief and unsatisfactory; to which I can only reply that very many actions, which appear of great importance to the actors, are not of much general interest. On the other hand, where our cavalrymen have done the most brilliant things, I regret to say that I have been unable, in some cases, to obtain truthful and detailed accounts with which to do them full justice.

CHAPTER 1

Formation

I shall attempt to write the *History of the United States Cavalry Service* under the present government, from the inauguration of President Washington in 1789 to this time, to show its rise from small and almost insignificant beginnings, until it has become one of the most powerful military arms the world has ever seen.

It is not my intention to go back to revolutionary times to recount the exploits of Lee's and Washington's legions in the South, or of Sheldon's light horse in the East during that period, but to give a clear view, of what has occurred since our regular army has been established. It would be impossible for me, even if I wished to do so, to give a history of the doings of the celebrated partisan officers before alluded to; and, in truth, our mounted service in the Revolutionary War accomplished no very not able work, and seems to have been considered as a secondary matter.

This fact holds good with regard to the second war with England; and, indeed, the cavalry service in this country was looked upon as comparatively worthless until a recent period.

The first mounted force which was organised under the present government was authorised by an Act of Congress of March 5th, 1792, which gave the President the power to raise at his discretion a "squadron" of cavalry to serve for three years, to be under a major commandant of cavalry. The squadron was made up of four troops, consisting each of one captain, one lieutenant, one cornet, six sergeants, six corporals, one farrier, one saddler, one trumpeter, and sixty-five dragoons. The pay allowed to the cavalry soldiers, or light dragoons, for these terms were at that time used synonymously, was not such as would at this day rouse the cupidity of our people. The major *commandant* received fifty-five dollars per month, captains forty dollars, lieutenants twenty-six dollars, cornets twenty dollars, sergeants six dollars, corporals five dollars, trumpeters four dollars, and privates *three dollars per month.*

This corps, under Major William Winston, of Virginia, was organised at Pittsburg, Pennsylvania, in the summer of 1793, and in the autumn of that year moved to Fort Recovery, in Ohio. There were some officers of much promise in this small force, among whom, conspicuous for their subsequent usefulness, were Leonard Covington, of Maryland, and Solomon Van Rensselaer, of New York, both of whom were subalterns, and both of whom rendered signal service.

This handful of men afterward bore an honourable part in the succeeding campaigns. The defeat of General Harmar in 1790, and of General St. Clair in 1791, had emboldened the Indians of the Northwest, and they considered themselves able to overthrow the whites.

It was reserved for Wayne to undeceive them, and in the victorious defence of Fort Recovery, on the 30th of June, 1794, and at the Battle of Maumee Rapids, August 20th, 1794, they were signally defeated.

In both of these actions the cavalry bore a conspicuous part; and Cornet Daniel Torrey was the first United States cavalry officer who gave his life for his country. He was killed at the defence of Fort Recovery. Captain Robert MisCampbell was killed at Maumee Rapids, and Captain Solomon Van Rensselaer was severely wounded at the same time. I give the following accounts of these battles:

On the 29th of June, 1794, Major McMahon marched with eighty riflemen, under the command of Captain Hartshorn, and fifty dragoons, under the command of Captain Taylor, for Fort Recovery, as an escort to three hundred pack-horses, loaded with flour for the garrison. On the morning following, after they had deposited their loading, and were preparing to set out on their return, they were attacked by a force of twelve hundred Indians.

Captain Hartshorn, who had advanced with the riflemen about a quarter of a mile into the woods, immediately took post on a very strong, commanding piece of ground near the garrison, and with great bravery maintained the unequal fight till Major McMahon, who had put himself at the head of the cavalry, was killed, as was Cornet Daniel Torrey and Captain Taylor, and many of the men wounded.

The enemy now attacked Captain Hartshorn, and, at the moment when they were pushing to cut off his communication with the garrison, Lieutenant Drake and Ensign Dodd sallied out at the head of twenty soldiers, who turned out voluntarily on the occasion, and joined him after beating the enemy at the point of the bayonet.

At this instant Captain Hartshorn received a shot which broke his thigh. Lieutenant Craig was killed, and Lieutenant Marks taken prisoner. Lieutenant Drake now ordered a retreat, and, on endeavouring to hold the enemy in check so as to give the men time to save Captain Hartshorn, he received a shot in the groin. The enemy now pressed so hard as to compel the men to leave their captain.

Great numbers of the Indians must have been killed, as they came forward in column up to the very muzzles of the guns. Lieutenant Mitchel, who was with Captain Hartshorn, but whom he had detached with a few active men to the flank of the enemy, was now missing; and while their companions in the fort were deploring their fate, and had given them up as lost, they saw him and Lieutenant Marks rushing through the thickest of the enemy at opposite directions, and although numbers of guns were fired at them, they got in safely. Lieutenant Mitchel lost every man of his party except three, and Lieutenant Marks got off by knocking down the Indian who took him.

The Indians were observed to carry off numbers of killed and wounded on pack-horses. The loss of the Americans was twenty-three killed and about forty wounded. The party commanded by Captain Hartshorn brought in ten scalps of the enemy.

I copy the following extract from General Wayne's official report of the Battle of Maumee Rapids to the Secretary of War, as I can show the doings of the cavalry in this way better than by attempting to write an account of the fight myself:

It is with infinite pleasure that I announce to you the brilliant success of the Federal Army under my command in a general action with the combined force of the hostile Indians and a considerable number of the volunteers and militia of Detroit, on the 20th of August, 1794, on the banks of the Miamis, in the vicinity of the British post and garrison at the foot of the Rapids.

The army advanced to Roche de Bout on the 15th, and on the 19th, we were employed in making a temporary post for the reception of our stores and baggage, and in reconnoitring the position of the enemy, who were encamped behind a thick, bushy wood and the British fort.

At eight o'clock on the morning of the 20th the army again advanced in columns, agreeably to the standing order of the march; the legion on the right, its right flank covered by the

Miamis; one brigade of mounted volunteers on the left, under Brigadier-General Todd; and the other in the rear, under Brigadier-General Barbee. A select battalion of mounted volunteers moved in front of the legion, commanded by Major Price, who was directed to keep sufficiently advanced, and to give timely notice for the troops to form in case of action, it being yet undetermined whether the Indians would decide for peace or war.

After advancing about five miles. Major Price's corps received so severe a fire from the enemy, who were secreted in the woods and high grass, as to compel them to retreat.

The legion was immediately formed in two lines, principally in a close, thick wood, which extended for miles on our left, and for a very considerable distance in front, the ground being covered with old fallen timber, probably occasioned by a tornado, which rendered it impracticable for the cavalry to act with effect, and afforded the enemy the most favourable covert for their mode of warfare.

The Indians were formed in three lines, within supporting distance of each other, and extending for near two miles at right angles with the river. I soon discovered, from the weight of the fire and extent of their lines, that the enemy were in full force in front, in possession of their favourite ground, and endeavouring to turn our left flank. I therefore gave orders for the second line to advance to support the first, and directed Major-General Scott to gain and turn the right flank of the Indians, with the whole of the mounted volunteers, by a circuitous route.

At the same time, I ordered the front line to advance and charge with trailed arms, and rouse the Indians from their covert at the point of the bayonet, and when up to deliver a close and well-directed fire on their backs, followed by a brisk charge, so as not to give them time to load again or to form their lines. I also ordered Captain R. M. Campbell, who commanded the legionary cavalry, to turn the left flank of the enemy next the river, which afforded a favourable field for that corps to act in.

All these orders were obeyed with spirit and promptitude; but such was the impetuosity of the charge by the first line of infantry, that the Indians and Canadian militia and volunteers were driven from all their coverts in so short a time that, although every possible exertion was used by the officers of the second

14

BATTLE OF FALLEN TIMBERS

line of the legion, and by Generals Scott, Wood, and Barbee, of the mounted volunteers, to gain their proper positions, but part of each could get up in season to participate in the action, the enemy being driven in the course of one hour more than two miles through the thick woods already mentioned by less than one half their number.

From every account, the enemy amounted to two thousand combatants. The troops actually engaged against them were short of nine hundred. This horde of Indians, with their allies, abandoned themselves to flight, and dispersed with terror and dismay, leaving our victorious army in full and quiet possession of the field of battle, which terminated under the influence of the guns of the British garrison.

The bravery and conduct of every officer belonging to the army, from the generals down to the ensigns, merit my approbation.

Lieutenant Covington, upon whom the command of the cavalry devolved (Captain Campbell being killed), cut down two Indians with his own hand, and Lieutenant Webb one in turning the enemy's left flank.

The wounds received by Captains Slough, Prior, Van Rensselaer, and Rawlins, and Lieutenants McKenny and Smith, bear honourable testimony of their bravery and conduct. In fact, every officer and soldier who had an opportunity to come into action displayed that true bravery which always ensures success. And here permit me to declare that I never discovered more true spirit and anxiety for action than appeared to pervade the whole of the mounted volunteers; and I am well persuaded that, had the enemy maintained their favourite ground for one half hour longer, they would have felt most severely the prowess of that corps.

But, while I pay this just tribute to the living, I must not neglect the gallant dead, among whom we have to lament the early death of those worthy and brave officers, Captain Campbell and Lieutenant Towles, who fell in the first charge.

Wayne's victory settled the Indians of the Northwest for a number of years; and the soldiers who had borne so honourable a share in the campaign were sent eastward, where the volunteers disbanded.

The term of service of the cavalry (three years) expired in 1795 and 1796, and on the 31st of October of the latter year, all of the regular light dragoons, with the exception of two small companies, were also disbanded.

On the 16th of July, 1798, the mounted force of the Federal Army was augmented by the addition of six troops of light dragoons, which, together with the two then in service, formed a regiment, which was placed under command of "Lieutenant-Colonel *Commandant*" John Watts, of Virginia, who received his appointment on the 8th of January, 1799. The men of this regiment were "to be enlisted for and during the continuance of the existing differences between the United States and the French Republic, unless sooner discharged."

By an Act of Congress of March 2nd, 1799, three regiments of cavalry were authorised to be raised for the United States. Each regiment was to have consisted of five squadrons of two companies each, but they were never filled up. On the 14th of May, 1800, Congress ordered the officers and men heretofore raised to be discharged, with the exception of the officers and men of two troops of dragoons; and on the 16th of March, 1802, under President Jefferson, these two companies were legislated out of service, and our army was left without any mounted men.

In the cavalry force organised in 1799 appear the names of several officers who subsequently gained distinction. Prominent among them is the name of Alexander Macomb, junior, who was born in Detroit on the 3rd of April, 1782. He entered the service as cornet of cavalry, January 10th, 1799, and became a Second Lieutenant in 1801. He was retained in service when the cavalry was disbanded, and, after a most honourable life, died while Major-General and General-in-Chief of the army, at Washington, June 25th, 1841.

John De Barth Walbach, born in Germany, and who had seen service as an officer in the Royal Alsace Regiment of France, and in the Rohan Hussars of Germany, left Europe during the French Revolution, and entered our service as first lieutenant and adjutant of cavalry, January 8th, 1799. He continued in it until the time of his death, in June, 1857, at which time he was a brevet Brigadier-General. George W. P. Custis, the *protégé* of Washington, also entered the service as cornet of cavalry in 1799, though he remained in it but a short time.

On the 12th of April, 1808, Congress ordered a regiment of light dragoons, of eight troops, to be raised, to serve as light infantry until mounted.

Wade Hampton, of South Carolina, was appointed colonel; Leonard Covington, of Maryland, was appointed lieutenant-colonel; and Electus Backus, of New York, was appointed major. The young Cornet Haxtun, of this regiment, was killed in a duel at Carlisle, Pennsylvania, December 29th, 1809.

This was the mounted force of the republic at the time of the commencement of the War of 1812. Hampton was promoted brigadier-general February 15th, 1809, when Covington became colonel; Backus, lieutenant-colonel; and Jacint Laval, of South Carolina, major. After the death of Backus and the promotion of Covington to the grade of brigadier-general, Laval became colonel; Major Nelson Luckett, of Virginia, lieutenant-colonel; and Captain Arthur P. Hayne, of South Carolina, major.

In Harrison's campaign against the Indians in 1811, a volunteer cavalry battalion was in service, and acquitted itself most admirably. This was Major Jo Daviess's battalion of Kentucky and Indiana cavalry. At the Battle of Tippecanoe, it rendered very important service; and Major Daviess was mortally wounded while leading it against the Indians, under Tecumseh, on the 7th of November, 1811. Jo Daviess, at the time of his death, was one of the most eminent men in the Western States, and his untimely fall cut short a career which would, no doubt, have been of the greatest benefit to his country. His bearing during the battle was gallant in the extreme, and he was ably seconded by the brave men of Kentucky and Indiana, who on that day won a renown which has since been cherished as one of the brightest pages of American history.

On the 11th of January, 1812, Congress ordered another regiment of twelve companies of light dragoons to be added to the army. James Burn, of South Carolina, was appointed colonel, and James V. Ball, of Virginia, major. On the 17th and 18th of December, 1812, Major Ball greatly distinguished himself, and was breveted Lieutenant-Colonel. This was at what is known as the actions on the Mississinewa, near the head of the Wabash River, in Indiana, fought by the United States Dragoons and a body of volunteer troops under Lieutenant-Colonel John B. Campbell against the Delaware and Miami Indians. First Lieutenant James Hedges, of the 2nd Dragoons, was wounded at this battle. On account of the lateness of the season, many of the men in this campaign were badly frostbitten, and the horses of the dragoons were completely broken down.

On the 12th of June, 1812, war was declared against Great Britain, and on the 29th of May, 1813, Sackett's Harbor was attacked by a British force under the personal command of Sir George Provost, governor of Canada. The garrison at that place consisted of about two hundred and fifty dismounted dragoons of the 1st Regiment, sixty artillery men, and about eighty recruits, the whole being under command of Lieutenant-Colonel Electus Backus, of the 1st Dragoons. As soon as Backus learned of the approach of the British, who were coming up on the water, he sent word to General Brown, who was some twelve miles distant, to come to his assistance at once. Brown immediately called together all of the available militia force, and upon reaching the town the fight commenced.

The militia soon gave way, and Backus was left to do the best he could. The fight was obstinate, and he soon fell mortally wounded. In the meantime, General Brown had used all his efforts, eventually with success, to reform a portion of the militia, and force the British back to their boats. They retreated, but had done considerable damage to our people, as during the fight the shipyard had been set on fire, and property worth more than half a million of dollars had been destroyed.

Backus's death was a severe blow, and our loss, considering the forces engaged, considerable.

The Battle of Stony Creek, Upper Canada, was fought on the 6th of June following. This was a most singular affair, and reflected no great credit either upon our troops or the enemy. It appears that Generals Chandler and Winder, of the United States Army, with about 1,300 men, were detached for the purpose of making an attack upon a British force under General Vincent. The latter, upon learning what was going forward, himself became the attacking party, and, with about 800 men, in the night made his way into Chandler's camp, capturing both Generals Chandler and Winder, five officers, and ninety-three men, besides four pieces of artillery.

In addition to this, we had seventeen killed and thirty-eight wounded. But our people, getting some insight into the state of affairs, drove the British off, they losing about two hundred and fifty, of which number one hundred were taken prisoners. Colonel Burn, with the whole of the 2nd Regiment of Dragoons, was nearby, but took no part in the action, though the command devolved upon him after the capture of the generals. He gave as his excuse for not pursuing the enemy his ignorance of knowledge of infantry tactics. On this account the British got off, though it is not at all certain what would have been the result had he followed even with a superior force. His excuse would not at this day be considered as exactly valid.

In the West the volunteer cavalry did well, particularly at the Battle of the Thames.

General Harrison had prepared himself for battle during the night, and early on the morning of October 5th, 1813, seeing the British infantry in front and on the right in open order, he gave the order to Colonel Richard M. Johnson to charge with his regiment of Kentucky cavalry. This was promptly executed; and the only movement worthy the name of a cavalry charge which occurred during the second war with Great Britain was gallantly carried out.

By it, in fact, Proctor's infantry force was entirely broken up and captured. Johnson then turned to the left, and attempted to charge a large Indian force which was stationed in the edge of a growth of timber, but he found the ground was swampy, and his horses commenced sinking. Seeing this, he ordered his men to dismount, and made the attack on foot.

Tecumseh, with his braves, was ready to meet him, and, uttering his Shawnee war-cry and discharging his rifle, the Indians and Kentuckians were soon mingled in mortal combat. Tecumseh was killed, and Colonel Johnson was dangerously wounded. The fight in the timber was picturesque as well as deadly, the Indians being dressed in their plumes and war-paint, and the Kentuckians dressed in hunting-shirts of jeans fringed with red, wearing round hats with long plumes of white tipped with red. Our victory was complete, and the volunteers soon afterward returned to Kentucky, where they were discharged.

Brigadier-General Covington, who had been Colonel of the 1st Regiment of Dragoons, was mortally wounded at the Battle of Chrystler's Field, on the 11th of November, 1813. At this battle a squadron of the 2nd Dragoons behaved with great gallantry, and rescued several pieces of cannon of ours which had been taken by the British, but they were unable to hold them, being too weak in numbers. After a severe struggle, however, they brought off all except one piece, which was kept by the enemy.

THE CREEK WAR.

In General Jackson's campaigns against the Creek Indians, the mounted volunteers from Tennessee behaved very well, particularly at Tallushatchee. The Creek War had its origin in the massacre of the whites at Fort Mims by the Indians, and Jackson was sent out to chastise them. The Battle of Tallushatchee, Alabama, took place on the 3rd of November, 1813. Here the mounted men of Jackson's army, under

Battle of the Thames

command of Brigadier-General John Coffee, behaved most admirably. In addition to his own men, Coffee had a band of friendly Creek Indians with him, wearing white feathers and white deers' tails, to distinguish them from their hostile brethren. In Coffee's official report to Jackson, he says:

I arrived within one mile and a half of the Indian town on the morning of the 3rd, at which place I divided my detachment into two columns, the right composed of the cavalry, commanded by Colonel Allcorn, to cross over a large creek that lay between us and the towns; the left column was of the mounted riflemen, under the command of Colonel Cannon, with whom I marched myself. Colonel Allcorn was ordered to march up on the right and encircle one half of the town, and, at the same time, the left would form a half circle on the left, and unite the head of the columns in front of the town, all of which was performed as I could wish.

When I arrived within half a mile of the town, the drums of the enemy began to beat, mingled with their savage yells, preparing for action. It was after sunrise an hour when the action was brought on by Captain Hammond and Lieutenant Patterson's companies, who had gone on within the circle of the alignment for the purpose of drawing out the enemy from their buildings, which had the most happy effect. As soon as Captain Hammond exhibited his front in view of the town (which stood in an open woodland), and gave a few scattering shot, the enemy formed and made a violent charge on him.

He gave way as they advanced until they met our right column, which gave them a general fire and then charged. This changed the direction of charge completely. The enemy retreated firing until they got around and, in their buildings, where they made all the resistance that an overpowered soldier could do. They fought as long as one existed; but their destruction was very soon completed. Our men rushed up to the doors of the houses, and in a few minutes killed the last warrior of them.

The enemy fought with savage fury, and met death, with all its horrors, without shrinking or complaining; not one asked to be spared, but fought as long as they could sit or stand. In consequence of their flying to their houses and mixing with the families, our men, in killing the males, without intention

22

killed and wounded a few of the squaws and children, which was regretted by every officer and soldier of the detachment, but which could not be avoided.

The number of the enemy killed was one hundred and eighty-six that were counted, and a number of others that were killed in the weeds, not found. I think the calculation a reasonable one to say two hundred of them were killed, and eighty-four prisoners of women and children were taken. Not one of the warriors escaped to carry the news—a circumstance unknown heretofore. We lost five killed and forty-one wounded, none mortally, the greater part slightly—a number with arrows. This appears to form a very principal part of the enemy's arms for warfare, every man having a bow with a bundle of arrows, which is used after the first fire with the gun, until a leisure time for loading occurs.

After the battle Coffee returned to General Jackson, thirteen miles distant.

While this affair was going on, a thousand hostile Creeks had got a body of friendly Indians penned up in a fort at Talladega, Alabama, situated on a branch of the Coosa River, in the midst of beautiful mountain scenery. Jackson heard of it, and also heard that the friendly Indians were suffering intolerably for want of water, which the hostiles had completely cut off. After a long and weary march, General Jackson, with eight hundred mounted men and twelve hundred infantry, arrived within six miles of the fort on the evening of the 8th of November, 1813.

Before four o'clock on the succeeding morning our army was in full march toward the enemy. A sudden and vigorous attack soon put the hostile Creeks to flight, and liberated the friendly Indians, who were overjoyed at regaining their liberty, and profuse in their demonstrations of gratitude. Fifteen minutes after the action became general the hostiles were flying in all directions, and falling beneath the sabre-strokes of our cavalry men, who followed them a long distance. The loss to the Indians was very severe, and the Creeks, seeing that they were likely to be overpowered, sent in to General Jackson, who had returned to Fort Strother, proposing to make peace.

General Jackson agreed to the terms, and sent back the messenger, assuring the Indians that the Creek War should cease; but unfortunately, while he was making this treaty, General White, with a body of East Tennesseans, without knowing what Jackson had done, fell upon the Creeks at the Hillabee and Autosse towns, and massacred many of them. The Indians, not being able to understand the difference between Jackson's troops and those commanded by General White, supposed that General Jackson had deceived them, and, as a matter of course, their hatred toward the whites became more deadly and intense than ever.

All hopes of making a peace being now at an end, Jackson prepared to follow the Indians again. He had had considerable difficulty with his own soldiers, whose term of service had expired, and many of them had gone home, in spite of all the general's efforts to retain them.

In January, 1814, Jackson, with his army, started to invade the Indian country in Alabama, and, after marching several days, encamped near the Indian town of Emucfau, near the bend of the Tallapoosa River. Here, during the night of the 21st of January, he was suddenly attacked by a large body of Indians, whom he succeeded in beating off, but was so severely handled that he started on his return to Fort Strother.

While on the march, and near the ford of the Enotachopco, on the 23rd, the Indians again fell upon him and his army with such terrible effect as to break his lines, put a portion of his troops to rout, and, had it not been for the steadiness of Jackson, Coffee, and a few daring spirits, no doubt the greater portion of them would have been massacred. It is impossible to state what the losses were on each side, but I am inclined to believe they were about equal, amounting to not more than a hundred killed and wounded on either side. The Creeks fought with great bravery, and the Tennesseans were only too glad to make their escape to Fort Strother. In these engagements, General Coffee, the cavalry leader, though wounded, behaved most gallantly, and left his litter to lead his men on horseback.

After his return to Fort Strother, General Jackson commenced making preparations for another and final campaign against the Creeks, who had assembled together under Weatherford, at Tahopeka, or the Horse-Shoe Bend of the Tallapoosa. Soon he was joined by a body of volunteers from East Tennessee, one from West Tennessee, the 39th Regiment of United States Regular Infantry, a part of Coffee's brigade of mounted volunteers, and a troop of dragoons from East Tennessee. After a weary march, he reached Tahopeka on the 27th of March, 1814, and commenced the attack upon the Indians, who had fortified their position in expectation of such an event.

24

Coffee, with his mounted men, was sent across the river to cut off the retreat of the Indians, and well did he do his work. In this battle there was a complete slaughter of the Indians, which is sickening in its details, as they would not surrender nor be taken alive. It is said that five hundred and fifty-seven were found dead on the peninsula. It was supposed that two hundred more had found a resting-place at the bottom of the river, and many more died while attempting to escape.

General Jackson's loss was fifty-five killed, and one hundred and forty-six wounded. General Jackson shortly afterward marched to Eccanachaco, or the Holy Ground, and the Creek War was ended. The chief, Weatherford, surrendered himself a prisoner; others gave themselves up, while others made their way to Florida, where they subsequently took part in the war against the whites. Weatherford, the chief, surrendered himself to Jackson only after he had seen nearly all his warriors sleeping beneath the ground which had belonged to the Creek nation for hundreds of years. No braver people ever lived.

The dragoon regiments having been very much reduced during the war, on the 30th of March, 1814, Congress enacted that they should be consolidated into one regiment This regiment was composed of eight troops, each one of which was to consist of a captain, one first lieutenant, one second lieutenant, one third lieutenant, one cornet, five sergeants, eight corporals, one riding-master, one master of the sword, two trumpeters, one farrier, one blacksmith, one saddler, and ninety-six privates, or a total of five officers and one hundred and sixteen enlisted men.

Colonel James Burn, of the 2nd Regiment, was retained as colonel, and Colonel Jacint Laval, of the 1st, was retained as lieutenant-colonel. A squadron of this regiment, under command of Captain Samuel D. Harris, served under Major-General Brown at the Battles of Chippewa and Niagara in July, 1814, where the dragoons did good service; and for his gallantry and bravery in these conflicts, Harris was made a brevet Major for Chippewa, and a brevet Lieutenant-Colonel for Niagara, or Lundy's Lane.

At the grand closing scene of the War of 1812, the Battle of New Orleans, none of our cavalry was present except Major Hinds's battalion of Mississippi mounted men, who had been drilled and disciplined but little, though they rendered such services as they were called upon to perform, and were of much benefit to Jackson in watching the movements of the enemy.

The truth is, that, in the last war with Great Britain, our dragoons were of no great use, and, having no friendly hand to help them, they fell into neglect, and the service became unpopular. There seems to have been no system about their organisation and ways of doing, and "light horsemen," so called by the people, were looked upon with fear, but with no great favour. The general officers knew little, and cared less about cavalry; and not many years have passed by since the then head of our army could not understand the use of it. But, thank Fortune, the cavalry have vindicated their own claim to being known, and now no branch of the service stands forth more proudly than this.

No cavalry was ever better than that which belonged to Wayne's army in 1794, and, I fear, no cavalry was ever much poorer than that which belonged to us in 1813 and 1814.

On the 15th of June, 1815, the dragoon regiment was disbanded by Congress, and our army was again left without mounted soldiers. The war with Great Britain had closed, and our government felt too poor to keep any more soldiers than could be got along with by the most rigid economy.

In the regiment of cavalry commanded by Lieutenant-Colonel John Watts, mentioned earlier, Solomon Van Rensselaer served as major. Watts had been a cavalry officer in the Revolutionary War, in which he was wounded three times.

The majors who were retained in the Light Dragoon Regiment until the close of the war were Major and Brevet Lieutenant-Col. James V. Ball and Major Thos. A. Helms. Lieutenant-Colonel Jacint Laval had been an officer in the French Army, and came to America in the Legion of the Duke of Lauzun during the Revolution. He commanded a squadron of dragoons at the Battle of Bladensburg.

CHAPTER 2

The Black Hawk War

Under President Jackson and on the 15th day of June, 1832, Congress ordered a battalion of mountain rangers to be raised for the protection of the Western frontier. "The Black Hawk War," so called, was then in progress, and it was supposed that a force of this kind, made up of officers and soldiers who had seen service on the frontier, would do much in bringing the Sauk and Fox Indians to peaceful terms. The battalion was composed of six companies, and Henry Dodge, of Wisconsin, was appointed major-*commandant*.

Dodge had commanded a company of mounted volunteers in the War of 1812, and had subsequently been a field officer in some militia organisation. Upon the breaking, out of the troubles with Black Hawk he had formed a company of volunteers, and had skirmished with the Indians successfully at Pickatolika, and at the Blue Mounds, in Illinois. On this account he was deemed by Jackson to be the most suitable person to command the rangers. As a partisan commander he was, no doubt, a good one, but as a colonel of a regular regiment, which he soon afterward became, there is no doubt that he was found wanting. This battalion appears to have done some service; but the good sense of those in power prevailing, the battalion was merged into the 1st Regiment of Dragoons by an Act of Congress of March 2nd, 1833.

From that hour the United States Cavalry Service has been most honourable, and from it must date the present organisation, and the school in which some as good officers as the world has ever seen have been trained.

As before remarked, Major Henry Dodge became colonel of this regiment. Major Stephen Watts Kearney, of the 3rd Infantry, was selected as lieutenant-colonel. It proved a most admirable selection, and the high character which the regiment subsequently attained was mainly due to him. Kearney was born in Newark, New Jersey, August

30th, 1794, and entered the army from New York as first lieutenant of the 13th Infantry in 1812. He was distinguished in the attack upon Queenston Heights, and bore an honourable part in the late war with Great Britain.

Captain Richard B. Mason, of the 1st Infantry, was appointed major, March 4th, 1833. He was from Virginia, and entered the army as 2nd Lieutenant in the 8th Infantry on the 2nd of September, 1817.

The regiment was composed of ten companies, which appears to be the favourite American organisation, and was to serve on horse or foot, as might be directed. Most of the officers who had served in the battalion of United States Rangers were retained in the regiment. The grade of cornet was not revived, but in lieu of it the junior commissioned officers were called second lieutenants. Among the captains were David Hunter, Nathan Boone, and Edwin V. Sumner.

The regiment rendezvoused at Jefferson Barracks, eleven miles below the city of St. Louis, Missouri, and was there organised during the summer of 1833. After its organisation it was employed in the West, and made several marches toward the Rocky Mountains, and south as far as Red River.

In the summer of 1834, it made a campaign far to the Southwest, the object being to cultivate an acquaintance with the Pawnees and Comanches, and to demand the surrender of an American boy, named Martin, whose father, Judge Martin, had been cruelly murdered by the Indians in the summer of 1833 while out buffalo-hunting west of Fort Gibson. Great sickness prevailed among both men and horses at the mouth of the False Washita; and to such an extent did it weaken the regiment that it was found necessary to form a camp there for the sick, which was left in command of Lieutenant-Colonel Kearney.

The regiment, when it left Fort Gibson, was about four hundred strong, and but about two hundred and fifty were able to go on with Colonel Dodge. Brigadier-General Atkinson accompanied the expedition, and died at the Cross Timbers, beyond the False Washita, on the 21st of July, 1834

The regiment marched due west from camp until it came to the great Comanche village, which numbered over six hundred lodges. After staying here for a time, it moved still farther west, until it came to the great Pawnee village on the banks of Red River, and ninety miles beyond the Comanche village. Here, after a great deal of trouble, the boy Martin was found and taken in charge by Colonel Dodge, and was eventually restored to his relatives.

BLACK HAWK

Catlin, the painter, accompanied the regiment in this campaign, and painted the portraits of many of the Indians of the Far West. His collection, which is now in London, was made in part while with the regiment. It is a lasting monument of the industry and talent of one of our countrymen, and a work which all Americans should feel proud of, and which it is wrong for our government to let remain in a foreign land.

While at the Pawnee village the officers and men were visited by bands of Kiowas and Wacos, and no doubt their presence had a salutary effect upon them. Still, the campaign was a most disastrous one, and, besides a large sum of money, cost the United States the lives of over one hundred dragoons and several valuable officers.

The regiment was afterward scattered over an immense extent of country, though but two companies of it served in Florida, and they but for a short time. One officer of it was killed there while serving on the staff of Major-General Gaines. This was First Lieutenant James Farley Izard, who was mortally wounded in the skirmishes which occurred at the ford of the Withlacoochee, on the 28th of February, 1836. He was a fine young officer, and was the only member of the 1st Dragoons killed during that war. He died at Camp Izard on the 5th of March, 1836.

On the 23rd of May, 1836, Congress passed a law authorising the raising of an additional regiment of Dragoons, which was organised, in all respects whatever, the same as the 1st Dragoons.

Lieutenant-Colonel David E. Twiggs, of the 4th Infantry, was promoted colonel of this regiment on the 8th of June, 1836. Wharton Hector, of Missouri Territory, was appointed lieutenant-colonel, June 18th, 1836, and Thomas T. Fauntleroy, of Virginia, was appointed major, June 8th, 1836. Rector declined the appointment, and Paymaster William S. Harney was promoted lieutenant-colonel, August 15th, 1836. Major Rector was appointed paymaster to fill the vacancy caused by the promotion of Harney.

Colonel Twiggs was born in Augusta, Georgia, in 1790, and entered the army as captain in the 8th Infantry on the 12th of March, 1812. He participated in several of Jackson's fights against the Creek Indians, and had the reputation of being a very shrewd officer.

Lieutenant-Colonel Harney was born in Louisiana in 1798, and entered the army as Second Lieutenant of the 1st Infantry on the 13th of February, 1818. He served through the various grades creditably to himself, bore a conspicuous part in the "Black Hawk" War, and

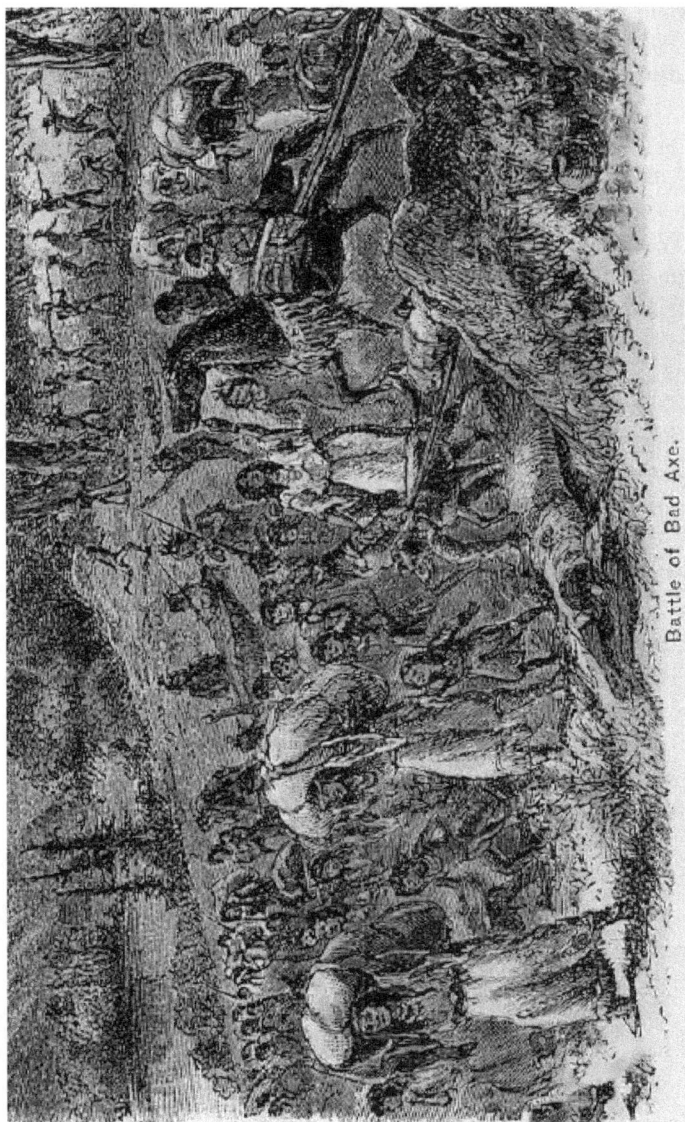

Battle of Bad Axe.

was considered one of the most athletic men in the service. He had a splendid military figure, and was, all in all, a "model dragoon."

The 2nd Dragoons was organised at Jefferson Barracks, Missouri, in the summer of 1836, and while it is fair to say that there was more *dash* about it than about the other regiment, the old 1st Dragoons had a steadiness of purpose and a determination which has made many an enemy quail on many a field.

The 1st Regiment was kept scouting in the Far West, and the 2nd was sent to Florida, where, among the swamps, live oak-trees, and mangrove bushes, it was kept at work for several years. Lieutenant John W. Scott McNiel, of this regiment, was mortally wounded, September 10th, 1837, while serving under Brigadier-General Hernandez, by the Seminole Indians, in action near Mosquito Inlet, and died on the following day.

On the 19th. of July of the same year Captain James A. Ashby, with sixty-two men of the 2nd Dragoons, had a fight at Welika Pond, where he succeeded in defeating a superior force of Seminoles. Ashby was severely wounded, and was breveted Major for gallantry and good conduct on that occasion.

Captain Lloyd J. Beall, of this regiment, with thirty dragoons, had a sharp skirmish with the Indians at Newnansville on the 17th of June, 1838, and gave them a good drubbing.

Harney himself had a most singular, and, to him, not very pleasant experience with the Indians at a trading-house on the Carloosahatchee, on the 23rd of July, 1839. He was there with nineteen dragoons, when in the night the Indians, who had appeared friendly enough, crept on them, and killed eleven and wounded two soldiers out of the nineteen.

Harney escaped with his negro man. In retaliation for this act of treachery on the part of the Seminoles, he, with a small party of dragoons and artillery-men, made an expedition into the Everglades in the month of December, 1840, and, falling upon a camp of them, committed dreadful havoc among them, so that his name became a terror to them far and wide. The negro interpreter, Sampson, who was taken prisoner by the Indians at the affair above mentioned, gives a most pathetic account of it, which I copy from Sprague's *History of the Florida War.* His account is also interesting, as giving an inside view of the condition of the Indians:

I belonged to Colonel Gad Humphries, and was captured by

the Indians at Micanopy in the year 1837. I lived with Osceola, who was my friend. He was a good Indian, and constantly urged the war-parties to spare women and children. After he was taken prisoner, I surrendered at Fort Mellon. I then was an interpreter for General Jesup, who commanded the army. In May, 1839, I was at Fort King when the treaty was made by General Macomb. In the December following, supposing peace was permanently made, I accompanied Lieutenant-Colonel Harney, 2nd Dragoons, to the Carloosahatchee River. He went there for the purpose of establishing an Indian trading-house.

He had with him twenty-seven dragoons, and Sandy, an old negro interpreter. Mr. Dalham and Mr. Morgan were also along with Indian goods. Three more white men were with us; one was a clerk (an Englishman); the other a carpenter; the third the captain of the sloop. The trading-house was established about half a mile from the dragoon encampment. I slept in the store; Mr. Dalham and Mr. Morgan were outside, one in a bunk, the other in a hammock. On the night of the attack (the third night after our arrival), we were about crossing the river to see an Indian dance, when the young Indians told us not to go, as the old men were all drunk.

Just at the break of day on the following morning, I heard the yell of Indians and discharge of rifles; and as I ran out, I found they were all around us. Mr. Dalham lay dead under his hammock. Mr. Morgan was dying, but continued to talk some minutes, when an Indian, placing a rifle close to him, fired. Still, he talked, when the Indian beat his brains out with the butt of his rifle.

As I ran for the river several rifles were discharged at me; a ball struck my leg, which threw me down, when the Indians brought me back to the store. They took Sandy, the carpenter, the clerk, and the captain of the sloop prisoners. The yelling and discharge of rifles continued more than an hour. When it had become quiet, I saw Holatter Micco, or Billy Bowlegs, approaching with Sergeant Simmons, whose life through his influence had been spared, and whom he protected three months, when, by a decree of the council, Sam Jones and the prophet, he was put to death in the most cruel manner.

The carpenter and the negro interpreter, Sandy, were allowed to live four days. They then tied them to a pine-tree, and inserted in their flesh slivers of light wood, setting them on fire, and at the same time placing torches at their feet. In this way it was five or six hours before they died. The fate of the clerk was never known. He accompanied a hunting-party for bear, and while in the swamp separated from the main body. Whether he joined the whites, or died in the swamp from hunger and fatigue, was never known. His wonderful tricks with cards gave him authority among the Indians, and induced them to believe him a second prophet.

The captain of the sloop made his escape. From conversations which I heard on the way to the Cypress Swamp, it appeared that the Indians designed killing Colonel Harney. Sho-nock-Hadjo, a sub-chief, said that the day before the massacre he counted every man in the camp, and took the precaution to see where and in what manner they slept at night. The camp and trading-house were attacked at the same moment.

Hospetarke led the party attacking the store; Chekika, a Spanish Indian, the one upon the camp. The number of warriors who participated was one hundred and sixty. One keg of powder was obtained, a large quantity of goods, and fifteen hundred dollars in specie. The rifles belonging to the soldiers, being of Colt's construction, were useless, and they left them on the ground after taking off the locks. The Indians crossed to the south bank of the river with their booty, where they continued intoxicated three days. No division of the plunder was made.

The most active and daring boasted of the largest quantity. The specie fell into the hands of one man. The powder was taken possession of by the chiefs. On the third day after the conflict a soldier gave himself up, exhausted from hunger, and his feet badly cut by oyster-shells. He was taken to the swamp, and for some months was required to do the humble offices of a squaw. The prophet's mandates caused his death. He was sent a short distance for wood, when the squaws fell upon him, and beat out his brains with pine-knots. Chekika came around the coast in canoes, and on the fourth day returned, entering the Everglades by the Malco River.

As we were returning to the swamp, it was proposed to burn me in the same manner as they had Sandy; but, through the interposition of Holatter Micco, or Billy Bowlegs, my life was spared. Three times the proposition was made while I was a prisoner. Once the prophet sent the order to my master. For two years I was watched constantly. I feared the whites would never come near enough for me to effect my escape. In April, 1841, a great council was held to prevent intercourse with the white men. A law was passed that, should any Indian, male or female, be found in communication with a white man, they should be put to death. Plans were concerted to convey information in the most rapid manner.

The canoes seen in the Everglades had determined them to keep within the swamp. It was understood in council that, being so reduced in numbers and in so confined a space, they must now ambush the enemy, fire, and then run. The powder was deposited with the chiefs. In all, they had five kegs, four of which were obtained at Indian Key when it was attacked by Chekika and the residents murdered. When going upon a *war-party*, each man drew a powder-horn full; but for the purpose of hunting, it was purchased, giving a hog for five charges.

In the centre of the swamp is the council-ground. South of this, within ten miles, is the village of Sam Jones. Otulke Thlocko (the prophet) lives within two miles of him. Hospetarke's town was near the Everglades, twenty miles from the council-house. Near him Passacka, his sub-chief, resided. *Trails*, or footpaths, communicated with all these places. No *trail* whatever is visible outside the swamp, as such would guide their pursuers. Within the swamp are many pine islands, upon which the villages are located. They are susceptible of cultivation; and between them is a cypress swamp, the water from two to three feet deep.

The Indians rely principally upon their crops, which, though small, add much to their comfort. Corn, pumpkins, beans, peas, and melons are raised. When these fail, roots, *coonta*, berries, wild potatoes, and cabbage palmetto afford subsistence. The scarcity of powder deprives them partially of game, though bears and turkeys are frequently killed with arrows. Discharging a rifle was forbidden, as in a country so flat and wet the reverberation is heard at a great distance. Fish and oysters on the coast can be obtained in abundance, but there they apprehend discovery. A few ponies, cattle, hogs, and chickens are owned by the chiefs. The dry goods obtained at the massacre clothes them as much as is necessary. The specie was sold and manufactured into silver ornaments. No community of feeling exists other than that which is necessary for mutual safety. Dissatisfaction has been often expressed by sub-chiefs, but no one had been bold enough to propose emigration or attempt to escape except Solo Micco, who came into Camp Ogden, on Pease Creek.

After his escape scouts were sent out in all directions, and the decrees of the council were enforced. If any were suspected, the prophet visited them; and by various dances, gestures, songs, etc., together with his blow-pipe, proclaimed their fate. Two Indians (a man and woman, with a child) were by his means immediately put to death. They were found following the family of Solo Micco. The prophet, they believed, could make known the approach of troops, find game, and control the seasons, heal the sick, or inflict disease upon anyone—even death.

Arpeika, or Sam Jones, is regarded as a medicine-man, or doctor. His advanced age (regarding such persons with reverence, as the Indians do) attaches to his advice and opinions much importance. At the commencement of the war, he planned attacks, fired the first gun, then retired to take care of the wounded. By certain medicines, and prayers offered to the Great Spirit, he infused into the young warriors a resolute daring. He instigated the attack upon Fort Mellon, fired the first rifle, and left Coacooche to fight the battle. The active *war-chiefs* in the Big Cypress Swamp were Holatter Micco, or Billy Bowlegs, Parsacke, Sho-nock-Hadjo, and Chitto-Tustenuggee.

They, together with the young sub-chiefs, headed the scouts, and executed with fidelity the mandates of the council, or the wishes of Sam Jones, or the prophet. The hanging of several Indians in the Everglades by the 2nd Dragoons and 3rd Artillery in December, 1840, fired the indignation of these chiefs. They declared eternal hostility and cruelty to the whites. We have 'given them heretofore,' said Jones, 'when prisoners, a decent death, and shot them instead of hanging them like a dog.' Sam Jones is a skilful navigator of the Everglades, knows all the secret passages, and cultivates fields in the most inaccessible and remote places. If the Indians are driven from the swamp they must suffer, and if besieged their supplies will soon be exhausted.

The services of the dragoons were of great benefit to the country, and they did much toward bringing the unruly and restless spirits of the wretched Seminoles to terms of peace. Our war in that section was always unpopular, and the "land of sun and flowers" proved the spirit land for many a noble soldier.

But, with all the hardships of a soldier's life in the Far South, there was some fun, and one of the officers wrote a song, which has been sung by many a dragoon with the voice of a stentor, and moistened with old Bourbon during the singing. The poetry is dragoon poetry, and must not be too closely criticised. The sentiment is good. It is called "*The Dragoon Bold*," and is as follows:

Oh! the dragoon bold he knows no care,
As he rides along with his uncropp'd hair;
Himself in the saddle he lightly throws,
And on the weekly scout he goes.

At night he camps in the old pine wood,
He lights his fire and cooks his food;
His saddle-blanket around him throws,
And on the ground, he seeks repose.

If an anxious care should cross his mind,
'Tis of the girl he's left behind,
When he parted from her in sorrow and woe,
And went to the wars a long time ago.

Then cheer, boys, cheer for the girls afar,
We'll all go home at the close of the war;
And, sadly tanned by a Southern sun,
We'll spin long yarns of the deeds we've done.

But the day of the 2nd Dragoons wrath was at hand, and Congress, with a most unwise piece of economy, ordered the regiment to be dismounted and to serve as riflemen. This was done by an Act of August 23rd, 1842, to take effect March 4th, 1843. The dragoons on this occasion composed another song, which was anything but complimentary to the members of Congress, and couched in language which they could not have failed to understand had they heard it.

But the Congressmen discovered their mistake, and gladdened the hearts of the regiment by remounting it, and restoring it to its original place. This Act was passed on the 4th of April, 1844.

Colonel Dodge, of the 1st Regiment, resigned in July, 1836, having been appointed governor of Wisconsin Territory. Kearney was promoted colonel; Mason, lieutenant-colonel; and Captain Clifton

Wharton, major.

Captain John F. Lane, of the 2nd Dragoons, acted as colonel of a regiment of Creek mounted volunteers in the Florida War. David Moniac, a Creek Indian, was major of this regiment. He was a graduate of West Point, where he stood well, but upon going South and getting among his old companions, true to his Indian instinct, he stripped off his uniform and changed it for a blanket His resignation was accepted December 31st, 1822. He again entered the service as above mentioned, and was killed while serving as major at the Battle of Wahoo Swamp, November 21st, 1836.

Lane was disappointed on account of some matters connected with the campaign against the Indians, and committed suicide by falling upon his own sabre at Fort Drane, Florida, October 19th, 1836. His regiment was led, at the Battle of Wahoo Swamp, by Lieutenant-Colonel Harvey Brown.

On the 8th of February, 1837, four companies of the 2nd Dragoons, under Lieutenant-Colonel Harney, participated in a fight with the Seminoles, near the site of Fort Mellon, Florida. The Indians were worsted with considerable loss. For gallantry in Florida, Harney was breveted Colonel; Captain Benjamin L. Beall, of the same regiment, was breveted Major; and Lieutenant Arnold, Captain.

The system of cavalry tactics adapted to the organisation of the dragoon regiments was authorised by Hon. J. R. Poinsett, Secretary of War, on the 10th of February, 1841. It is mainly a translation of the tactics of the French service, and has not as yet been improved upon, though several attempts have been made, but they have all proved failures. I believe almost every cavalry officer of experience considers the tactics of 1841 as far superior to anything which has yet been introduced into our service.

The 1st of Dragoons, as before stated, was principally employed west of the Mississippi River. Jefferson Davis became a first lieutenant in the regiment on the 4th of March, 1833, and adjutant during 1833 and 1834. It would, no doubt, have been much better for the country had he been killed during that period; but it was designed to be otherwise, and he resigned on the 30th of June, 1835. Davis, as a cadet, manifested a proud, haughty, and cold disposition, which he seems to have retained through life. He is eminently selfish, and has no friends aside from those who can be of use to him. Nevertheless, it must be admitted that he was a good officer, and gained the respect of those with whom he was thrown in contact.

It is exceedingly difficult at this day to note all of the changes of station which were made by the dragoons. In fact, it is impossible, and is of no great consequence at best. They established several forts and encampments, roamed about from Fort Snelling in the Far North to Fort Jesup on Red River, and westward to the base of the Rocky Mountains. Their presence, particularly that of the 1st Regiment, among the tribes of the Upper Missouri, exerted a salutary influence, and protected the frontier settlers in their homes.

A body of Texans, under Colonel Jacob Snively, during their war for independence, invaded our territory for the purpose of capturing a train of Mexican traders who were wending their way from Santa Fé to St. Louis. Captain P. St. George Cooke, of the 1st Dragoons, over-took these marauders, disarmed them, and sent them to their homes south of the Red River, and let the unarmed merchants pursue their course unmolested. This occurred on the banks of the Arkansas River on the 30th of June, 1843. For this act Cooke was never popular among the Texans, though there is no doubt but his course of conduct was perfectly proper, and served to show that he was an officer who understood his duty, and was determined to do it

The Florida War was a most deplorable affair, and a vast amount of suffering sprang from it. For years the Indians clung to the homes of their forefathers, and it was at the cost of much blood and treasure that they were finally expelled from that country. Captain Benjamin L. Beall's company killed Waxehadjo, a celebrated chief, which no doubt had a good effect upon the people, and conduced toward bringing about a peace.

Five companies of the 2nd Dragoons left Florida on the 17th of October, 1841, and moved to Fort Jesup and Fort Towson, west of the Mississippi River; the remaining five companies were sent to join them on the 29th of May, 1842. The regiment had served in Florida since its organisation in June, 1836. Its duties were incessant and labo-rious, and were performed at all times in the most creditable manner. One officer was killed in action, and five died from the effects of the climate. Twenty non-commissioned officers, musicians, and privates were killed in action, and one hundred and ninety-two died from disease incident to the service.

I cannot leave Florida without making the following extract from Coacoochee, or Wild Cat's *narrative* of his life, given after he had sur-rendered to the whites. The language and imagery are to me most beautiful, and seem well worthy of a child of the Land of Flowers. He said:

In leaving Florida I leave behind me the spirits of the Seminoles. Their spirits have taken care of me all my life. And the spirit of my twin sister I leave behind. When I am laid in the earth I shall go to and live with her. She died suddenly. I was out on a bear-hunt, and, when seated by my camp-fire alone, I heard a strange noise; it was something like a voice, which told me to go to her.

The camp was some distance, but I took my rifle and started. The night was dark and gloomy; the wolves howled about me as I went from hummock to hummock; sounds came often to my ear—I thought she was speaking to me. At daylight I reached her camp: she was dead. When hunting sometime after with my brother Otulke, I sat alone beside a large oak. In the moss hanging over me I heard strange sounds; I tried to sleep, but could not. I felt myself moving, and thought I went far above to a new country, where all was bright and happy. I saw clear water-ponds, rivers, and prairies, on which the sun never sets.

All was green; the grass grew high, and the deer stood in the midst of it looking at me. I then saw a small white cloud approaching; and, when just before me, out of it came my twin-sister, dressed in white, and covered with bright silver ornaments. The long black hair, which I had often braided, hung down her back. She clasped me around the neck, and said, 'Coacooche! Coacooche!' I shook with fear. I knew her voice, but could not speak. With one hand she gave me a string of white beads; in the other she held a cup sparkling with pure water, which she said came from the spring of the Great Spirit, and if I would drink from it, I should return and live with her forever.

As I drank, she sang the peace-song of the Seminoles, and danced around me. She had silver bells on her feet, which made a loud noise. Taking from her bosom something, I do not know what, she laid it before me, when a bright blaze streamed far above us. She then took me by the hand, and said, 'All is peace here.' I wanted to ask for others, but she shook her head, waved her hand, stepped into the cloud, and was gone.

Wild Cat died at Laguna de Leche, not far from New Laredo, in

Mexico, in the summer of 1857.

The uniform of the dragoon soldiers of the United States Army during the Florida and Mexican Wars was a blue fatigue jacket trimmed with yellow lace, a flat forage cap with a wide yellow band, and sky-blue trowsers re-enforced, or, as the soldiers call it, with a "saddle piece," with two yellow stripes up outside seam. The dress uniform was a short coat trimmed with yellow, and a heavy dress cap, with a long, drooping white horse-hair pompon. The sash worn by dragoon officers was of silk net, of a deep orange colour; and that worn by the non-commissioned staff and first sergeants was of yellow worsted. The dress cap and coat, in active service, was seldom if ever worn.

From 1842 until the breaking out of difficulties on the Rio Grande frontier, the cavalry had a comparatively easy time. The Florida War was closed, though there were some disturbances in that region as late as 1856, but these were of minor importance. They were at liberty once more to sing the songs of peace, and to enjoy their ease by their camp-fires. Peace spread her soft wings over the land, and Plenty smiled upon America.

Secure Arachne spread her slender toils o er the worn buckler;
Eating rust consumed the vengeful swords and once far-gleaming spears;
No more the trump of war swelled its hoarse throat,
Nor robbed the eyelids of their genial slumber.

★★★★★★★★★★

For further reading on The Black Hawk War see *Black Hawk's War, 1832*: Autobiography of Ma-Ka-Tai-Me-She-Kia-Kiak, or Black Hawk dictated by Himself & Wakefield's *History of the Black Hawk War* by Frank Everett Stevens also *Narratives of Black Hawk's War*, 1832 by Henry Smith, C. R. Green, Benjamin Drake & William Edwards; Leonaur 2018.

★★★★★★★★★★

41

CHAPTER 3

The Mexican War

But the storm now commenced gathering in the Far South, where the first real fame of the dragoons was to be won. It is true, they had done their whole duty in Florida, and on the wide plains which stretch from Missouri River to the Rocky Mountains, but they had yet to go through the baptism of blood. The fields were waiting for them, and the sabre, which for a long time had lain idle, was to be drawn and sharpened ready for the foe. The two regiments had confidence in themselves, and the country had confidence in them. They were about to prove that this confidence was not misplaced, and the dull war-drum was about to awaken the nation from its peaceful dreams.

Our dragoons were not only good they were excellent; and the thorough training which they had received was perfected by constant drill and attention to discipline, and the most trifling neglect met with summary punishment. They were supplied with everything which could add to their efficiency, though no luxuries were allowed them, and the officers which were left had been winnowed out of an immense amount of chaff, which had at one time, through political favouritism, been put into the army to get rid of it. But both Twiggs and Kearney understood their professions, and many a worthless wight was cut loose by them.

It is not my intention to recount the causes which led to the Mexican War; it is sufficient to know that they existed, and that the government thought proper, by "the act of Mexico," to commence it. I am simply dealing with facts which grew out of the war, and shall attempt to detail the part borne by the cavalry in that struggle.

In the year 1845 Brevet Brigadier-General Zachary Taylor had assembled quite a respectable United States force at Corpus Christi, on the coast of Texas, and early in the spring of 1846 moved on to the Rio Grande, and threw up a field work, which has since been known as Fort Brown, on the banks of that stream. Arista, the Mexican commander, hearing of this, sent a force of twenty-five hundred men, under General Torrejon, to the Texas side of the Rio Grande, with a view of commencing hostilities against the Americans, and plainly stated such to be his intention to General Taylor.

The latter sent Captain Thornton, with a squadron of the 2nd Dragoons, to watch his movements. He proceeded about sixteen miles above the fort, when his guide refused to proceed farther; but Thornton, wishing to carry out the full instructions of his general, and learn as much as possible of the enemy, whom he believed had not yet crossed from the Mexican side of the river, continued on. He proceeded about three miles farther, when, halting near a ranch, he sent his men inside of an enclosure, or corral, as it is called, to feed their horses, and soon followed himself.

At the farther end the Mexicans were discovered, when the dragoons attempted to get outside, but found the entrance closed upon them. Thornton was severely wounded, and his horse was shot under him by the first fire of the Mexicans, and he lay under him. After a sharp firing from the enemy, which the dragoons were unable to return with effect, as the Mexicans were outside the pickets of the enclosure, Captain Hardee, who took command on the fall of Thornton, surrendered. This occurred on the 24th of April, 1846.

Second Lieutenant George T. Mason was killed in this affair, and sixteen dragoons were killed and wounded. The prisoners were taken to Matamoros, and were subsequently exchanged. This seemed rather an unfavourable commencement of hostilities, and had a dispiriting influence upon the army; and General Taylor himself was considerably annoyed by it.

The fort was completed, and Taylor, leaving a sufficient force to guard it, started for Point Isabel to obtain supplies and then return. He took with him the greater part of his army, as the Mexicans had by this time crossed the Rio Grande in large numbers, and a battle was considered imminent. Taylor obtained his supplies, and started on his return to Fort Brown on the 7th of May, having with him a train of three hundred wagons. On the 8th of May the battle of Palo Alto was fought.

In this action Captain Croghan Ker's squadron of the 2nd Dragoons guarded the train, and the colonel of that regiment (Twiggs) acted as Brigadier-General commanding one of the wings of the American Army. The dragoons did their duty well; but there was nothing particularly devolved upon them, and their prowess was not put to the test. Darkness put an end to the conflict, and the Mexican Army during the night changed its position, and retired somewhat nearer Fort Brown, and about seven miles from the first battlefield.

Sending his wounded to Point Isabel, and leaving his train with a sufficient guard at Palo Alto, Taylor moved forward with his army, and came up with the Mexican force at a place known as Resaca de la Palma. Here he found it necessary to attack the enemy under most disadvantageous circumstances, but knowing it would not do to falter, he sent his troops forward, and the action commenced. A deep ravine separated the two armies, which was defended on the Mexican side by a number of pieces of artillery, which kept up a heavy firing upon the Americans as they advanced.

The American infantry was broken up in small parties trying to force the passage of the ravine, when Taylor ordered Captain Charles A. May's squadron of the 2nd Dragoons forward to charge a battery which annoyed our people excessively. May's squadron consisted of his own and Lawrence Pike Graham's companies, and moved forward down the road at a gallop, and pulling up for a moment when near Ridgely's battery of artillery, the latter poured a heavy fire into the Mexicans, and May went thundering forward with the dragoons under cover of the smoke.

On they went among the Mexicans, who, frightened by their impetuosity, broke in all directions, and their guns were captured. But in the *mêlée*, of course, the dragoons were greatly scattered, and riding about furiously amid the smoke of battle. May, however, rallied a party, and, taking General La Vega prisoner, carried him off under a severe fire from the Mexican infantry. Ridgely had meanwhile galloped forward with his guns, and, halting for a short time for the dragoons to get out of the way, poured a terrible fire into the Mexicans, who had again formed near their guns. The 8th Infantry and a portion of the 5th came down the road at double-quick under Colonel Belknap, crossed the ravine, and the battle was won.

Some parties kept up the firing some time longer, and the Mexicans gradually faded away in the distance. This was a fine cavalry charge; in fact, one of the finest ever made in America. First Lieutenant Zebulon M. P. Inge was killed, as well as several dragoons, and quite a number were wounded. May was breveted Lieutenant-Colonel for his conduct in this battle; Captain Graham was breveted Major; First Lieutenants Ripley, A. Arnold, and Oscar F. Winship, were breveted Captains;

BATTLE OF RESACA DE LA PALMA, MEXICAN WAR—MAY CHARGING WITH HIS DRAGOONS.

and Second Lieutenants Alfred Pleasanton and Delos B. Sackett were breveted First Lieutenants—all of them of the 2nd Dragoons. The fame of this charge added greatly to the reputation of the dragoons, and they were popular with the army from that day.

After the battle Taylor's force continued its course toward the Rio Grande, and reached Fort Brown in safety. He prepared to cross that river, and by the 20th of May his whole force, except the garrison at Fort Brown and a small party at Point Isabel, was on the soil of Mexico. In crossing the river on the 18th of that month, Second Lieutenant George Stevens, 2nd Dragoons, an officer of promise, was drowned.

Taylor's army did not remain long at Matamoros, but gradually worked its way up the Rio Grande. Boats were brought from the United States, and means of transportation were accumulated before a forward movement was attempted, and twelve months volunteers were called for by the President. In response to this call, besides the infantry which flocked round the old flag, Kentucky sent one regiment of cavalry, under Colonel Humphrey Marshall; Tennessee one, under Colonel Jonas E. Thomas; Missouri two, under Colonels Alexander W. Doniphan and Sterling Price; Arkansas one, under Colonel Archibald Yell; Eastern Texas one, under Colonel George T. Wood; and Western Texas one, under Colonel John C. Hays.

Congress also passed a law by which both Colonel Twiggs and Kearney, of the dragoon regiments, became Brigadier-Generals; whereupon Mason became Colonel of the 1st Dragoons, and Harney Colonel of the 2nd. Captain Eustace Trenor was promoted Major of the 1st, and Captain Edwin V. Sumner, Major of the 2nd.

On the 19th of May, 1846, a law was passed by Congress to provide for establishing military stations on the route to Oregon, and to raise a regiment of mounted rifle men. It was raised accordingly, though it was not sent to Oregon, but upon its completion was sent to Mexico, where (with the exception of two companies which were mounted) it did a great deal of good service as *foot* riflemen, the horses of the regiment having been lost by shipwreck in the Gulf of Mexico, and no opportunity occurring for getting a re-mount.

Colonel Persifer F. Smith, of Louisiana, was selected for colonel of this regiment. He was a lawyer of New Orleans, but had seen service as colonel of a regiment of Louisiana volunteers during the Florida War, and, as Brigadier-General of a brigade of six regiments of Louisiana six months men, who first went to re-enforce General Taylor. He was a good soldier, having given a great deal of attention to military affairs while a citizen; and soon after being appointed was placed in command of a brigade of regulars.

Brevet Captain John C. Fremont, of the Topographical Engineers, was selected as the Lieutenant-Colonel. He was born in South Carolina, had seen considerable service, and was mainly known at that time on account of his explorations to and beyond the Rocky Mountains. At the time of his appointment, he was among the mountains, and led a battalion of mounted California volunteers, mostly American mountaineers, in the conquest of California. He never served with his regiment.

George S. Burbridge, of Kentucky, was appointed major. His service was of an unimportant character, and he resigned on the 8th of January, 1848.

General Taylor, after leaving suitable garrisons at different points on the Rio Grande, moved up that stream with a majority of his army to Camargo, and on the 19th of August set out for Monterey, where it was known a large force of Mexicans had assembled, and had fortified the town to a very considerable extent. By this time many of the volunteers had arrived from the North, and had been organised into a division under General Butler, of Kentucky.

The mounted force which accompanied the army consisted of four companies of the 2nd Dragoons, under Brevet Lieutenant-Colonel May, who had distinguished himself at Palo Alto and at Resaca de la Palma; Colonel Jack Hays's and Colonel Woods's regiments of Texans, or, as they were called, "Texas Rangers." These rangers were good troops for reconnoissances and for scouting, but were not of the best class for anything like regular movements. The march was not opposed in any manner, though parties of Mexican lancers were frequently seen ahead on the road; but they did not interfere, being thrown out by their own commander to watch our operations.

On the 19th of September Taylor arrived in front of Monterey. This city, the capital of the State of Nuevo Leon, is situated on the little river San Juan, in the midst of a delightful plain, which is shut in on the west by lofty spurs of the Sierra Madre Mountains. Pure streams of fresh water trickle down the mountains, and in the irrigated bottom lands the finest crops can be raised without difficulty. It was at that time a town of about ten thousand inhabitants, and, though far away on the frontier, possessed some fine buildings and a good population.

Ampudia, the Mexican *commandant*, had used every means in his power to strengthen the place, and had assured his own government that he was able to check the farther advance of the Americans into the interior. His force was made up of regular and irregular Mexican soldiers, and, on the whole, was a very respectable army.

General Taylor arranged his plan of attack on the morning of the 20th. General Worth, with his division, was ordered to move round to the right of the town through the cornfields, and gain, if possible, the Saltillo road above it, and thus cut off supplies and re-enforcements which were expected to arrive for the Mexicans from the interior.

Twiggs's division was to attack in front, together with the volunteers under Butler. The mounted force which accompanied Worth in his detour to the right consisted of Hays's rangers; but Taylor, thinking this not strong enough, sent May's four companies of dragoons and Woods's regiment to re-enforce him. The attack upon the town had by this time commenced, and the Mexicans were returning our fire in the most determined and spirited manner.

Upon arriving in the vicinity of the Hill of Independence, on his way to join Worth, May found the fire of the guns upon its summit too hot for him, and halted out of range of them. General Henderson soon arrived with Woods's regiment, when he assumed command, and sent back to Taylor for instructions as to what he should do; but the cavalry arrived too late to be of any service on the east.

Meantime Twiggs and Butler were working away at the city, and Worth was moving round. On the 21st, as Hays's regiment was passing a spur of the mountains, it came suddenly upon a Mexican regiment of Guanajuato lancers, supported by an infantry force. As soon as they were discovered, Hays halted his regiment, deployed, and moved down to a cornfield, where two companies were dismounted, and placed in ambush amid the thick bushes and fences of the field. One company pushed forward, fired, and returned toward the main body, pursued by the lancers, who came on in fine style. The lancers galloped on, but were met by Smith's battalion of infantry, which was advancing in open order.

The skirmishers opened a scattering fire, but the lancers, under Lieutenant-Colonel Don Juan Najira, seemed not disposed to halt or give way. At this moment, however, the Texans, who were dismounted and concealed in the bushes, opened a most deadly fire upon them, when they turned, and tried to get back to the Saltillo road. Their efforts in this direction were foiled, when they attempted to cross over the hill, which was clear of our men, and presented their only chance of escape. None succeeded; and the gallant young Colonel Najira, who refused to surrender although left alone, was struck by a bullet, and rolled off his horse dead. His behaviour in this fight elicited the admiration of everyone.

The Mexican infantry fell back, and Worth pushed his men forward toward *La loma Federation*. The fight above described was the only one which occurred during the attack upon Monterey, which was carried on by the cavalry alone. The Texas troops dismounted, and fought their way into town on foot with the other troops; but it is not my province to do with the operations of infantry, which would lead me into giving almost endless details.

After a most sanguinary conflict of three days duration, the Mexican force capitulated and surrendered the city to the Americans. During the morning of the 25th the Mexican garrison evacuated the citadel, and on successive days the different corps left the town and marched to Saltillo. On the 28th the last corps left the town and Worth occupied it with his division.

While these events were transpiring on the soil of Northern Mexico, events of the most startling character, and which have been of the greatest importance, were being carried on in California, and on the plains between the Mississippi River and the Pacific. Captain Fremont, with a command made up of mountaineers and back woodsmen well mounted, had made his way beyond the Rocky Mountains, and had visited a portion of the Territory of Oregon; but the winter approaching, and he seeing no safe and secure place in which to pass it, pushed his way south, and in the month of January, 1846, arrived within one hundred miles of Monterey, California, which is situated on the Pacific Ocean.

As his animals needed recruiting, he determined to halt in the valley of the San Joaquin, which was filled with game, and which he had previously explored. Besides this, he found good water and abundance of grass, articles which he mostly stood in need of. To avoid trouble, he left his party in the valley of the San Joaquin, and proceeded in person to Monterey to visit General De Castro, the military *commandante*, where he explained his wants, and, as his was purely an expedition of a peaceful character, he having been sent out in the first instance by our government to make explorations of roads and routes leading from our Western settlements to the then far-off country of Oregon, De Castro, after some demur, gave his sanction to Fremont's remaining for a time, and the latter left to join his little command of mounted men, thinking all was right, and that he would have no trouble. In this, however, he was mistaken.

Scarcely had he left De Castro before that wily Mexican sent out his messengers calling upon the people to rise and expel Fremont and his little band of Americans. This news was immediately transmitted to Fremont, when he moved with his command within thirty miles of Monterey, and took a position on the San Juan Mountain, commonly called "*Gavilan*," where he was enabled to overlook an immense extent of country, and here he unfurled the United States flag, determined to stand or fall in its defence. De Castro approached with his forces, but did not attack Fremont; and, after remaining in a threatening attitude for several days, the Americans abandoned the mountain, and started for Oregon. De Castro followed with a force, which outnumbered Fremont's six times over, and continued to dog his trail for several days.

Finally, however, De Castro gave up the pursuit, and Fremont continued on his course, his progress north being impeded by natural obstacles, and by the hostility of the Klamath Indians, who attacked him, and killed and wounded several of his men.

On the 9th of May he was overtaken by Lieutenant Gillespie, of the Marine Corps, who had made his way across the Republic of Mexico from Vera Cruz to Mazatlan. From him he learned the condition of affairs in the States, and the likelihood of a war with Mexico. Determining, therefore, to return and face the danger which threatened him in rear, and to protect the American settlers who lived on the banks of the Rio de los Americanos, whom De Castro had proclaimed his intention of expelling from the country, he returned to the Bay of San Francisco with his party.

The security of his own men, and of his countrymen living in California, made it necessary that decided and prompt measures should be taken at once, and, after due deliberation, he determined to overthrow the Mexican authority in California. This took place on the 6th of June, 1846.

Fremont commenced operations by seizing, on the 11th of June, a drove of two hundred horses, which was on its way to De Castro's camp in charge of an officer and fourteen men. He next attacked the military post of Sonoma, which was taken on the 15th of the same month, together with the garrison, consisting of General Vallejo, several officers and men, nine brass cannon, and two hundred and fifty stand of arms. Leaving a small guard at Sonoma, Fremont set out for the Rio de los Americanos, where he assembled the American settlers, and gained several volunteers from among them, for his party had up to this time been made up of but few men, but they were brave and determined.

Hearing that De Castro intended to attack Sonoma during his absence, he started immediately on his return. He received this news on the afternoon of the 23rd of June, and before two o'clock on the morning of the 25th he was again at Sonoma, with ninety men, having ridden the intervening distance during that time. It must be admitted that this was *fair* cavalry marching. He attacked the Mexicans under De la Torre, one of De Castro's subordinates, defeated him near Sonoma, and he escaped after losing his boats and artillery, which had been spiked.

Having succeeded in driving the Mexicans from the northern shore of the bay, Lieutenant-Colonel Fremont (for he had been promoted, as before stated, as Lieutenant-Colonel of the Mounted Rifle Regiment) returned to Sonoma July 4th. He called the Americans together, and, after explaining the state of affairs to them, a declaration of independence from Mexico was agreed upon, and Fremont was chosen as the director of affairs. De Castro meantime had established himself at Santa Clara, where he had intrenched himself on the south side of the bay, with two pieces of cannon and four hundred men.

The Americans decided to attack him, and, moving forward, they travelled one hundred miles in three days, and, reaching the American settlements at the forks of the Sacramento, learned that De Castro had abandoned his works at Santa Clara, and retreated to the Cuidad de los Angeles on the Pacific, which was the place of residence of the governor general of the Californias, and about four hundred miles south of San Francisco.

Everything was prepared for following De Castro, when news of the declaration of war between the United States and Mexico reached Fremont, and that Commodore Sloat, who commanded the American squadron on the Pacific, had taken the different Mexican ports. Commodore Sloat, Commodore Stockton, and Lieutenant-Colonel Fremont met together at Monterey in July, and soon after Sloat, whose health was very much impaired, returned to the United States. Stockton was left in command of the squadron, and co-operated heartily with Fremont.

On the 25th of July Fremont's battalion was taken on board the United States ship *Cyane*, and started for the Cuidad de los Angeles, where Governor Pico and General De Castro had assembled a large

Mexican force. The force of Fremont was landed in due time at San Diego, but there he found it extremely difficult to procure a re-mount of horses. However, after much labour, he succeeded, and then started to join Stockton, who had landed at San Pedro, and who was drilling his sailors and marines for duty on land. While these officers were preparing themselves for battle, Stockton received some messages from De Castro.

To these he replied, telling him he would attack him as soon as he had prepared his forces. Stockton started for the Cuidad de los Angeles, and sent word to Fremont to join him *en route*. The Americans, as they neared that place, learned that the Mexican leaders had become frightened, and were on their way to the Mexican state of Sonora, which was farther south.

Upon learning this, Stockton and Fremont entered the city on the 15th of August, and on the 17th, Stockton issued a proclamation announcing the conquest of California, and promising a government similar to that of the American Territories as soon as it could be established. Stockton announced himself as governor, and Lieutenant-Colonel Fremont military *commandant*.

In the meantime, Colonel Kearney (he had not yet received his promotion) had started from Fort Leavenworth with a force of eight companies of dragoons and some volunteers for the conquest of New Mexico. He was followed on his way by a band of Mormons, who were mustered into the service, and formed into a battalion under command of Lieutenant-Colonel P. St. George Cooke, who was then a captain in the 1st Dragoons.

Lieutenant-Colonel James Allen, the first commander of this battalion, was also a captain in the 1st Dragoons, but died at Leavenworth on the 23rd of August, 1846. The regular dragoons were commanded by Sumner. Pursuing the military road to the westward, the "Army of the West" crossed the grassy prairies which lie between the Missouri and Kansas Rivers, which are in summer clothed with the most luxuriant verdure, and gemmed with flowers. On the 4th of July they struck the main road leading from Independence to Santa Fé at Elm Grove, and were soon upon the great plains, which extend for miles and miles in every direction, giving pasture-ground to the buffalo and elk, and whose solitary echoes had then but infrequently been broken by the sound of human voices.

Occasionally they passed small water-courses, which were wending their way toward the great "Father of Waters," and then upon the sandy plains, where the short, dry grass was interspersed with stunted bushes. Trees were scarce, and only seen at long intervals. The army reached the Arkansas on the 19th of July, and continued its march along the northern bank to Bent's Fort, which was a small post erected by some citizens for a trading post with the Indians. This was the rendezvous of the different detachments, and here a large amount of provisions had previously been stored for Kearney's force.

At this place Kearney rested his men, and supplied his artillery with mules, his horses having become completely broken down. He then pushed forward toward New Mexico. After leaving the valley of the Arkansas he came into a mountainous country. His road lay along the spurs of the Rocky Mountains, near the head waters of the Cimaron and Canadian Rivers, and those of the Rio Grande.

Colonel Kearney reached Santa Fé on the 18th of August without any incident occurring worthy of note, and assumed control of affairs. He issued a proclamation declaring New Mexico to be a part of the United States, and absolving the inhabitants from their allegiance to the Mexican Government, and claiming them as American citizens. A civil government was organised, and the proper officers appointed.

Seeing everything in a fair way of doing, Kearney set out for California on the 25th of September, to assist, if necessary, in the conquest of that country. On the 5th of October, 1846, he met an express from Commodore Stockton and Lieutenant-Colonel Fremont reporting that they were already in possession of that country, and that the war in that section was ended. On receiving this welcome news, General Kearney, who had received his promotion, directed Major Sumner, with a portion of the dragoons, to return to the States, and he, with his dragoon escort, pushed forward for California.

After a long and most tedious journey, he entered the Territory of California in November, and halted a short time to rest in the frontier settlements. Here he learned that a counter-revolution had broken out in California, and sent word to Commodore Stockton to open communications with him. Without waiting for a reply, he pushed forward on the 5th of December, and about forty miles from San Diego met Captain Gillespie, who had come from the shores of the Pacific Ocean to meet him.

It appears that after Stockton and Fremont had taken the Cuidad de los Angeles (City of the Angels), and Governor Pico and De Castro had retreated to Sonora, they went north to San Francisco, at which place they designed to make arrangements for an attack upon Acapulco and Mazatlan, on the Pacific side of the Mexican Republic. While doing this, however, a revolt was brought about among the Mexicans, who did not seem inclined to acquiesce at once in the newly-made government.

A fight had taken place between the sailors and marines of the Pacific squadron and the Mexicans a short distance from San Pedro, which did not prove very sanguinary, as the Mexicans kept retreating; and another uprising of the people took place at Santa Barbara, which was easily put down. Fremont came down the coast with his men, and, landing at Monterey, after some difficulty succeeded in providing horses for them, and then marched toward the capital. Matters were in this condition when Kearney reached the Territory.

On his way to join General Kearney, Captain Gillespie learned that a large force of Mexicans was at San Pascual, about fifteen miles from his camp, on another road leading to San Diego. Lieutenant Hammond was sent forward to make a reconnaissance in the evening, and returned about two o'clock on the morning of the 6th of December. He reported that he had found the enemy, but that they had made no effort to pursue him. Upon learning this, General Kearney determined to attack them. Captain Johnston, 1st Dragoons, with twelve soldiers, led the advance; they were mounted on the best horses.

Captain Moore followed with fifty dragoons, who were mostly mounted on mules, their horses having been broken down in the long march from Santa Fé. Captain Gillespie's volunteers came next; then two mountain howitzers, manned by dragoons, and under command of Lieutenant Davidson; the rest of the troops, including the men from the Pacific squadron under Lieutenant Beall and Passed Midshipman Duncan, of the navy, remained in rear with the baggage, under Major Swords.

At daybreak on the 6th of December, the enemy was discovered, about one hundred and sixty strong, under Andres Pico, brother of the governor. Captain Johnston immediately charged upon them, and they gave way. General Kearney followed, with Captain Moore and the other dragoons, when, becoming somewhat scattered, the Mexicans turned rapidly and unexpectedly upon their pursuers, and a most bloody conflict ensued, the Mexicans inflicting dangerous wounds with their long lances, and having an immense advantage over our men in the fact that their horses were fresh, whereas those of our dragoons were nearly broken down by the long march which they had made.

For five minutes the conflict was terrible; but on the approach of the forces in rear, the Mexicans gave way, carrying most of their killed and wounded with them. Lieutenant Davidson was unable to bring his howitzers into action, as at the commencement of the fight the mules before them became frightened and unmanageable.

In this action our country lost three most valuable officers of the 1st Regiment Dragoons, who were killed. They were Captain Abram R. Johnston, of Ohio; Captain Benjamin D. Moore, of Illinois; and Second Lieutenant Thomas C. Hammond, of Pennsylvania. Sixteen non-commissioned officers and privates were also killed or mortally wounded. Brigadier-General Kearney was twice severely wounded, besides several officers and soldiers. For his gallantry at this action, he was made a brevet Major-General. Having inflicted this loss upon our soldiers, the Mexicans retired.

A large body soon after showed itself in rear of the Americans, which created some uneasiness for the safety of the train, but it was safely brought up, and the Americans encamped near the scene of the fight. On the following day the last sad rites were performed for the dead; the wounded were cared for, and the survivors wended their way sorrowfully toward the Pacific. Captain Henry S. Turner, 1st Dragoons, took command after General Kearney fell wounded, and he subsequently was breveted Major for gallantry during that battle, and others in which he afterward participated.

The enemy appeared in front on the day after the battle, and took post at San Bernardino among the hills, where they seemed inclined to make a stand; but our advance drove them from their position, and then halted. The affairs of General Kearney's command were now in a most critical state. A number of them were wounded; they were all poorly provided for, and surrounded by enemies who were determined to cut them to pieces, if possible.

At the *rancho* of San Bernardino Captain Turner collected some cattle, and sent an express to Commodore Stockton at San Diego for assistance. Lieutenant Godey, of the volunteers, the messenger, started in the night, but was captured when in sight of the American flag which was waving over that town. Pico's cavalry still hung round, and in the night drove away the cattle which Turner had collected upon which to subsist his men. This occurred a short distance beyond the *rancho*. The situation of the Americans was becoming desperate.

The provisions were gone, the mules "given out," and the horses were dead; and from the celerity of Pico's movements, Kearney was convinced he could not move with his mounted men and baggage. Kearney determined to remain upon the hill of San Bernardino. The fattest mule was killed for meat, and holes were bored for water, and in this way enough was obtained to last two days. On the night of the 8th of December, Kit Carson, Lieutenant Beall, of the navy, and an Indian servant, volunteered to go to San Diego to ask for assistance from Commodore Stockton. The expedition was one of extreme peril, as the enemy had possession of all of the roads; but, after a night of great hazard and a day of concealment, they reached San Diego, twenty-nine miles distant, in safety.

On the morning of the 10th Pico attacked Kearney's camp, driving in front of him a drove of horses to protect his men. A few horses were killed, and the Mexicans were driven back. It was determined to push on to the ocean on the following day at all hazards, but during the night Lieutenant Grey, of the navy, arrived with, re-enforcements, and the Americans were relieved. It was time, as our people were nearly *in extremis*. They had no provisions; their baggage was gone, for they had burned a portion of it in anticipation of a forward movement; they were without animals, for most of them had been turned loose for want of forage; and with a large number wounded, considering the strength of the party. It is difficult to conceive how they could have escaped, had it not been for the opportune arrival of Lieutenant Grey. Pico retired on the junction of Grey's party with Kearney's, and, after a weary march, they arrived at San Diego on the 12th of December.

After resting for a time at San Diego, Stockton and Kearney prepared an expedition against the capital; and Stockton, who had been acting as governor, offered to turn over the whole charge of affairs to General Kearney, but this he refused at that time to accept. From this circumstance as to who was in reality the true governor of California there was afterward much trouble, and many bitter enmities were created. I do not pretend to give an opinion as to the rights or wrongs of that matter.

Everything being prepared, Stockton and Kearney set out to capture the Cuidad de los Angeles, Kearney acting as commander of the troops, and Stockton accompanying the expedition in the character of governor.

On their approach to the San Gabriel River the enemy was discovered on the opposite bank. This was on the 8th of January, 1847. Here the dragoons, who were serving on foot, behaved well, and the enemy was routed. The next day the force, which consisted of dragoons, sailors, marines, and volunteers, again met the enemy on the Plains of Mesa, near the capital, where another skirmish took place. In this the enemy was again worsted, and on the 10th the American force entered the city.

In the meantime, Fremont, who was in the northern portion of California, had organised a body of volunteers, and, after a secret march of one hundred and fifty miles, surprised the Mission of San Luis Obispo, capturing the *commandant* and thirty-five others. The *commandant*, Don Jesus Pico, was a prisoner on parole at the time of his capture. He was tried by a court-martial and sentenced to death, but this was remitted by Fremont.

After this Lieutenant-Colonel Fremont marched to the Cuidad de los Angeles, where he met Stockton and Kearney. The Mexicans by this time saw the futility of their efforts, and, at the convention on the Plains of Couenga, the leaders of the revolt capitulated, and quiet was re stored to California. When the troubles with the Mexicans ceased, our own officers commenced quarrelling, and a most serious misunderstanding took place as to who was the actual governor.

Charges were preferred against Fremont for not obeying Kearney, and both of those officers returned to the States, leaving Colonel Richard B. Mason, 1st Dragoons, acting as governor, to which place he had been appointed by the President.

Fremont was tried and found guilty of the charges preferred against him, and was sentenced to be dismissed; but the President, in consideration of his valuable services to the country, remitted the sentence. Lieutenant-Colonel Fremont was stung by what he considered the injustice done him, and resigned on the 15th of March, 1848.

CHAPTER 4

Third Regiment of Dragoons Formed in 1847

While these events were transpiring on the shores of the Pacific, Brigadier-General John E. Wool was organising a force at San Antonio, Texas, for the purpose of marching upon and capturing the city of Chihuahua, which is the most considerable city in Northwestern Mexico. This force started from San Antonio on the 26th of September, 1846, and contained, besides the regular artillery under Captain Washington, two regiments of Illinois Volunteer Infantry, one battalion of regulars, four companies of the 2nd Dragoons, under Colonel Harney, and the Arkansas cavalry, under Colonel Yell.

General Wool proceeded to the Rio Grande, and crossed that stream near the old Presidio, below Laredo; thence, taking a northwesterly course, he passed through Nava and San Fernando to Santa Kosa. At this place he found his progress impeded on account of the bad state of the roads, and the uninhabited condition of the country between that place and Chihuahua. There are long stretches of country almost destitute of water, and the grass almost burned out by the intense heats of the summer sun. This tract is inhabited by roving bands of Comanche and Apache Indians, who move about from the headwaters of the Arkansas to the Pacific Ocean, their wealth consisting of immense herds of wild horses.

Upon consultation, Wool turned to the left and marched to Monclova, whence he sent word to General Taylor at Monterey, stating his reasons for not moving forward. Taylor agreed with his views, and, sending a letter to the Secretary of War, asked to have the force under General Wool added to his own, and the expedition to Chihuahua abandoned for the present. The Secretary of War assented to this, as the benefits which it was supposed would be derived from the expedition were found to be not at all commensurate with the cost to the government, and Wool's column was added to Taylor's.

Major-General Scott visited the Rio Grande in the month of January, 1817, and, preparatory to his march into the interior, found it necessary to withdraw from General Taylor some of his best troops, leaving enough, however, to protect the valley of the Rio Grande. It was hard for Taylor to part with these men, but the exigencies of the service demanded it, and they started for Tampico and other places *en route* for Vera Cruz. The greater portion of the dragoons were sent with Scott.

After their departure, Taylor, although suffering from mortification at what he supposed was an injustice to him, put his army in the best condition he was able, and advanced to Saltillo. A large Mexican force was believed to be marching upon that place, but as yet no positive evidence of it had been obtained. Before the arrival of the general at Saltillo, a small party of the Arkansas cavalry had been sent out to make such discoveries as were possible, under command of Major Borland. He proceeded some distance, and was about to return, when he was joined by another party of the 1st Kentucky Cavalry, under Major Gaines and Captain Cassius M. Clay.

The parties moved forward to a place called Encarnacion. This was on the night of the 21st of January. General Miñon, of the Mexican Army, with a large force, was nearby, and, learning the exact position of the Americans, quietly surrounded the *hacienda* where they were encamped, and the next morning all of them were taken prisoners. Two majors, two captains, one lieutenant, and sixty-six cavalry men were captured, and sent as prisoners to the city of Mexico. On the morning of the 26th of January, another party of the Kentucky cavalry, consisting of seventeen men, under Captain Heady, was captured by Lieutenant-Colonel Cruz, and was likewise sent to the city of Mexico.

The only man who made his escape at the time Borland's party was taken was Captain Dan Drake Henrie, of Texas, acting as interpreter, who had previously been a prisoner in the hands of the Mexicans, and who believed he would be murdered as soon as he became known to them. When the Americans found they were surrounded, Henrie made known his fears to Major Gaines, and asked him to let him mount his mare, which was known to be very fleet, and a most excellent animal. As the Mexican lancers crowded round, Henrie pretended to be trying to hold the mare, but was, in reality, pressing her against them.

They gave way a little for her, which he, discovering, sprang upon her back and darted off. Several volleys were fired after him, but the mare was true as steel, and away she went to the mountains. They both escaped, but, having no water, this beautiful animal fell dead, and Henrie was obliged to make the best of his way alone. He dared not visit any of the farmhouses along the route, and, after almost unheard-of sufferings, reached our army three days after his escape, having had nothing to eat except a mouse or two which he had caught while far off the main road. When found by our people he was almost deranged, and it was a long time before he recovered from the effects of his trials. His escape was one of the most remarkable ever known.

General Taylor arrived at Saltillo, and, after staying a short time, moved his force past the *rancho* of Buena Vista and the pass of L'Angostura to Agua Nueva, where he had a better drill-ground for his volunteers than he could find elsewhere. In going forward, he had made up his mind, in case of an action coming on, to fall back to the pass of L'Angostura, which was narrow and easily defended, and there give battle to the enemy. Up to this time it was uncertain what the Mexicans intended to do, and no knowledge of the force in front was in Taylor's possession. To make everything secure, and learn as much as possible of the enemy, he sent Brevet Lieutenant-Colonel May, with one squadron of the 1st, one squadron of the 2nd Dragoons, and some volunteer cavalry, to the *rancho* of La Hedionda and beyond, to try and discover the enemy.

He reached that place on the afternoon of the 20th of February, and thence sent out several parties to scour the country in all directions. In the distance signal fires were seen rising up from the tops of the hills, and to the east clouds of dust indicated the movement of a large body of troops. Second Lieutenant Samuel D. Sturgis, of the dragoons, was sent to the top of a hill to obtain a better view, accompanied by only one dragoon, when both were captured by the enemy and carried off.

May remained out all night, and next morning returned to General Taylor, and announced that the enemy was advancing in force. Upon the receipt of this information his soldiers fell back, as had been his intention before, from Agua Nueva, to a position in front of the *rancho* of Buena Vista. Leaving his army for a short time, Taylor, with a squadron of the 2nd Dragoons and a, regiment of volunteers, went back to Saltillo to satisfy himself that all was right there, and to keep the garrison of that place, which was very small, in as good spirits as possible. This was on the night of the 21st of February. The next morning, he returned to the field, but, in the meantime, the battle had commenced under orders of Generals Wool and Lane.

The attack was made by a heavy column of Mexican lancers and infantry, who pushed a portion of our volunteer infantry back, and then attacked the cavalry regiments of Kentucky and Arkansas in the most determined manner; but they with stood the shock, and night put an end to the first day's conflict. On the 23rd another and the final battle was fought, and Santa Anna was forced back, with his Mexican hordes, never to appear again on the northern frontier in any very considerable numbers. The fight on this day between our cavalry and the Mexican lancers was most deadly, and several of our cavalry officers fell. Colonel Yell and Captain Porter, of the 1st Arkansas Cavalry, were killed, and Lieutenant Reeder was wounded. Adjutant Vaughan was killed, and Captain Shawhan, and Lieutenants Brown, Merrifield, and Conn, of the 1st Kentucky Cavalry, were wounded.

In the 1st Regiment of Dragoons Captain Steen was wounded, and was made a brevet Major for gallantry; Captains Chilton, Rucker, and Carleton were made brevet Majors; Lieutenant Abram Buford, brevet Captain; and Second Lieutenants Whittlesey and Evans, brevet First Lieutenants.

In the 2nd Dragoons Brevet Lieutenant-Colonel May was made a brevet Colonel; First Lieutenant Reuben P. Campbell, brevet Captain; and Second Lieutenants Givens and Wood, brevet First Lieutenants.

This battle, particularly in the West, has been always looked upon as the most severe one ever fought on American soil, and no doubt it was true until the breaking out of the Rebellion; still, officers differed in opinion, and many considered Molino del Rey a much more severely contested action. The cavalry made one most gallant charge against the enemy on the 23rd of February, and cut their way through them; but the Mexican lancers were far from being a contemptible enemy, and many of them were admirable horsemen.

Our people had the advantage of larger horses and heavier men as a general thing, but the Mexicans were much more agile, and could handle their horses as well perhaps as any people on earth. With the lance they were greatly our superiors, and used that weapon with great effect both at Buena Vista and at San Pascual. We have yet to make good lancers in the United States, as experiments, even on a small scale, have proved failures among the Americans.

Torrejon and Miñon were both good cavalry officers in the Mexican Army, and could handle their troops easily. Their forces greatly exceeded ours in numbers, and their irregular troops were no doubt better, as the Mexicans, accustomed as many of them are to a life on horseback, and all of them feeling a pride in owning horse flesh, it did not take so long a time to train them as it did ours, who, particularly those from the older states, know little or nothing about riding or managing horses. The Mexicans are most relentless riders, and their poor horses sometimes suffer dreadfully at their hands.

On the 11th of February, 1847, Congress passed what was known as the "Ten Regiment Bill," by which one regiment (the 3rd) of Dragoons was ordered to be raised "for and during the war with Mexico," and giving two majors to each regiment of the line. Major Eustace Trenor, of the 1st Dragoons, died in New York city on the 16th of February, 1847. Nathan Boone, Senior Captain of the 1st Dragoons, and a son of Daniel Boone, of Kentucky, was promoted in place of Trenor. Captain Benjamin N. Beall, of the 2nd Dragoons, was promoted Major of the 1st; and Captain Philip St. George Cooke, of the 1st, Major of the 2nd Regiment. Captain William W. Loring was promoted Major in the Mounted Rifle Regiment.

Edward G.W. Butler, of Louisiana, a graduate of West Point, was appointed Colonel of the 3rd Dragoons; Thomas P. Moore, of Kentucky, was appointed Lieutenant-Colonel; Lieutenant William H. Emory, of the Topographical Engineers, and Lewis Cass, junior, of Michigan, were appointed Majors on the 9th of April, 1847. Emory declined, whereupon William H. Polk, a brother of the then President, was appointed, August 31st, 1847.

Major-General Scott landed with his army of invasion near Vera Cruz, Mexico, in March, 1847, and, after a somewhat protracted investment and bombardment, that city, with the Castle of San Juan d'Ulloa, fell into the hands of the Americans. While the bombardment was going on the dragoons arrived, and refitted at Vergara, above the city, and on the shores of the Gulf of Mexico. The horses were many of them lost in crossing the Gulf, and for many days a portion of the dragoons were dismounted.

A fight took place, however, between them and a party of the enemy at the Medelin River, on the 25th of March, 1847. The enemy had been prowling about for several days, when Colonel Harney determined to beat the bush for them. Accordingly, he started, with Thornton's squadron of dragoons and fifty dismounted men, under Captain Ker, in the direction of the river above named, and continued without opposition until near the stone bridge of Morena, which he found fortified, and protected by a force of lancers, with two pieces of artillery.

Seeing this, Harney fell back, as he had not force enough to fight the enemy successfully. As soon as this was known in camp, Captain Hardee, who was disembarking his horses, started with what men he could gather to go to Harney's assistance. Both Thornton and Hardee had been prisoners among the Mexicans, and had been exchanged. Harney, having increased his force by the addition of some volunteers and two pieces of artillery, started on his return to the attack.

He formed his infantry on the right and left near the bridge, and Lieutenant Judd, with the cannon, opened fire upon the barricades. This was returned for some time, when he ordered the infantry and dismounted dragoons to charge, and those who were on horseback to follow. The barricade was quickly leaped, but the Mexicans fell back and formed beyond the bridge. Harney ordered it cleared, and sent Sumner with the dragoons across it at a gallop. On their approach the footmen fled into the woods, and the lancers were met and completely routed. Lieutenants Lowry and Oakes pursued a party of lancers some distance, and killed and wounded several of them. Major Sumner and Lieutenant Sibley, with another party of dragoons, pursued another body of lancers, killing and wounding several, as far as the village of Madeline, six miles distant.

Lieutenant Neill, in advance, came up with two lancers, who turned upon him, and inflicted two severe lance wounds upon him, from the effects of which he fell from his horse. Neill behaved most gallantly, and Colonel Harney complimented his whole command for their good conduct in this affair. Our loss was trifling, and that of the Mexicans did not amount to anything very serious; but it was a fine race after a party of the enemy who had ventured too near our people, and were consequently worsted. Captains William J. Hardee and Henry H. Sibley were made brevet Majors for their conduct, and Second Lieutenants Lewis Neill and James Oakes were made brevet First Lieutenants all of the 2nd Dragoons. Second Lieutenant Orren Chapman, 1st Dragoons, was also breveted First Lieutenant.

After this the regiments were put in the best shape possible, and the army started on its way to the interior. The progress was slow, as our people were obliged to wait for supplies of every kind to be received from the States, and it was nearly a month before they made much progress. In April it was known that Santa Anna had taken command of the Mexicans in front of General Scott's army, and had been engaged in throwing up various defences at Cerro Gordo, on the road to the city of Mexico. He had with him a portion of the Mexican forces which had fought at Buena Vista, and had reorganised an army, which, considering the opposition he had to contend with among his own people, was really remarkable, and proved him to be, what many have been unwilling to admit him to be, a most able and talented man, and a soldier by no means to be despised. Had he commanded American troops, and had the resources which the United States could command, the story of the Mexican War would read differently.

In the Battle of Cerro Gordo, on the 17th and 18th of April, 1847, the dragoons did not play a conspicuous part, as they were not called upon to do anything until the enemy was retreating, when a squadron under Captain Blake, and some companies under Major Beall, pursued the enemy far out on the Jalapa road, and took some prisoners; but the Mounted Rifle Regiment behaved most admirably, and won a proud name for itself on that occasion. It was commanded in the commencement of the action by Major Sumner, of the 2nd Dragoons, when, he falling from a severe wound in the head, the command devolved upon Major William W. Loring. As before remarked, the regiment served on foot at this battle.

On the 17th of April the first squadron of the regiment, after moving up, was halted about four hundred yards from the point of attack, partly under cover from the enemy's batteries. While waiting thus, it was fired upon by the batteries and the skirmishers of the enemy. The squadron was deployed, and a charge ordered; at the same time, the rest of the regiment and a company of infantry attacked the enemy on the summit and farther slope of the hill, and they were driven from their position.

In this attack Major Sumner was wounded, and was carried to the rear. The Rifles were then deployed, and, with the 1st Artillery, drove the enemy from their position. The regiment was then employed in sustaining a battery of mountain howitzers, and in preventing the enemy turning our left. It remained here during the night of the 17th, and assisted in placing the heavy guns which were brought up in position. At dawn of day, it was ordered to prepare for battle. Loring, in his report says:

At an early hour, and before the attack upon the main work, a large succouring force was seen advancing on the Jalapa road.

The Rifles were ordered to pass to the left, attract the attention of the enemy, and keep them in check until the storming of the heights commenced, in which the regiment was to join on the left flank. During this diversion it was exposed to a galling and destructive fire of round, grape, canister, and musketry, upon its front and both flanks, from the enemy's three main intrenchments and batteries, from which it suffered great loss. In this movement a large force of the enemy was held in check, which, from its position, would have been able to have turned the assaulting column.

The general assault having been ordered, a portion of the regiment joining in it, the works having been carried before the whole line, which was necessarily extended to the left, could possibly reach the heights: this being effected, the regiment, with others, was placed in position on the heights. In a very short time, the enemy surrendered. The regiment of Mounted Riflemen followed, in company with others, the retreating army to within ten miles of Jalapa.

Lieutenants Thomas Ewell and Thomas Davis were killed while displaying the greatest gallantry. Captain Stevens T. Mason had his leg carried off by a round shot, and died soon after.

Lieutenant Dabney H. Maurey was severely wounded, as were Lieutenants Alfred Gibbs and George H. Gordon.

Major Sumner was breveted Lieutenant-Colonel, and Second Lieutenants Frost, Maurey, Gibbs, and Gordon were breveted First Lieutenants for gallantry and meritorious conduct in this battle. The total loss to the regiment was seventy-eight killed and wounded. Colonel Harney, of the 2nd Dragoons, commanded the brigade to which it was attached, and he was breveted Brigadier-General for his good conduct.

The immediate results of this battle were the possession of the city of Jalapa by the Americans, the abandonment of the works and artillery at La Hoya, and the occupation of the Castle of Perote, which was nearly as large as the Castle of San Juan d'Ulloa, and which contained a vast amount of ordnance and ordnance stores.

Scott's army continued to march to Puebla. In the meantime, the term of service of many of the volunteer regiments was expiring, and it became necessary to wait for re-enforcements from the States, which were expected in the shape of the new regiments which had been a thorised by Congress. It was not until the summer had set in that these began to arrive in sufficient numbers to do much good. While one of these columns of new troops was on its way up from Vera Cruz to Puebla, it was greatly annoyed by the guerrillas, which commenced swarming along the way.

Captain Charles F. Ruff, with his company of Mounted Rifles, they having by good fortune secured horses, and one company of the 2nd Dragoons, were sent out against a party of them at San Juan de los Llanos, on the 1st of August, 1847. Their den was found not far from the main road, when a most spirited skirmish took place, and they were badly used up. The Rifles dismounted, and drove them out of a *hacienda* by sharp-shooting through the windows. For gallantry in this affair Ruff was made brevet Major; First Lieutenant John G. Walker, of the Rifles, brevet Captain; and Second Lieutenant James M. Hawes, 2nd Dragoons, brevet First Lieutenant. Their loss was forty or fifty killed and wounded.

A company of the 3rd Regiment of Dragoons had a fight at the National Bridge while they were on their way up from the sea-coast, and behaved well. A barricade had been erected on the bridge to stop their progress, but General Pierce ordered our men to carry the work at once. Lieutenant-Colonel Bonham, of the 12th Infantry, at the head of his battalion, rushed forward under a heavy fire from the enemy's *escopets*, followed by Captain Duperu, with his company of the 3rd Dragoons, sword in hand. The men leaped over the barricades, and the horsemen followed, when, after a spirited fight of ten minutes, the enemy were seen flying in all directions, and did not again make their appearance while that column was nearby.

The Mexican guerrillas were bodies of men formed, it is believed, by their own government, or sometimes self-constituted, who thought their mission was to annoy and harass our troops as much as possible. They were led by men of the most unscrupulous character, and all laws of war were set aside and disregarded by them. They were most relentless foes, and their operations were carried on with the greatest cruelty toward those who were unfortunate enough to fall into their power. Our men preferred death to getting into their hands, and in our fights with them no quarter was expected on either side.

The costume of these guerrillas was picturesque, and they were generally mounted on horses which, though small, possessed much spirit, and were capable of enduring great fatigue. These horses were descended, no doubt, from those which were brought to that country by the Spaniards during and soon after the conquest of Mexico, and many of them bore traces of Arabian blood. Their progenitors had some of them escaped, or had been reared on the immense plains of Northwestern Mexico or Texas, where to this day large herds of them, perfectly wild, may frequently be seen.

Some of the horse-raisers of Mexico have great numbers of horses; and it is related of one widow lady, who had a *hacienda* near the city of Durango, that she fitted out a Mexican colonel's regiment with a full supply of horses which were perfectly white, all of which was a free gift. This story is so well authenticated as to leave no doubt about it. Their horse furniture consisted of a bridle made of white leather or horsehair, some of which were very beautiful, with an immense bit and curb, which was capable of breaking a horse's jaw by one jerk of the rider. The saddles were also very tastefully ornamented, generally with silver, with a high pommel and cantle. They also carried a long rope, or lasso, called by them a *riata*, and by our people a lariat.

The men wore large broad-brimmed hats, which are most unpleasant things to wear in a wind, but which, are excellent to shield against the sun's rays. Their jackets were made of leather, velvet, or cloth, and generally embroidered most elaborately by some fair *senorita*. Their trowsers were wide open at the sides, which were buttoned up by long rows of silver or even gold buttons, and sometimes little bells. They had also tiny bells on their hats and on their immense spurs. Their weapons were a sword, carried under the left leg, whereby it was prevented from dangling about; a pistol or two; an *escopet*, or short musket, not generally very available; and their lasso, which they could throw with amazing dexterity and effect.

They prowled about the American Army, annoyed our trains, murdered our soldiers when straggling, and cut to pieces such small parties as they were able to overpower.

General Scott marched on with his army, and entered the broad and beautiful valley of Mexico in August. This beautiful spot was soon to be the scene of great deeds, and the American soldiers were to win a lasting fame. To give a clear and concise view of the part taken by the dragoons at the Battles of Contreras and Churubusco on the 20th of August, 1847, I copy Colonel Harney's report, he being Commander of the Cavalry Brigade.

In proper order, however, ought to be mentioned the cavalry skirmish at San Augustine on the 17th of August, on account of which Captain Blake, of the 2nd Dragoons, was made a brevet Major; Hardee, a brevet Lieutenant-Colonel; and Second Lieutenant Richard H. Anderson was made a brevet First Lieutenant. It was a skirmish of some importance, and the Mexicans were defeated, as usual.

Colonel Harney says, in writing at Tacubaya, Mexico, August 24th, 1847:

> The cavalry force being necessarily weakened by detachments to the different divisions of the army, I found myself, on the morning of the 19th instant, in the immediate command of nine companies only, consisting of six companies of the 2nd Dragoons, one company of Mounted Riflemen, and two companies of Mounted Volunteers. With this force I was ordered by the general-in-chief to report to Brigadier-General Twiggs, who was at this time covering Major-General Pillow's division in an effort to make a road through the ridge of lava which forms the pass of San Antonio. Owing to the nature of the ground, I was compelled to halt within range of the enemy's shells, and to remain in this position for several hours, an idle spectator of the action which ensued. After night I returned with my command to San Augustine, and remained there until the enemy's position at Contreras was carried on the morning of the 20th.
>
> As soon as the road was ascertained to be opened and practicable for cavalry, I was directed by the general-in-chief to proceed, with two squadrons and Captain McKinstry's company of volunteers, to the field of battle, and to take charge of the prisoners which had been captured. While in the execution of this order, I received instructions from the general-in-chief to leave one squadron in charge of the prisoners, and to report to him in person with the other three companies. Captain Blake, with his squadron, was directed to perform this duty; while Major Sumner and myself, with Captain Ker's squadron and Captain McKinstry's company of volunteers, joined the commanding general near the field of Churubusco just after the engagement at that place had commenced.
>
> The reports of Major Sumner, commanding 1st Battalion, and Lieutenant-Colonel Moore, commanding 2nd Battalion, which I have the honour to forward herewith, will show in what manner the other troops and squadrons of my command were employed. The three troops of horse brought by me on the field

being ordered away in different directions, Major Sumner and myself soon found ourselves without commands.

I then employed myself with my staff in rallying fugitives and encouraging our troops on the left of the main road. Major Sumner, toward the close of the engagement, was placed by the general-in-chief in charge of the last reserve, consisting of the rifle regiment and one company of horse, and was ordered to support the left. This force was moving rapidly to take its position in line of battle, when the enemy broke and fled to the city. At this moment, perceiving that the enemy were retreating in disorder on one of the main causeways leading to the city of Mexico, I collected all the cavalry with in my reach, consisting of parts of Captain Ker's company of 2nd Dragoons, Captain Kearney's company of 1st Dragoons, and Captains McReynolds and Duperu's companies of the 3rd Dragoons, and pursued them vigorously until we were halted by the discharge of the batteries at their gate.

Many of the enemy were overtaken in the pursuit, and cut down by our sabres. I cannot speak in terms too complimentary of the manner in which this charge was executed. My only difficulty was in restraining the impetuosity of my men and officers, who seemed to vie with each other who should be foremost in the pursuit. Captain Philip Kearney gallantly led his squadron into the very entrenchments of the enemy, and had the misfortune to lose an arm from a grape-shot fired from a gun at one of the main gates of the capital. Captain McReynolds and Lieutenant Graham were also wounded, and Lieutenant Ewell had two horses shot under him.

Great praise is due to Major Sumner, commanding 1st Battalion, for his zeal, energy, and promptitude, and for the gallant manner in which he led up the last reserve of the general-in-chief.

It is much to be regretted that the 2nd Battalion, under the command of Lieutenant-Colonel Moore, was so cut up by detachments as to materially weaken its efficiency, and to impair the usefulness of that officer, who was always at the post of danger, and anxious to participate in the conflict. My warmest thanks are due to my brigade staff, consisting of Captain Wood, A. Q. M., Lieutenant Steele, A. A. Gen., and Lieutenant Julian May, my *aide-de-camp*, who were actively employed on the morning of the 20th in rallying our men, and who exhibited the utmost coolness and bravery under a heavy fire of the enemy. The two last-named officers were foremost in the pursuit, and Lieutenant Steele cut down three of the enemy with his sabre. In conclusion, I beg leave to state that the dragoons, from the commencement of the march from Puebla, have been engaged on the most active and laborious service.

These duties have been the more arduous in consequence of the small force of cavalry compared with the other arms of service. Small parties being constantly engaged in reconnoitring and on picket guards, the utmost vigilance and precaution have been required to prevent surprise and disaster. The gallant Captain Thornton, while reconnoitring the enemy near San Antonio on the 18th instant, was shot through the body by a cannon shot, and instantly killed. His death is much to be regretted. On the 20th, although I had but four companies of my brigade with me on the field, the remainder were actively employed in the performance of important and indispensable duties. Captain Hardee, while watching the enemy with his company near San Augustine, was attacked by a band of guerrillas, but the enemy was promptly and handsomely repulsed, and a number of their horses, with arms and accoutrements, captured.

The Mounted Rifle Regiment, under Major Loring, bore a conspicuous and honourable part in the Battles of Contreras and Churubusco, and Lieutenant Michael E. Van Buren was reported severely wounded in the former action. It served on foot, not having yet procured horses, with the exception of two companies, one of which at that time was not in the valley.

The following brevets were conferred on account of these battles in the mounted regiments, but it must be borne in mind that some of them were not given until a year or two afterward. In the 1st Dragoons, Captain Philip Kearney, who lost his left arm, was made a brevet Major; First Lieutenants Richard S. Ewell and Lorimer Graham were made brevet Captains.

In the 2nd Dragoons, First Lieutenants William Steele and Philip W. McDonald were made brevet Captains; and Second Lieutenant Arthur D. Tree was made a brevet First Lieutenant,

In the 3rd Dragoons, Captain Andrew T. McReynolds was made a brevet Major; and First Lieutenant Herman Thorn a brevet Captain.

In the Mounted Rifle Regiment, Captains Winslow F. Sanderson,

George B. Crittenden, Jacob B. Backenstoss, and Andrew Porter, were made Majors by brevet.

First Lieutenant Michael E. Van Buren was made a brevet Captain; and Second Lieutenants McLane, May, Hatch, Granger, Palmer, Stuart, were made brevet First Lieutenants from Churubusco.

Second Lieutenant Robert M. Morris was made a brevet First Lieutenant from Contreras.

Captain Seth B. Thornton, 2nd Dragoons, was killed by the first cannon shot which was fired at San Antonio, near the city of Mexico, by the Mexicans. It literally tore him to pieces. There was something very sad in the fate of this daring and high-toned officer. He was first to meet with a reverse before the Battle of Palo Alto, in which he was severely wounded, and was the first officer who fell in the valley of Mexico. His defeat by the Mexicans preyed upon his spirits, and, though suffering from ill health, he continued to do his duty until stricken by the fatal shot. His loss was deplored by the whole army.

After the Battles of Contreras and Churubusco, an armistice was agreed upon by the authorities, and our army drew its supplies for a time from the city of Mexico itself, pack-mules going in at night and returning laden with rations, etc. This was, of course, done by consent of the Mexican general, and was an understanding at the time the armistice was entered upon. This armistice continued until the 7th of September, when General Scott, believing the Mexicans were acting in bad faith, ordered it to be brought to an end.

Hostilities of an active character commenced soon afterward, and on the 8th of September, 1847, was fought the Battle of Molino del Rey. As to the part enacted by the mounted men in that battle, I subjoin Major Sumner's report:

My command, consisted of six troops of the 2nd Dragoons, one troop of the 1st Dragoons, a part of a troop of the 3rd Dragoons (under the command of Lieutenant C. D, Williams, 3rd Dragoons), and Captain Ruff's company of Mounted Riflemen—in all, about 270 men. My orders were to take a position on the left of our line, to hold in check the enemy's cavalry, and to give a blow to their horse or foot if an opportunity should offer. In taking up my position I was compelled to pass within pistol-shot of a large body of the enemy, who were protected by a ditch and breastworks. This exposure of my command was entirely unavoidable in consequence of a deep ditch on my left, which was impossible to cross until I got very close to their line; and I could not pause at that moment, as a very large body of the enemy's cavalry was advancing toward the left of our line. After passing through this fire and crossing a ravine, I formed my command in line facing the enemy's cavalry, on which they halted, and shortly afterward retired. I continued to hold my command on the left flank of our line until the enemy's infantry broke and retired, changing my position from time to time in order to face their cavalry whenever they advanced. I should have joined in the pursuit of their infantry when they broke; but in doing this I should have uncovered our left, and their large cavalry force was still maintaining a menacing attitude, covered and protected as it was by a large *hacienda* filled with troops.

My loss in passing their line of fire was severe, *viz.*, five officers and thirty-three soldiers wounded, and six soldiers killed; twenty-seven horses killed, and seventy-seven wounded. Captain Ker, of the 2nd Dragoons, First Lieutenant Walker, of the Rifles, and Second Lieutenants Smith and Tree, of the 2nd Dragoons, and Second Lieutenant C. D. Williams, of the 3rd Dragoons, were wounded, but, I am happy to state, not dangerously. My officers and men maintained their character for steadiness and confidence throughout the action. They all did well; but I must notice, in particular, the successful efforts of Captain Hardee in maintaining order in his squadron during the many evolutions that it was necessary to make with great rapidity. I have also to state that Assistant Surgeon Barnes was very assiduous in his duties, and took such measures that our wounded men received prompt attention. I have also the pleasure to report that I received effective aid from my adjutant, Lieutenant Oakes.

Lieutenant-Colonel Moore, of the 3rd Dragoons, joined me after the action commenced, and did me the great favour to abstain from assuming the command. His presence, however, was of great service to me, and his example of the most perfect coolness under fire had a favourable influence upon my command.

Colonel Harney, who was quite unwell, also came upon the field during the action, and, after observing my measures for some time, expressed himself satisfied with them, and said to me that he would not assume the command, for which I am deeply obliged to him.

Lieutenant Herman Thorn, of the 3rd Dragoons, was also wounded. The Mounted Rifle Regiment did not participate in this battle, which was fought almost entirely by Worth's division. Sumner was made a brevet Colonel, and Oakes a brevet Captain, for good conduct. No other mounted officers were breveted.

The storming of Chapultepec, which was a strong castle near the city of Mexico, and used as a military school, occurred on the 13th of September, 1847. In this action, as well as along the causeways leading toward the city, and entering it by the Belen Gate, the Mounted Rifle Regiment displayed the greatest gallantry. The city was entered and captured on the 14th of the same month.

The dragoons had no opportunity of doing much service on entering the city. The loss to the Rifles was, in killed and wounded, seventy-nine. Colonel Persifer F. Smith, of this regiment, had received the brevet of Brigadier-General for his conduct at Monterey, and was afterward breveted Major-General for Contreras and Churubusco.

Major Loring, who commanded the Rifles, was breveted Colonel for good conduct, and lost an arm at the assault on De Belen Gate. Captain Simonson was wounded, and made brevet Major at Chapultepec; Captain Backenstoss was wounded, and made brevet Lieutenant-Colonel; Captain Tucker was wounded, and made brevet Major; Captain Roberts, brevet Major; Captain Andrew Porter, brevet Lieutenant-Colonel; Lieutenant McLane, brevet Captain; Lieutenant Morris, brevet Captain; Second Lieutenant Russell, wounded, brevet First Lieutenant; Lieutenant Hatch, brevet Captain; Lieutenant Granger, brevet Captain; Lieutenant Palmer, wounded, brevet Captain; Lieutenant Stuart, brevet Captain. Lieutenant Gibbs, brevet Captain from De Belen Gate.

Lieutenant McDonald, of the 2nd Dragoons, serving as *aide-de-camp* to Major-General Twiggs, was made brevet Major from Chapultepec.

On the morning of the 14th the citadel was taken possession of by General Quitman's division. Here, understanding that great depredations were going on in the National Palace and public buildings, he moved his column in that direction through the principal streets to the great square, where he formed it in front of the palace. Captain Roberts, of the Mounted Rifle Regiment, who had led the advance company of the storming party at Chapultepec, and had greatly distinguished himself during the preceding day, was detailed by the general to plant the star-spangled banner of our countrymen upon the National Palace. This flag, the first strange banner which had ever waved over that palace since the conquest of Cortez, was displayed, and saluted with enthusiasm by the whole command.

General Quitman, in his report, pays the following high compliment to the Rifles:

> This report, has already shown the prominent part taken by the regiment of Mounted Riflemen, under the command of the brave and intrepid Major Loring, who fell severely wounded by my side while receiving orders for the final charge upon the Gate of Belen. After the taking of the batteries of Chapultepec, in which portions of this corps took an active part, this efficient and splendid regiment were employed as sharp-shooters in the advance, through the arches of the aqueduct, where their services were invaluable. My only concern was to restrain their daring impetuosity.

Major-General Scott and his staff, in full uniform, entered the capital at eight o'clock, escorted by Major Sumner with his battalion of cavalry. It was a most imposing spectacle, and one which has been, and will for years to come be celebrated in song and story. The pages of romance furnish no parallel to the conquest of the beautiful and lovely land of Mexico. It is emphatically the chosen place of God, and is without equal on earth. Its fair plains covered with matchless verdure; its uplands teeming with abundant harvests; and its glorious old mountains piled up among the fleecy clouds. How much—how very much the Almighty has done for that fair land, and how little has man seconded His efforts!

When all of the troops had made their way into the city, they were sent to their several stations, and the cavalry brigade, under Colonel Harney, was ordered to occupy the cavalry barracks near the National Palace. The city of Mexico was in possession of the Americans. It is the most ancient as well as the most splendid capital on the American continent, and contained at that time about two hundred thousand inhabitants, and teemed with the white domes of churches and shady *pascos*. A beautiful *alameda*, or public garden, was within its limits; a magnificent cathedral; and the "Halls of the Montezumas," or National Palace, which, though not lofty or imposing in appearance, was well arranged, and had cost an immense sum of money.

CHAPTER 5

Third Regiment of Dragoons Disbanded, 1848

While the events recorded had been transpiring in the valley of Mexico and along the Rio Grande, Colonel Doniphan, with his regiment of Missouri cavalry, had been invading Mexico, and had made a famous march.

When General Kearney left Santa Fé, Doniphan was left at that place with orders to make a campaign against the Navajo Indians, and afterward to join General Wool's column at Chihuahua; it being, of course, then unknown to both these officers that the proposed expedition to that place under General Wool from San Antonio, Texas, had been broken up, and his forces transferred to General Taylor.

On the 26th of October, 1846, he started from Santa Fé for the invasion of the country occupied by the Navajo Indians. This is a semi-civilized tribe inhabiting the country west of a range of mountains bounding the Rio Grande, and extending down the tributaries of the Rio Colorado to near the Pacific Ocean. The country was invaded by three routes. Every portion of their country was visited; and, after near three fourths of them were collected together, a treaty was made with them.

It was late in the season; the cold weather came on, and Doniphan's men were obliged to march over a ground covered with snow, and suffering much from intense cold. Finally, however, he reached Valverde, a town on the Rio Grande, in New Mexico, where he refitted, and prepared to set out on his march to Chihuahua.

On the 18th of December, 1846, he left Valverde with his command, which did not exceed eight hundred and fifty-six men, including two small parties which had preceded him. At Donna Aña his whole force, including Clarke's battery of artillery, was consolidated.

On the 25th, when near Brazito, as he was about to encamp for the night, and the men were bringing in wood and water, the enemy was reported advancing.

Soon a messenger, bearing a black flag, from the Mexicans, came into his camp, and demanded his surrender. This was declined, when a smart skirmish took place, and the enemy was beaten back and retired. The loss to both sides was trifling. On the evening of the 27th of December, he entered the town of El Paso, where he remained until the following February, waiting the arrival of his artillery, with his baggage and provision train. It is hardly fair to call this a battle, but Doniphan and his men considered it so, though his own loss was "none killed, seven wounded, all since recovered." Still, it was a gallant affair, and the Missourians were entitled to much credit.

On the evening of the 8th of February, he left El Paso with a large train for Chihuahua, his own force numbering but little more than one thousand men. His march was undisturbed for several days; but on the 28th, when near the pass of Sacramento, he learned that the enemy in considerable force was waiting for him. This pass is formed by the spur of the mountains which juts down into the plain on the right, and the dry bed of a creek, deep and full of ravines, on the left.

The enemy had considerable artillery well posted, and redoubts had been thrown up under direction of General Garcia Conde, ex-minister of war of Mexico, who was a scientific man, and who had some military knowledge. The artillery was mostly behind these redoubts. The action was commenced by the firing of cannon into the Mexicans, who were drawn up in front of their works. This fire was returned, and the Mexicans retired behind their redoubts. A charge was now ordered by Colonel Doniphan, in which the mounted companies of Captains Reid, Parsons, and Hudson participated, accompanied by two twelve-pounder howitzers under Captain Weightman.

The remainder, who had dismounted, followed on foot, and the enemy was soon put to flight. There is no doubt but this was a daring and gallant charge, and entitled the men to great credit; but the Mexicans gave way at once, not being able to stand the sabres of our men and the scattering fire of the howitzers.

Captain Philip R. Thompson, of the 1st Dragoons, accompanied Doniphan, and acted as his *aide* during the fight. For his good conduct he was made a Major by brevet. Lieutenant Crockett Harrison, of Doniphan's regiment, was wounded.

The loss to the Americans was small considering the number engaged, while that of the Mexicans was very considerable.

The Mexican force consisted of some irregular cavalry from the Mexican states of Durango and Chihuahua, some Vera Cruz dragoons, a corps of artillery, and a body of *rancheros*, or Mexican farmers and labourers, "badly armed with lassos, lances, and *machetos*, or corn-knives," all under the command of Major-General Heredia, assisted by Brigadier-Generals Justiniani and Garcia Conde.

All of their artillery, consisting of two nine, two eight, four six, and two four pounders, and six culverins, or rampart pieces, was captured, but it does not appear that any of this was *very* serviceable.

The victory being complete, the Americans entered the city of Chihuahua on the 1st of March, 1847. Here Doniphan remained for some time regulating the affairs of the Mexicans, and resting from his long and tedious march. He moved from this place to Monterey, Mexico, thence to the mouth of the Rio Grande, and thence by water home to St. Louis, Missouri.

After Doniphan started from Santa Fé, Colonel Sterling Price, of the 2nd Regiment of Missouri Cavalry, was left in command. A revolution broke out among the Mexicans, and Governor Charles Bent, and most of the civil officers of the Territory, were most basely and cruelly murdered by them. These murders occurred at the town of Taos, and Price, upon hearing of them, determined not only to punish the rebels, but to capture and put to death the murderers.

Starting from Santa Fé on the 23rd of January, 1847, with a battalion of Missouri cavalry, some Santa Fé infantry under Captain St. Vrain, and two howitzers under Lieutenant Dyer, he continued his course toward Taos until the afternoon of the 24th, when, near the town of Canada, he discovered the enemy in front. Preparations were immediately made for action. Seeing the enemy had possession of a range of hills beyond a creek nearby, he ordered his howitzers to open upon them, and followed with his men at a charge. The enemy gave way, and retreated toward Taos, after having made an unsuccessful attempt to capture the baggage train. The loss to the Americans was not material, and that of the enemy did not appear to frighten them.

Oh the 27th Price was joined by Captain Burgwin's company of the 1st Dragoons, serving on foot, and a company of Missouri cavalry. With these he continued his march. On the 29th the enemy again made their appearance near the pass of Embudo. They were well posted on the slopes of a steep mountain, whose sides were covered with a thick growth of cedars. Our men climbed the mountain sides, and, upon their approach, the enemy gave ground, retreated across the mountains through the pass, and were followed by our men; but the enemy made good their escape, after suffering the loss of some twenty killed and several wounded.

On the 30th and 31st the column continued its march, and on the 1st of February reached the summit of the Taos Mountain, which was covered with two feet of snow, and on the 2nd encamped near a small village called Rio Chiquito, in the entrance of the valley of Taos.

The march had been severe, most of the men had been frostbitten, and all were jaded by the exertions necessary to travel over unbroken roads, which they had necessarily to do to make a path for the baggage-wagons and artillery. The men bore everything without a murmur, and on the 3rd marched through Don Fernando de Taos to the Pueblo de Taos, which was found to be a place of great strength, surrounded by *adobe* walls and strong pickets.

Within the enclosure were two large buildings, eight stories high, each capable of sheltering five or six hundred men. Besides these there were several smaller buildings and a large church. The walls were pierced for rifles, and the town was well adapted for defence, every point being flanked by projecting buildings.

On the 4th of February, 1847, after a careful reconnaissance, the attack on the town was commenced by a cannonade of the town from the artillery under Major Clark, Lieutenant Dyer, of the Ordnance, and Lieutenant Hassendaubel (the latter was afterward killed at the siege of Vicksburg, while colonel of a loyal Missouri regiment), who kept up a brisk and effective fire.

At a given signal, Captain Burgwin, at the head of his own company and that of Captain McMillan, 2nd Missouri Cavalry, charged the western flank of the church where the enemy had taken a stand, while another party charged the northern wall. As soon as the troops had reached the western flank, axes were used in the attempt to break it; and a temporary ladder having been made, the thatched roof was fired.

About this time, Captain Burgwin, at the head of a small party, left the cover afforded by the flank of the church, and, penetrating into the corral in front of that building, endeavoured to force the door. In this exposed situation he was severely wounded, and died from its effects three days after. Lieutenants McIlvain, of the 1st Dragoons, and William B. Royall and Lackland, of the 2nd Missouri Cavalry, accompanied Captain Burgwin into the corral; but the attempt proved a failure, and they were forced to retire. In the meantime, holes had been cut in

78

the walls of the church, and shells had been thrown in by hand, doing good execution. The enemy had all this time kept up a brisk fire.

About half past three o'clock p.m., a six-pounder was run up within sixty yards of the church, and after ten rounds, one of the holes which had been cut by the axes was widened into a practicable breach. The gun was now run up within ten yards of the wall, a shell was thrown in, followed by three rounds of grape, when the storming-party entered without opposition. The interior of the church was full of smoke, which shielded our men from view of the enemy. They ran out of the church, and many of them fled to the mountains; others took refuge in one of the large houses, and next morning surrendered. The murderers of Governor Bent were captured and punished, as were the leaders of the insurrection.

This was a hard and well-fought affair, and our men deserved great credit. Burgwin, who was a noble man, was shot, as before mentioned, and the 1st Dragoons lost in him one of its best officers. Our men all behaved admirably; and Second Lieutenants Wilson and O. H. P. Taylor, 1st Dragoons, were made brevet First Lieutenants. Lieutenant Joseph McIlvain, of the 1st Dragoons, greatly distinguished himself, and would no doubt have been breveted, but, unfortunately, he accidentally shot himself at Albuquerque, New Mexico, and died on the 12th of July, 1847.

Lieutenant John Mansfield, of the 2nd Missouri Cavalry, was mortally wounded, and died on the 16th of February. Captain Samuel H. McMillan, and Lieutenant Thomas G. West, of the same regiment, were wounded.

Colonel Price's total loss was fifty-two killed and wounded. The enemy lost about one hundred and fifty, as nearly as it could be ascertained.

Captain Israel R. Hendley, of the separate battalion of Missouri Volunteers, was killed at Mora on the 24th of January by a party of insurgents whom he had attacked in a house. Four of his men were killed at the same time.

Colonel Price returned to Santa Fé, but the rebels continued to annoy our people for some time longer. On the 20th of May they surprised Captain Robinson's camp, of the separate battalion of Missouri Volunteers and stampeded and drove off two hundred horses and mules.

At Las Vallas they fell upon Lieutenant Robert T. Brown, of the 2nd Missouri Cavalry, and murdered him and his whole party on the

27th of June; and again, on the 6th of July, at the grazing camp of the separate battalion of Missouri Cavalry, Captain Morris's company was attacked, and Lieutenant John Larkin and four men killed, and nine wounded. These operations were carried on by the half-breed Indians and Mexicans, who possess a most malignant and cruel disposition, and are always ready to commit any act of treachery in their power. The forces under Price were so much diminished by the term of service of the volunteers having expired that he was obliged to keep most of his troops in Santa Fé.

Rumours of insurrections were rife, and it was said that a large force of Mexicans was marching on Santa Fé from Chihuahua. Price, in his letter to the adjutant-general, said:

> I am unable to ascertain, whether these rumours are true or false, but it is certain that the New Mexicans entertain deadly hatred against the Americans, and they will cut off small parties of the latter whenever they think they can escape detection.

It is now time to return to General Scott's line of operations. He was in the city of Mexico; Colonel Childs, with a small garrison, was in the city of Puebla; and all communication with the sea-board was cut off. In this condition of things, it was necessary that something should be done.

Major Folliot T. Lally, of the 9th Regiment of Infantry, left Vera Cruz on the 6th of August, 1847, with a mixed command of recruits and parts of regiments, on his way to join General Scott, but his march was harassed at all points by the guerrillas, and he lost many men; finally, after much peril, he reached the city of Jalapa, where he was forced to halt until re-enforcements could be sent to him. This force was a little over one thousand strong, and contained two companies of horse, *viz.*, Captain Loyall's company of Georgia cavalry, and Captain Besançon's company of Louisiana cavalry. During the march they could not be of much service, though several of the men were picked off by the enemy.

Brigadier-General Joseph Lane, with his brigade, left Vera Cruz on the 19th of September, 1847, for the city of Mexico. The weather was intensely hot, and his men made slow progress. A party of guerrillas attacked the column on the 20th, and a company of Louisiana Cavalry, under Captain Lewis, which was his only mounted force, easily routed them, killing and wounding several. On the 22nd, as the command was about starting in the morning, another attack was made by the guerrillas, and a fine young officer named John Kline, who was Second Lieutenant in Lewis's company, was killed. The guerrillas were again driven off, and did not molest the column any more.

Lane's men were without tents, and in the rains which fell during the latter part of September and in October, they suffered very much. At Jalapa his command was increased by that of Major Lally, and again pushed on, the cavalry companies of Besançon and Loyall joining that of Lewis.

At Perote his force was again increased by Captain Samuel H. Walker's company C, Regiment of Mounted Riflemen, which was splendidly armed and equipped, and a battalion of infantry. He learned on the 8th of October, while at the *hacienda* of San Antonio Tamaris, that Santa Anna, with a large Mexican force, was at Huamantla, some twelve miles distant. This Mexican general, after his defeat at the capital, had escaped with a large number of soldiers, and had fallen upon Colonel Childs's garrison at Puebla, which he had been besieging since about the 15th of September.

Hearing of Lane's approach, he moved down the Mexican road and fortified the pass of El Pinal, determined to arrest his farther progress. The ground was admirably chosen, being a high bluff or side of a hill on the left, and a steep declivity on the right of the road; but General Lane did not allow himself to be caught in this very nice trap which had been laid for him. Learning that Santa Anna was off the road at Huamantla, where he could more easily subsist his troops, Lane determined to give him battle there, and thus prevent the Mexican soldiers from guarding the Pinal Pass.

I was a subaltern in Lane's command at the time, and well recollect the enthusiasm which prevailed among the soldiers at the idea of meeting Santa Anna. Captain Walker, who had had considerable experience, was ordered to take command of the four companies of cavalry, which was really a very respectable body of men. He had orders to lead off, and, when he came in sight of the Mexican forces, to wait until the infantry support could come up. The heat was overpowering, but still everybody kept up as well as possible; and when within three miles of the city, Walker discovered a body of Mexicans which he supposed was about equal to his own, and, ordering his men to follow, away he went at a gallop.

The Mexicans fled toward the town, with Walker and his men streaming after them. The charge of our cavalry was most splendid, and it is no disparagement to anyone to say that it has had few equals in our country. The Mexicans could not withstand it, though they fought with their lances with considerable effect; but the Rifles were determined to beat them, and they scattered in all directions. Walker's company did the whole thing, and suffered in consequence most severely.

At this time Walker supposed that all was over, and the Mexicans conquered; but in this he was mistaken. A large force of lancers came rolling into town before the American infantry column could get there, and, falling upon Walker's company, some of whom had dismounted to save some pieces of artillery, it was, in effect, cut to pieces. Walker himself was shot down, and died in a few minutes, and his whole cavalry force took refuge in a churchyard. This column of lancers numbered between two and three thousand, and, had it not been for the opportune arrival of the infantry, it is a question whether any of the cavalry would have escaped.

The fight was now soon over, and the Mexicans, with Santa Anna, started off on their way to Queretaro. This was the last time he ever met the Americans in battle, and Lane's infantry had the honour of finishing the military career of this celebrated officer. In the fight, Walker, Lewis, and Besançon behaved admirably, as did Lieutenants Claiborne, of the Rifles, and Anderson, of the Georgia Cavalry. In the action Walker's company had thirteen men killed and eleven wounded.

On account of this action Lieutenant Thomas Claiborne was made a brevet Captain.

The Mexican lancers I saw that day made a most splendid appearance, with their flashing lances, bright pennons, and green uniforms. They were in sight of our column for a considerable time as we were approaching the town at right angles to each other, and each was striving to get there first.

In the night Lane's command returned to the *hacienda*, and on the 12th of October reached the beautiful city of Puebla.

After Lane had been here several days, he learned that General Rea, of the Mexican Army, was at Atlixco, a town some thirty miles distant, with a large force of Mexican soldiers, and determined to attack him. Captain Lemuel Ford, with his company of the 3rd Dragoons, had been with Colonel Childs during the whole siege of Puebla, and he was put in command of the cavalry, Lieutenant Martin commanding his company. Walker's company was left in Puebla, as it was so cut up as to be of little use.

On the 19th of October, the column, with the cavalry in advance, left Puebla. It was a fine day, but was again most intensely hot, and our Northern soldiers suffered accordingly. Lane had a due proportion of artillery and infantry, and two companies of cavalry—one of the 3rd Dragoons, and one of Louisiana.

Though I was myself in this action, I copy portions of Lane's report, which gives a very fair account of the fight. He says:

About four o'clock p.m., when near Santa Isabella, seven leagues from this place (Puebla), the advance guard of the enemy was discovered. A halt was ordered until the cavalry (which had previously been detached to examine a *hacienda*) should arrive. The enemy, with his accustomed bravado, came to the foot of the hill in small parties, firing their *escopetas* and waving their lances. On the arrival of the cavalry, a forward movement was made by the column. A large, deep ravine appearing on the left of the road, Lieutenant-Colonel Moore, with his Ohio regiment, was ordered to flank it, Major Lally, with his battalion, leading the advance.

Our column had scarcely commenced its movement when signs of confusion were visible among the enemy; in consequence of which, the cavalry was ordered to charge, follow them up, and engage them until the infantry could arrive. Lieutenant Pratt, with his battery, was ordered to follow in rear of the dragoons at a gallop. Had this movement been performed, the whole force would have been ours. But, by an order from Major Lally, Lieutenant Pratt was taken from the place assigned him by me, and, in consequence, detained until a greater portion of the column had passed; then, owing to the nature of the ground, it was impossible for his battery to proceed with rapidity.

The cavalry pursued the retreating enemy for about a mile and a half, skirmishing with them. On arriving at a small hill, they made a stand, and fought severely until our infantry appeared, when they took flight. Our artillery fired a few shots as soon as it came up, but without effect, as, by their rapid retreat, they had placed themselves at long range. The dragoons were again ordered to follow and keep them engaged. After a running fight of about four miles, and when within a mile and a half of Atlixco, the whole body of the enemy was discovered on a side hill, covered with *chaparral*, forming hedges, behind which they had posted themselves.

Our cavalry dashed among them, cutting them down in great numbers. So thick was the *chaparral*, that the dragoons were ordered to dismount and fight them on foot. A most bloody conflict ensued, fatal to the enemy. Our infantry for the last six miles had been straining themselves to the utmost to overtake the enemy, pressing forward most arduously, notwithstanding the forced march of sixteen miles since eleven o'clock. Owing to the nature of the road, almost entirely destroyed by gullies, the artillery could only advance at a walk. As soon as the infantry again appeared in sight, the enemy again retreated.

So worn out were our horses (the sun having been broiling hot all day) that they could pursue the enemy no farther. The column was pressed forward as rapidly as possible toward the town; but night had already shut in, giving us, however, the advantage of a fine moonlight. As we approached, several shots were fired at us, and, deeming it unsafe to risk a street-fight in an unknown town at night, I ordered the artillery to be posted on a hill near to the town and overlooking it, and open its fire. After firing three quarters of an hour, and the firing from the town having ceased, I ordered Major Lally and Colonel Brough to advance cautiously with their commands into the town. On entering, I was waited upon by the *ayuntamiento*, desiring that their town might be spared. After searching the next morning for arms and ammunition, and disposing of what was found, I commenced my return.

General Rea had two pieces of artillery, but, as soon as he was aware of our approach, he ordered them with haste to Matamoros, a small town eleven leagues beyond. The enemy state their own loss in this action to be two hundred and nineteen killed and three hundred wounded. Scarcely ever has a more rapid forced march been made than this, or productive of better results. Atlixco has been the headquarters of guerrillas in this section of the country, and of late the seat of government in this state. From thence all expeditions have been fitted out against our troops. So much terror has been impressed upon them at thus having war brought to their own homes, that I am inclined to believe they will give us no more trouble.

The loss to Lane's command was very small, and I think the number of their killed may have been overestimated. But I saw many of their dead lying along the road.

In consequence of good conduct in this affair, Captain Ford was breveted Major, and Lieutenant Martin, of the 3rd Dragoons, was breveted First Lieutenant

Lane's command returned to Puebla, and a few days afterward he went to the city of Mexico.

One battalion of the 3rd Dragoons was sent to the Rio Grande after it was raised, and served there, under command of Colonel Butler and Major Cass, until the close of the war. This battalion had no opportunity to distinguish itself particularly, though it was a fine body of men and was well disciplined. Adjutant Edward McPherson, of this regiment, was killed in a duel at Mier, Mexico, March 16th, 1848.

General Lane, with a cavalry command, did much good service toward the closing scenes of the Mexican War, which I will attempt to give in the order in which the fights occurred. On the 22nd of November, 1847, he moved with a command of Texas cavalry under Colonel Hays, Lewis's company of Louisiana cavalry, and one piece of artillery, to Matamoros, about fifty-four miles from Puebla, which distance he marched in twelve hours. Here he made an attack upon a party of Mexicans, defeated them, and destroyed a quantity of ammunition, stores, etc.

When returning, on the 24th, he was in turn attacked by the Mexicans, and, after a severe fight, drove them off, but his command suffered a good deal. This is known as the fight at the Pass of Galaxara. Lane's losses in these affairs were inconsiderable, though in the latter his acting assistant adjutant general, Henderson Ridgely, First Lieutenant 4th United States Infantry, was killed. The Mexicans suffered to a greater extent than did our troops. The command returned to Puebla, and Lane then marched to the city of Mexico.

On the 18th of January he again started from the capital with one company of Mounted Riflemen, two of the 3rd Dragoons, and four of Texas Rangers, his object being to capture General Santa Anna, who was known to be in the city of Tehuacan, many miles away. He travelled by night in order to deceive the enemy. On the second night out from Puebla he encountered a coach with an armed escort. This he halted, but the owner producing a safeguard from the Governor of Mexico, he was obliged to release him. No sooner had Lane left than this Mexican put one of his servants on a mule, and sent him with all haste to Santa Anna, who, being apprised of Lane's approach, started from Tehuacan at once.

Lane's party entered the city, but the bird had flown; and, after a fruitless search of some hours, he was found to have been too quick for the Americans. This was a sore disappointment, but the soldiers made the best of it by capturing all of Santa Anna's military property, which they carried away as legitimate spoil. Lane captured the town of Tehuacan, the city of Orizaba, and the town of Cordova, killing several enemies, and doing much service. Upon his return, the dragoons, under Major Polk, had a skirmish with a body of guerrillas under Don Manuel Falcon, who were signally defeated.

Learning that a body of guerrillas was infesting the country north and northeast of the capital, he determined, upon his return, to go out and attempt their capture, or, at least, to break up their rendezvous; accordingly, he started on the 17th of February, 1848, with a command of Mounted Rifles, 3rd Dragoons, and Texas Rangers, Major Polk again commanding the regular cavalry. Lane found a large body of guerrillas, under Padre Jarauta, at the town of Sequalteplan, and, after a spirited skirmish, succeeded in defeating them. Padre Martinez, the second in command, was killed, together with many others. In all of these affairs the mounted men behaved well, and gained considerable reputation. This was the last fight of any importance which occurred in the vicinity of the city of Mexico.

On General Taylor's line, another dragoon fight of some importance took place at Agua Fria on the 2nd of November, 1847. The dragoons were commanded by Captain Reuben P. Campbell, of the 2nd Regiment, and acquitted themselves with their usual gallantry.

In New Mexico trouble was again brewing, as the country was left nearly barren of mounted men by the expiration of the term of service of the Twelve Months' Volunteers. Colonel Price had returned to Missouri with his regiment, but, being appointed Brigadier-General of Volunteers, again went to New Mexico in the autumn of 1847. In the neighbouring state of Chihuahua, a Mexican force had been gathered, for the purpose, it was supposed, of attacking the towns of El Paso and Santa Fé.

In anticipation of this, Price determined to attack the city of Chihuahua. The enemy was met at Santa Cruz de Rosales, sixty miles from Chihuahua, and the town was stormed on the 16th of March, 1848. Price's command consisted of portions of the 1st Regiment United States Dragoons, and of detachments of Missouri cavalry. The American loss was not great, though. Lieutenant George O. Hepburn, of the Missouri cavalry, was killed, besides several men, and a number of dragoons and volunteers were wounded. This was the last act in the war with Mexico, and our soldiers were allowed a period of rest.

Major Benjamin L. Beall, of the 1st Dragoons, was breveted Lieutenant-Colonel for this action; Captain William N. Grier, of the same regiment, was breveted Major; First Lieutenants John Love and O. H. P. Taylor were breveted Captains; and Second Lieutenant John Adams First Lieutenant.

Lieutenant William B. Royall, while escorting Major Bryant, paymaster, on his way to Santa Fé from Fort Leavenworth, had a fight with a party of Indians, in which he succeeded in giving them a severe chastisement. This occurred on the 18th of June, 1848.

When the Mexican War closed, the 3rd Regiment of Dragoons, which had been raised to serve during the war, was disbanded. It had done some good service, though nothing to greatly distinguish itself.

CHAPTER 6

Fights with the Apaches

At the close of the Mexican War, in the summer of 1848, the troops left the territory of that republic. Our own country obtained a large accession of territory as a result of the war, and California and New Mexico had been retained by us. The 3rd Regiment of Dragoons was sent to Jefferson Barracks, Missouri, where it was disbanded; and it was deemed advisable to discharge the enlisted men of the regiment of Mounted Riflemen, who had found some pretext, through the medium of certain legal advisers, to annul their obligations with government. As a consequence of this, it required some time to again fill up that regiment.

Lieutenant-Colonel Clifton Wharton, of the 1st Dragoons, died at Fort Leavenworth on the 13th of July, 184:7. Major Edwin V. Sumner, of the 2nd Dragoons, was promoted in his place; and Captain Marshall S. Howe, of the 2nd Dragoons, was promoted Major, *vice* Sumner.

Major Burbridge, of the Mounted Rifles, resigned on the 8th of January, 1848, and Captain Winslow F. Sanderson was promoted in his place.

I had failed to notice in the proper order that Lieutenant Colonel Philip St. George Cooke, commanding the Mormon battalion (captain in the 1st Dragoons), had the honour of making the first wagon road from the streams of the Atlantic to the Pacific Ocean. This was a great undertaking at that time, which was in the autumn and winter of 1846-47, and entitles him to much credit. In his report to General Kearney, he recounts the hardships endured by himself and his men, and says that the general's letters to him made it almost a point of honour to take the wagons through to the Pacific, and he was much retarded in making and finding the road. The breaking the track, often through thickets of *mesquit* and other thorny bushes, although worked on by pioneers, was so laborious that it was necessary to relieve them every hour.

In this expedition Cooke was accompanied by Lieutenants Andrew J. Smith and George Stoneman, of the 1st Dragoons, who were of much assistance to him, and who now rank in our service among our very best officers.

Cooke was breveted Lieutenant-Colonel for meritorious conduct in California.

The close of the year 1848 found our mounted force scattered far and wide. There was one company at each of the posts of Fort Leavenworth, Fort Scott, and Fort Washita, belonging to the 1st Dragoons; three companies in New Mexico; three in California; and one on the Mississippi River, above Fort Snelling. Of the 2nd Dragoons, six were in Texas, two in New Mexico, and two *en route* for California. The Mounted Rifle Regiment was being recruited, and was under orders for Oregon.

The gold mines had been discovered in California, and a new fever had attacked the Americans. Colonel Mason, of the 1st Dragoons, had a most difficult task in controlling the restless spirits which flocked to the new-found land of gold, and desertions became so frequent as to render his soldiers of no avail; companies dwindled away in a single night; and it was a serious question in his mind whether all the enlisted men would not desert in a body. And, indeed, this is not to be wondered at, as the pay of infantry soldiers at that time was but seven dollars per month, and cavalry soldiers eight, and in the mines, they could easily make from twenty to thirty dollars per day.

Colonel Mason's administration of affairs in California was successful, and he was made a Brigadier-General by brevet for meritorious conduct in that Territory.

The stations of troops through the year 1849 remained substantially the same as the dispositions which were made at the close of the war. There were as yet no Indian depredations of any magnitude, and our soldiers had a time to rest.

In Texas, the commander of the department had authority to mount, when necessary, a portion of the infantry force, which enabled him, with a proper disposition of the regular cavalry, to concentrate six mounted companies at any point on short notice. But the troops suffered exceedingly from the effects of cholera, which for a time threatened to cut them off entirely.

The positions at Eagle Pass, near the high road from San Antonio to Chihuahua, at Ringgold Barracks, and at Fort Brown, had larger garrisons than the frontier posts, because, being the keys to the upper provinces of Mexico, they must necessarily have a strong influence in maintaining peaceful relations along the boundary-line, and in protecting the revenue laws. The Texans had taken every foot of land from the Indians, as they had done from the Catholic Church.

The Mounted Riflemen moved westward by detachments from Fort Leavenworth in May, 1849, and were ordered to establish a chain of posts along the route to Oregon Territory, one being at Fort Kearney, another at Fort Laramie, three hundred and fifty miles west, and another was to have been on the head waters of the Columbia River, near Fort Hall, or in that vicinity; but, on account of a scarcity of forage, etc., it was not located at that point. This was at that time like finding a new world, though the golden attractions of California drew the young and adventurous in that direction, and there was far less enthusiasm about going beyond the Rocky Mountains than there otherwise would have been.

The soldiers would desert in spite of every precaution, and wend their way to the gold-fields, which had then so recently been discovered. It was a gay, wild, roving life, and the *genii* of the mines enticed many a young man to ruin.

The Mounted Rifles were marched to Oregon, under command of Lieutenant-Colonel Loring, Fremont having resigned, and Loring having been promoted in his place. This vacancy was filled by the promotion of Captain George B. Crittenden to the majority. He was a son of the Hon. John J. Crittenden, of Kentucky. During the winter of 1849-50 desertions were very common, and at one time more than one hundred deserted in a body. Loring pursued them, and captured over seventy, having made a march in midwinter, going and coming, of over one thousand miles.

While these events were transpiring in and on the route to Oregon, the Indians of Texas and New Mexico had commenced their depredations upon the settlers. There was wrong, no doubt, on both sides, although I am personally far from believing the Indians themselves to be saints, and cannot join the very good people of the quiet settlements in believing "the Poor Indian" is incapable of doing harm, and that all the fault is on the side of the white people. I have seen too much of their cruelty to believe that; but, at the same time, I think they were sometimes—not often—imposed upon.

Major Steen, of the 1st Dragoons, had a fight with a party of Apaches on the 15th of August, 1849, in which he was severely wounded.

In the spring and summer of 1850, the Indians, principally Comanches, became quite troublesome, and three companies of Texas Rangers were called out to assist the regular cavalry. One of these was commanded by Captain John S. Ford, who was a good Indian fighter—a brave man—and one who, in two minor conflicts with the savages, defeated them, and otherwise did good service.

Brevet Lieutenant-Colonel Hardee, with a portion of the 2nd Dragoons and some Rangers, in the months of July and August, 1850, organised a campaign against them. His command met the Indians on several occasions, and in one of them Brevet Captain James Oakes, of the 2nd Dragoons, was severely wounded in the breast by an arrow, from the effects of which he has never recovered. This happened in August.

In New Mexico Major Steen and Major Grier, both of the 1st Dragoons, had severe skirmishes with the Indians, and captured some of their property. Steen's pursuit of them, which occurred in February, was most exciting. After he had followed one party many miles, he came upon another after passing through a *cañon* above the San Diego. The Indians were in full sight of Steen's command, not more than a mile ahead, and on a level plain, both parties at the top of their speed, and thus was the chase continued over thirty miles until the horses were completely broken down. Toward the last, the Indians were to be seen throwing away blankets, provisions, and everything but their arms, rendering themselves as light as possible. Three of Steen's best horses were left dead on the route.

Major Grier killed several of the enemy, and lost some of his own command. He captured sixty horses and mules, eighty head of cattle, one hundred and fifty sheep, and a quantity of provisions and camp materials. This was on the 26th of July, 1850.

Colonel Richard B. Mason, of the 1st Dragoons, died at Jefferson Barracks on the 25th of July, 1850. Lieutenant Colonel Fauntleroy, of the 2nd, was promoted in his place. Major Nathan Boone became Lieutenant-Colonel of the 1st, and Captain George A. H. Blake, of the 2nd, became Major. Captain Croghan Ker, of the 2nd Dragoons, resigned on the 10th of November, 1851. Brevet Lieutenant-Colonel Backenstoss, and Brevet Major Tucker, of the Mounted Rifles, resigned on the 30th of June, 1851.

In the summer of 1851, the Mounted Rifle Regiment left Oregon, and, going by sea to San Francisco and Panama, returned to Jefferson Barracks. The reason for this movement was the fact that the regiment was almost reduced to nothing by desertions, and the Indians of Oregon had promised to remain at peace with the whites. Notwithstanding this, Captain James Stuart, of this regiment, was mortally wounded in a skirmish with the Indians on Rogue River on the 17th of June, 1851, and died on the following day. He was a most excellent officer, and those who knew him loved him for his many good qualities and dauntless courage.

The years 1851 and 1852 do not appear to have been at all eventful in the history of the cavalry, and, with the exception of Colonel Sumner's somewhat celebrated march to the *cañon* of Chelly, in New Mexico, there is little to be found of interest to cavalry men. This was an expedition against the Navajoes, a tribe inhabiting the country west of the Rio Grande, semi-civilized, and, perhaps, in the same condition the Aztecs were in when the valley of Mexico was invaded by Cortez.

In the canon of Chelly Sumner's dragoons did not gather many laurels, though they did their duty; but the Indians were too wily for them, and, lining the sides of the pass, or *cañon*, they rolled down rocks, fired guns, and shot arrows at our troops, until they were glad to re trace their steps.

It was, I believe, on this march that the song was composed by a soldier, which nearly all cavalry men know, and which is sung to the tune of "*Stable-call*." It runs thus:

"*Come off to the stables, all if you are able,*
And give your horses some oats and some corn;
For if you don't do it the colonel will know it,
And then you will rue it as sure's you're born."

On the 15th of July, 1853, Lieutenant-Colonel Nathan Boone, of the 2nd Dragoons, resigned. He was quite old, having served as a captain of Rangers during the War of 1812. His last entrance into the service was as captain in Dodge's battalion in 1832. He was a most finished woodsman, and it is doubtful if he had any superior in that respect in our army. The paths leading out on the plains of the Great West were familiar to him, and he was able to pilot parties in any direction. He was a worthy son of Daniel Boone, of Kentucky. Major Philip St. G. Cooke was promoted Lieutenant-Colonel, and Captain Enoch Steen, of the 1st Dragoons, Major, *vice* Cooke.

This year there were several fights of considerable importance with the Indians, which I shall write of in the order in which they occurred. I had failed to mention that after the regiment of Mounted Riflemen had recruited at Jefferson Barracks in 1851, it was sent to

Texas, and its Colonel, Brevet General Persifer F. Smith, was commanding that department.

Before commencing the detail of Indian fights, it may be well to state that brevet Major Kipley A. Arnold, of the 2nd Dragoons, was killed at Fort Graham, Texas, on the 6th of September, 1853, by Assistant Surgeon Steiner, United States Army. A private quarrel was the cause of this sad occurrence.

The Indians, as before mentioned, had become very daring in their depredations in Texas, and several parties of mounted riflemen were sent out against them during the month of May, 1854, from Fort Merrill, on the Nueces River. One party, supposed to have been composed of Lipans and Seminoles, crossed into Texas from Mexico, and was fallen in with by one of these detachments of rifles, near Lake Trinidad, about forty miles northwest of Corpus Christi. It was composed of Lieutenant George B. Cosby, two non-commissioned officers, and eighteen men.

The Indians numbered about forty. After a most gallant skirmish, they were driven off, though in doing so Cosby's command was scattered and somewhat worsted. Lieutenant Cosby was severely, though not dangerously, wounded in the sword-arm. Shortly afterward, Lieutenant Roger Jones, with a party, appeared and continued the pursuit.

Second Lieutenant Jerome Napoleon Bonaparte, junior, of the Mounted Rifles, also joined in the pursuit, but was unable to overtake the enemy. General Smith, who commanded the department of Texas, and whose headquarters were at that time at Corpus Christi, says, "I have no terms to speak my sense of the gallantry and coolness displayed by Lieutenant Cosby in this affair."

Another party, under command of First Sergeant C. H. McNally, with First Sergeants John Green and John Williams, of the Rifles, were successful in a scout against the Indians, and all of them were promoted to second lieutenancies on account of good conduct. Lieutenant Williams, who was put in the 2nd Cavalry, was afterward murdered by a soldier at a camp on Limpia Creek, Texas, June 30th, 1855.

Another scout was sent out, which resulted sadly. I give General Smith's account of it, under date of July 15th, 1854, from Corpus Christi. He says:

Preparatory to moving the regiment of Mounted Riflemen from the Nueces to the Rio Grande, in conformity with the instructions of the War Department, the companies were ordered to be got ready, and Brevet Lieutenant-Colonel Roberts, commanding Fort Ewell, called in all the detachments from that post, thus uncovering the Rio Grande from Loredo down. Lieutenant-Colonel Seawell, at Ringgold Barracks, and Colonel Loomis, at Fort McIntosh, immediately reported that small parties of Indians were crossing the river at various places, and committing robberies and murders.

I immediately ordered some companies to the river again, and directed the detachment from Fort Merrill, that had been withdrawn from Santa Gertrude's (forty miles from this) on account of the men having the scurvy, to be replaced there; but at three o'clock a.m. on the 14th, an express from up the road informed me that the Indians had killed some persons at 'Proscenius,' twenty-five miles north of Santa Gertrude's. I then ordered another detachment from Fort Merrill toward the former place.

In the meantime, on the 4th of July, Captain Van Buren took up the trail, and followed it to the southward with unsurpassed diligence and under great difficulties, until, on the 11th, in the evening, he met them, about thirteen miles from 'Proscenius,' toward the south west. They were thirty, and he had thirteen men in all. He attacked them boldly, and the Indians at first stood their ground. Their chief, however, was killed, and his body remained in Captain Van Buren's possession.

Four other Indians fell, but were picked up by their companions. Captain Van Buren was badly wounded in the arm, but dismounted his men to use their rifles more effectually. He soon routed the Indians, who fled, leaving some horses, many lances and shields, and other trophies; but I regret to say that Captain Van Buren himself was shot through the body with an arrow, entering just above the sword-belt, and coming out *through* it behind. His wound is very dangerous. He had two men wounded, and his horse shot in the head. In this situation he could not pursue, but sent a corporal and two men to Fort Ewell for a surgeon and ambulance.

As these did not arrive, next day he dispatched two other men to meet and bring them in; but these got lost, and, finding a trail, followed it until they reached Palo Alto, twenty-five miles from here. From this place they came here, and I immediately dispatched Second Lieutenant Roger Jones, with nine riflemen that were waiting as escort for my departure for El Paso.

Dr. McParlin, who was here also to accompany me, went with them with an ambulance.

The poor captain was brought into Corpus Christi, and breathed his last soon afterward.

General Smith visited El Paso in the month of August and September, 1854. He left that place on the 28th of September. On the 1st of October he reached Eagle Spring, which is on the road. About fourteen miles from the Rio Grande a party of citizens was met who were driving cattle, who reported that on the previous day the Indians had robbed them of sixty or one hundred cattle.

Finding the trail, General Smith sent a portion of his escort, under Captain John C. Walker, of the Rifles, to overtake, if possible, the Indians, and recover the cattle before they could cross the Rio Grande. In the night Walker lost the main trail, though accompanied by one of the best guides in Texas, Polycarpio Rodriguez, but next morning found another, which was evidently leading to the principal haunts of the Apaches in the mountains. Walker met the Indians, and General Smith says:

> His spirited action there is highly to his credit and that of his command. His own conduct is spoken of in the highest terms by all present; and his clothes, which are cut in more than one place by the Indian arrows, bear testimony of his having been in the thickest of the fight.
>
> Lieutenant Carr's gallantry before he was wounded, and his coolness afterward, were admired by all, and the whole command did their duty in the most praiseworthy manner. Captain Walker lost one man killed, and Lieutenant Eugene A. Carr and the guide wounded. Several of the horses were wounded, one fatally, but it was brought off. The necessity of seeking surgical aid for Lieutenant Carr, whose wound was thought dangerous, if not fatal, put an end to farther search for the stolen cattle, which were not at this camp.
>
> The chief and six other Indians were killed, and several wounded; but as these, with some neighbouring bands of the same tribe, have been committing constant depredations on this road, I propose to send up some of the Texas Volunteers and other mounted troops to drive them out of the county.

In New Mexico a spirited affair took place on the 5th of March,

1854, some sixty miles from Fort Union, between the Jicarilla Apaches and a detachment of the 2nd Dragoons, commanded by Second Lieutenant David Bell. The parties were about equally matched—twenty-four warriors each—and both ready to measure strength. The result of the conflict was that the Indians lost five killed and several wounded, and the dragoons two killed and four wounded.

The Indians fled in great disorder to the *cañons* in the gorges of the Canadian. This was a part of the band which captured and killed Mrs. White, whose fate was most revolting, and worse than death itself. To this poor lady death was indeed a relief. Lieutenant Bell killed the chief, Lobo, with his own hand, and, during the whole affair, managed it with great discretion and gallantry.

During the same month the Indians, Jicarilla Apaches and Utahs, managed to combine a force of two hundred and fifty warriors, and unexpectedly attacked a company of dragoons, sixty strong, about twenty-five miles from Fernandez de Taos, under command of Lieutenant John W. Davidson, 1st Dragoons, and succeeded, after a desperate conflict, in overwhelming it. Lieutenant Davidson and Assistant Surgeon Magruder, both wounded, returned from the battlefield with about seventeen men, most of them wounded.

General Garland, commanding the Department of New Mexico, pays the following high compliment to Davidson. He says:

> The troops displayed a gallantry seldom equalled in this or any country, and the officer in command, Lieutenant Davidson, has given evidence of soldiership in the highest degree creditable to him. To have sustained a deadly contest of three hours, when he was so greatly outnumbered, and then to have retired with the fragment of a company crippled up, is amazing, and calls for the admiration of every true soldier.

When Lieutenant-Colonel Cooke, 2nd Dragoons, heard the news of the disaster which had befallen Lieutenant Davidson, he organised a force of about two hundred men, and, after a march of four days, overtook the Indians on the upper branches of the Aguas Calientes, gave them battle, and killed six of them. This prompt and energetic action on the part of Cooke reflected the highest credit upon him, and prevented the Utahs from making common cause with the Jicarilla Apaches against the whites.

Portions of Cooke's command followed the Indians a long distance, and broke them up completely. Major Blake attacked one party,

Captain Carleton another, and Lieutenant Randall another. All did well, and received the thanks of the general commanding. Kit Carson, the celebrated guide and mountaineer, accompanied one of these parties in the pursuit, and aided very much by his knowledge of woodcraft and the habits of the Indians. Carson was at one time a lieutenant in the Mounted Rifle Regiment.

It is necessary to state here that Lieutenant John L. Grattan, of the 6th Infantry, and twenty-nine enlisted men of the same regiment, were massacred by the Brulé band of the Sioux nation, near Fort Laramie, on the 19th of August, 1854. In this instance the Indians were the aggressors, and were alone to blame. In retaliation for this massacre, General Harney was sent out against them the next year, an account of which will be given in proper order.

The first fight of any moment which occurred during the year 1855 was that of Lieutenant Samuel D. Sturgis, 1st Dragoons, against a party of Mescalero Apaches, who had been committing depredations near the town of Galisteo, in New Mexico. This was on the 13th of January. Sturgis and his dragoons pursued the Indians rapidly, and the result was most satisfactory. One hundred and sixty miles were accomplished in two days and three hours; the Indians overtaken and attacked, and three left dead on the field; four others were badly if not mor tally wounded. The morning of the fight was intensely cold—so much so that after the first fire the men had to use their sabres, their fingers being too stiff to load readily. One dragoon was killed and two wounded.

On the 18th of January, Captain Ewell, of the 1st Dragoons, had a fight with the Mescalero Apaches on a stream called the Peñasco, which rises in the Guadelupe Mountains and empties into the Pecos. His command consisted of one hundred and ten dragoons and fifty infantry. During the whole of the 17th the march of the column was disputed by the Indians, they coming at times under cover within arrow-shot. On the 18th the first of their abandoned camps was discovered, and the command was halted, about 3 o'clock p.m., for the night. Captain Stanton, of the 1st Dragoons, was directed to take his company, with some additional men, and examine a valley to the right where there were some abandoned lodges, about five hundred yards distant, and endeavour to find the direction taken by the Indians when they left.

This officer, after reaching the place designated, charged after some Indians he saw in front, and in following up the steep hill-sides, in the ardour of the chase became separated from some of his men, badly mounted, which were unable to join when he sounded the rally. After rallying about a dozen of his men, he proceeded up the valley until he became satisfied that the Indians had not retreated in that direction, and he started back, leading his horses. About three fourths of a mile from camp the valley narrowed, with trees, and here he was ambushed and fired into, the first fire killing one of his men. He ordered his party to take to the trees; but the Indians being in too great force, he mounted, and directed his party to retreat, remaining in the rear himself, firing his Sharp's carbine, when he received a shot in the head, and was instantly killed. One of the men with him when he first charged was dismounted, surrounded, and lanced after killing an Indian.

Ewell sent Lieutenant Moore to the assistance of Stanton, and upon his approach the Indians dispersed. They scattered into the mountains, and the guides were unable to trail them. In this affair the Indians retained the advantage.

Colonel Fauntleroy, 1st Dragoons, had a most successful fight with the Utahs, about twenty miles from the Punche Pass, up the Arkansas River. He fell suddenly upon a camp of twenty-six lodges, and estimated to contain about one hundred and fifty fighting men. He made the attack at daylight, and, after a fight of twenty-five minutes, carried the camp, killing forty and wounding a large number of others. Several children were taken, with a herd of horses, sheep, and goats. This was on the 28th day of April, 1855. Colonel Fauntleroy had another fight with them on the 1st of May, and again defeated them. His operations were very successful, and he gained much credit.

CHAPTER 7

Distinctions Between Heavy and Light Cavalry

A most important piece of legislation was carried through Congress on the 3rd of March, 1855, which authorised the raising of two regiments of cavalry. This was an unheard-of thing in the history of the United States the raising of two regular mounted regiments at one time and was looked upon as almost a miracle; but the necessities of the country demanded it, and our law-makers wisely acquiesced.

The annexation of Texas, and the conquest of New Mexico and California, had increased the area of the Republic fully one third. Much of this was in a wild state, inhabited by predatory bands of savages, who roamed from near the waters of the Mississippi far beyond the Rocky Mountains, and from the boundary-line of British America to the plains which border on the Rio Grande. Our settlements were stretching westward; the families of the pioneers needed protection, and the trains of emigrants passing from east to west had to be escorted through the Indian country, which for centuries had been their homes, and over which they considered the white man had no *right* to cross.

Cavalry was the only force that could combat with the Indians of the plains, as they themselves are reared on horseback, and move across them fleeter than the wild deer. The raising of these regiments was forced upon us by the circumstances of the country, and I think no one now doubts its having been a wise measure. In the selection of officers for these regiments great care was taken, and many meritorious men were placed in them.

Lieutenant-Colonel Edwin V. Sumner, of the 1st Dragoons, was made Colonel of the 1st Regiment of Cavalry. Sumner was born in Massachusetts, and entered the army as Second Lieutenant in the 2nd

A Cavalry charge in the Civil War

Infantry, in March, 1819. He became a First Lieutenant in 1823, and Captain in the 1st Dragoons in March, 1833. His history while in the Dragoons has already been given in the pages of this work. Sumner was a capital soldier. He was thoroughly devoted to his profession, and manifested it in almost every action and gesture. Upon being presented to Louis Napoleon, while he was on a visit to France, the emperor remarked to our minister that he saw in Sumner a finished soldier, and one who had evidently spent much of his life in camp.

He gave great attention to the minutiae of his profession, perhaps too much so, and never suffered himself, or those under his command, to neglect even the most trifling duties. But he is gone—honourably gone—and mine is not the pen to write even the slightest word which can be construed into censure of that most noble and gallant soldier.

Joseph Eccleston Johnston was selected as Lieutenant-Colonel. He was born in Virginia, and graduated at West Point in 1829; he served in the 4th Regiment of Artillery until 1837, when he resigned. In 1838 he re-entered the service as First Lieutenant in the Topographical Engineers. He was breveted Captain for gallantry in Florida, and attained the full grade in 1846. In 1847 he was made Lieutenant-Colonel in the *Voltigeurs*, one of the "Ten Regiments," and was severely wounded at the battle of Cerro Gordo. He was distinguished at Molino del Rey, and at Chapultepec, in which battle he was again wounded.

At the close of the war his regiment was disbanded, but he was retained as captain in the Topographical Engineers. Joe Johnston was considered a good officer, and for some years after the close of the Mexican War was engaged in making roads and examining routes across the plains of the far Southwest.

Ben McCulloch, of Texas, was made a Major; but he, thinking it was not sufficiently high for him, declined the appointment. Ben had proved himself a good partisan officer in Texas and Mexico, but he did not make a good general. I was with McCulloch in New York City in 1858, when on one occasion he visited a fortune-teller. His fate was then clearly told to him, as the witch, wizard, or impostor, whatever he might be, told him that he would die by a bullet on the battlefield. I know this to be truth.

Captain William H. Emory, also of the Topographical Engineers, was promoted Major. He had served in the army since 1837, engaged in making surveys, etc. He was with Kearney at San Pascual, and had served as Lieutenant-Colonel of the Maryland and District of Columbia Volunteers during a portion of the Mexican War.

John Sedgwick, of Connecticut, was the other major. He graduated at West Point in 1837, and was made a Second Lieutenant in the 2nd Artillery, in which regiment he continued to serve until his promotion. He was made a brevet Captain for gallantry at Contreras and Churubusco, and brevet Major for Chapultepec, and was also distinguished in the attack on San Cosme Gate. He became a Captain of Artillery in January, 1849. Sedgwick was considered, and proved himself to be, a very superior officer, and gave his life for his country on the 9th of May, 1864, in Virginia. At the time of his death, he was Colonel of the 4th United States Cavalry and Major-General of Volunteers.

Deles B. Sacket, a First Lieutenant in the 1st Dragoons, was made senior captain in this regiment. He was a New Yorker by birth, had graduated at West Point, and was a skilful cavalry officer. He had served as Instructor of Cavalry at the Military Academy, and had perfected himself in the details of the mounted service. Robert S. Garnett had been appointed senior captain of the cavalry, but was promoted to a majority in the 9th Infantry, and never served with the regiment.

First Lieutenant Thomas J. Wood, of the 2nd Dragoons, was made the next Captain in rank. He was a native of Kentucky, had graduated at West Point, and had served with credit at Palo Alto and Buena Vista, as before narrated.

Captain George B. McClellan, of Pennsylvania, graduated at West Point in 1846, and entered the Engineers as Second Lieutenant. He was breveted First Lieutenant for his gallant conduct at Contreras and Churubusco, and brevet Captain for gallantry at Chapultepec. He served with the company of Sappers and Miners, and at the close of the war was placed in command of it. After his appointment as Captain of Cavalry, he visited Europe for the purpose of making observations in reference to the different organisations of the cavalry in the Armies of Europe.

It is to be regretted that McClellan had not himself had more experience in the cavalry before going there; but as it is, his work was of some benefit to our service, and contains some information of value. He resigned in January, 1857, and was engaged in civil pursuits until the breaking out of the rebellion, when, after a series of rapid promotions, he became Major-General and Commander-in-Chief of the United States Army. He is a good soldier, and many think he has no superior in this country. In the army, while he was a captain, he was considered one of its brightest ornaments.

Samuel D. Sturgis, the next captain, was also from Pennsylvania, and after graduating at West Point, entered the 2nd Dragoons, was transferred to the 1st Regiment, and had proved himself an active and zealous officer.

Captain William D. De Saussure, of South Carolina, was appointed from civil life. He had been a Captain in the South Carolina Regiment of Volunteers during the Mexican War, and had distinguished himself at Churubusco (where he was wounded), and at the De Belen Gate. He was a good soldier.

Captain William S. Walker, of Mississippi, was also appointed from civil life. He had been a First Lieutenant in the Voltigeur Regiment in Mexico, and was breveted Captain for gallantry at Chapultepec.

Captain Edward W. B. Newley, of Illinois, had served in the war with Mexico as Colonel of the 5th Regiment of Illinois Volunteers, and was stationed for some time at Santa Fé, New-Mexico.

Captain George J. Anderson, from Georgia, was next. He had served through the Mexican War creditably as lieutenant in Loyall's Company of Georgia Cavalry, and captured Colonel La Vega and Major Iturbide (a son of the ex-Emperor Iturbide, of Mexico) at the Battle of Huamantla. He did not remain long in the regiment.

Captain John T. Coffee, of Missouri, had been a member of the Legislature of that state. He was not a military man, and "could not see the necessity of drilling men." He remained in service but a short time. During the rebellion he has gained a most unenviable reputation as chief of "Coffee's Guerrillas."

Among the lieutenants appointed in this regiment were William N. R. Beall, of Arkansas, who shortly became a captain, and is now a Confederate general; George H. Stewart, also a Confederate general; McIntosh, Eugene A. Carr, United States Brigadier-General of Volunteers; Ransom, Bell, Perkins, Iverson, Wheaton; Stanley, Major-General United States Volunteers; Stockton; James E. B. Stuart, the famous Confederate *raider*; Otis, McIntyre, Crittenden, Riddick, Church, and Colburn. Ingraham, Long, Bayard, Lomax, Taylor, and Fish, joined it afterward.

In the 2nd Regiment of Cavalry, Colonel Albert Sidney Johnston was appointed. He was a most brave and skilful soldier, though his last days were tarnished by a treason which covered like a pall his many virtues. Johnston was a native of Kentucky, and after graduating at West Point, became adjutant in the infantry. While stationed at Jefferson Barracks, Jefferson Davis, who was then a lieutenant of dragoons, was stationed there. On account of some detail which was made by

Johnston, Davis became very angry, and challenged him; the challenge was accepted, and it was only through the mediation of Lieutenant Alexander that a duel between them was prevented.

They were ever after the warmest personal friends. He resigned and went to Texas, where he offered his services to that republic. They were accepted, and he passed through the various grades of Brigadier-General, Commander-in-Chief, and Secretary of War. On account of some misunderstanding with Felix Houston in regard to the command of the army, a duel was fought by them, in which Johnston was severely wounded, and ever afterward walked a little lame. He became a planter in Texas, but upon the breaking out of the Mexican War he was chosen Colonel of a Texas Infantry Regiment, and served some time.

The regiment was disbanded, and he continued to serve on the staff of Major-General William O. Butler as acting inspector-general. While thus serving he participated in the Battle of Monterey, and shortly after was appointed paymaster in the regular army, with the rank of major. In 1855 he was appointed Colonel of the 2nd Cavalry, and although afterward breveted Brigadier-General for his services in Utah, was in fact the head of the regiment when the rebellion broke out, and when he resigned. He was killed while in command of the Confederate Army at the Battle of Shiloh. General Johnston was a very gentlemanly and kind man in the private walks of life, though he had been for years a secessionist at heart He, like most soldiers, was an in different speaker, though a chaste and fluent writer. He had a fine military presence and carriage, with the most gentle and winning manners.

Robert E. Lee, the Lieutenant-Colonel of this regiment, and since Commander-in-Chief of the Rebel Army, a son of "Light-horse Harry Lee" of the Revolution, was born in Virginia, and graduated at the West Point Military Academy. He was first in the Engineers, and gained a fine reputation during the Mexican War, at the close of which, although but a captain, he had the brevet rank of Colonel. For some years he was superintendent at West Point, and held that position when he was promoted Lieutenant-Colonel of the 2nd Cavalry. He served some time with the regiment in Texas, and for a time had command of that department.

Lee was not a secessionist at heart, and deplored the sad state of things brought about by the then approaching attempted dissolution of the Union. In a letter to me shortly after the Presidential election in 1860, in referring to it, he says, "I fear the liberties of our country will be buried in the tomb of a great nation." His heart was sore over disunion, but this strong man gave way before the tempter, and he, too, took the fatal step which led to the abodes of darkness. Lee was a refined American gentleman, courteous and affable in his deportment, and kindly in his feelings. His personal appearance was striking, and impressed one with the idea that he was a great soldier, which he proved himself to be. He was wounded at Chapultepec.

Brevet Lieutenant-Colonel William J. Hardee was promoted Major from a captaincy in the 2nd Dragoons. He got his brevets at two mere skirmishes, those of Medelin and at San Augustine, as has been shown heretofore. He was born in Georgia, and, having graduated at West Point, entered the 2nd Dragoons at the time when Twiggs was colonel. Twiggs was also a Georgian, and, of course, Hardee was a pet, and a worthy one he was, too, of that notorious officer. Hardee's principal military exploit during the Mexican War was his being taken prisoner at the *ranche* on the Rio Grande.

He is known as the author of *Hardee's Tactics*, so called, which were mainly a translation from the French made by some junior officers for Hardee's glory, and it is safe to say that he knew as little about them as almost anyone else. His career in the regiment was unmarked by a single thing which could go to show that he was anything more than a vain and conceited martinet, who had been pushed forward to the manifest injustice of braver and better men. He was a man of mediocre talent, joined to sobriety, and an industry carried on at the expense of others. He is now a lieutenant general among the rebels, and seems to suit their style admirably.

Major George H. Thomas, formerly of the artillery, was breveted for gallantry in Florida, at Monterey, and at Buena Vista. He was born in Virginia, and graduated at West Point in 1840. Major Thomas is one of the best of men, and has proved himself, as a soldier, to be made of the most unyielding material. His conduct as a major-general at the Battles of Mill Spring and at Chickamauga is beyond all praise, and is what all who knew him believed of him.

In danger he is cool and self-possessed to a remarkable degree, and has a mind which is never led astray. He was wounded in Texas while leading his cavalry against the Indians. Thomas was beloved by every honest man in the regiment, and I have since had the pleasure of serving under his command at the siege of Atlanta and at Nashville.

The next in rank was Captain and Brevet Major Earl Van Dorn. This man's career astonished friends as well as foes. He was considered at one time as being the very embodiment of all that was chivalrous, brave, kind, and gentle, but the curse of secession swept like a *sirocco* over his breast and withered every manly principle. Van Dorn was a failure. His domestic life was unhappy, and he fell most in gloriously. He was born in Mississippi, and graduated at West Point, and, though never considered a man of profound wisdom, his personal courage was undoubted, as was shown in the Mexican War, and in two of the most successful Indian fights with the Comanches in the Witchita Mountains which have occurred in the history of our country.

In one of these fights, he was seriously wounded. Van Dorn was one of Davis's especial pets, and joined secession with a zeal and heartiness worthy of a better cause. He subsequently became a rebel general, and his whole course was a series of remarkable failures. His death was a most disgraceful one, but was a fitting close to his traitorous and unfortunate career.

The other captains were Edmund Kirby Smith, a Floridian by birth, and a graduate of West Point. In the Mexican War he won distinction as a lieutenant, and on that account was promoted to a captaincy in the 2nd Cavalry. He was wounded by the Indians in Texas. He joined the rebels, though with reluctance, his family (mother and sisters) having had the miserable satisfaction of forcing him out, when his own good judgment revolted against it. At the Battle of Bull Run he was severely wounded. Smith was a kind-hearted man, and a man of sound judgment and much intelligence. He has risen to the grade of lieutenant general among the Confederates, and commands the trans-Mississippi country.

Captain James Oakes was from Pennsylvania, and a graduate of West Point. He was a man of most determined purpose; had served with distinction in the 2nd Dragoons in Mexico; and, as before related, was wounded by the Indians in Texas. On account of this wound he was obliged to decline the Brigadier-General's commission tendered him by the President.

Captain Innis N. Palmer, of the Mounted Rifles, was next. He was from New York; had graduated at West Point; had been breveted Captain for his services in Mexico, and had been wounded at Chapultepec. He was made a Brigadier-General of Volunteers during the rebellion.

George Stoneman, of New York, was promoted from a first lieutenancy in the 1st Dragoons. He had served for several years in California, and had established a good reputation as an officer. He graduated at West Point in 1846, and had done much service on the frontiers. He has since risen to the position of a Major-General of Volunteers, and Chief of the Cavalry Bureau.

Theodore O Hara and Charles E. Travis were originally appointed in the regiment from citizen life, but served in it only a short time. The former was from Kentucky; had been an assistant quartermaster and brevet Major in Mexico, and was severely wounded in Lopez's Cuban Expedition, being an intense filibuster. He served as Sidney Johnston's *aide-de-camp* at Shiloh. Travis was the only son of Colonel Travis, the hero of the Alamo, and died in 1860. He had resided for several years in Texas, and the summer before had commanded a company of Texas Rangers on the frontier.

Captain William R. Bradfute, of Tennessee, had served in a Tennessee regiment in the Mexican War as a Captain. At the Battle of Monterey, he did very well. At the breaking out of the rebellion he joined the rebel cause, and was advanced to a field office.

Captain Albert G. Brackett was born in New York, and appointed from Indiana. He had served as First Lieutenant in an Indiana Regiment of Volunteers during the Mexican War, and was at the fights of Huamantla and Atlixco. During the rebellion he became colonel of a regiment of volunteer cavalry, and was severely wounded by the rebels in Arkansas.

Captain Charles J. Whiting, of California, was born in Massachusetts. He graduated at West Point in 1835; served sometime in the artillery in Florida; resigned, and was afterward surveyor general of California. He is now out of service.

Captain Richard W. Johnson, of Kentucky, also a West Point man, is now a Brigadier-General of Volunteers. He was considered a good officer in Texas, and has proved himself so during the rebellion.

Captain Nathan G. Evans, of South Carolina, graduated at West Point in July, 1848. He did well in Texas, but was always a red-hot fireeater. Of course, he joined the rebels. He fought us at Bull's Run and Ball's Bluff. Evans had many good traits of character, but he was too intensely Dixiefied to be at all times agreeable.

Among the lieutenants were McArthur, Charles W. Field, a rebel general, Garrard, now a Union general, Jenifer, Royall, Chambliss, Lowe, John B. Hood, the rebel commander-in-chief in Georgia, Witherell, Minter, Phifer, and Van Camp. Afterward Lieutenants Harrison, Porter, Owens, Major, Fitzhugh Lee, the rebel cavalry general, and Kimmel, joined, as will be seen.

The first regiment was organised during the summer of 1855, at Fort Leavenworth, and the second at Jefferson Barracks. While these regiments were being organised, our other mounted men were working in the field. In the month of August, Lieutenant Horace Randall, of the 1st Dragoons, had a fight with the Indians, and acquitted himself very creditably. It took place in the gorges of the mountains near the Rio Grande. The prompt and well-devised plans of the lieutenant met with perfect success. But by far the most important Indian fight which occurred this year was that fought by General Harney, Colonel of the 2nd Dragoons, against the Sioux Indians. I give his report entire of this action.

Writing to the adjutant general from his camp on Blue Water Creek, N. T., under date of September, 1855, he says:

> I have the honour to report, for the information of the general-in-chief, that, on my arrival at Ash Hollow, on the evening of the 2nd instant, I ascertained that a large portion of the Brulé band of the Sioux nation, under '*Little Thunder*,' was encamped on Blue Water Creek (*Mee-na-to-wah-pah*), about six miles northwest of Ash Hollow, and four from the left bank of the North Platte.
>
> Having no doubt, from the information I had received from the people of the country I had previously met on the road, and from the guides accompanying me, of the real character and hostile intentions of the party in question, I at once commenced preparations for attacking it. I ordered Lieutenant-Colonel P. St. George Cooke, 2nd Dragoons, with companies 'E' and 'K', of the same regiment, light company 'G,' 4th Artillery, and company 'E,' 10th Infantry, all mounted, to move at three o'clock a.m. on the 3rd instant, and secure a position which would cut off the retreat of the Indians to the Sand Buttes, the reputed stronghold of the Brulés.
>
> This movement was executed in a most faultless and successful manner, not having apparently attracted the notice or excited the suspicion of the enemy up to the very moment of the encounter.
>
> At half past four o'clock a.m. I left my camp, with companies 'A,' 'E,' 'H,' 'I,' and 'K,' 6th Infantry, under the immediate command of Major Cady, of that regiment, and proceeded toward the principal village of the Brulés, with a view to attacking it openly, in concert with the surprise contemplated through the cavalry. But, before reaching it, the lodges were struck, and their

Ash Hollow Massacre, Indian fight on the Blue Water

occupants commenced a rapid retreat up the valley of the Blue Water, precisely in the direction from whence I expected the mounted troops.

They halted short of these, however, and a parley ensued between their chief and myself, in which I stated the causes of the dissatisfaction which the government felt toward the Brulés, and closed the interview by telling him that his people had depredated upon and insulted our citizens while moving quietly through our country; that they had massacred our troops under most aggravated circumstances, and that now the day of retribution had come; that I did not wish to harm him personally, as he professed to be a friend of the whites, but that he must either deliver up the young men whom he acknowledged he could not control, or they must suffer the consequences of their past misconduct, and take the chances of a battle.

Not being able, of course, however willing he might have been, to deliver up all the butchers of our people, '*Little Thunder*' returned to his band to warn them of my decision, and to prepare them for the contest that must follow.

Immediately after his disappearance from my view I ordered the infantry to advance, the leading company (Captain Todd's) as skirmishers, supported by company ('H,' 6th Infantry (under Lieutenant McCleary), the remaining companies of the 6th being held in hand for ulterior movements. The skirmishers, under Captain Todd, opened their fire, crowned the bluffs on the right bank of the stream (where the Indians had taken up their last position) in a very spirited and gallant manner, driving the Indians therefrom into the snare laid for them by the cavalry, which last troops burst upon them so suddenly and so unexpectedly as to cause them to cross, instead of ascending the valley of the Blue Water, and seek an escape by the only avenue now open to them through the bluffs of the left bank of that stream.

But, although they availed themselves of this outlet for escape from complete capture, they did not do so without serious molestation, for the infantry not only took them in flank with their long-range rifles, but the cavalry made a most spirited charge upon their opposite or left flank and rear, pursuing them for five or six miles over a very rugged country, killing a large number of them, and completely dispersing the whole party.

This brilliant charge of cavalry was supported, as far as practicable, by the whole body of the infantry, who were eager from the first for a fray with the butchers of their comrades of Lieutenant Grattan's party.

The results of this affair were eighty-six killed, five wounded, about seventy women and children captured, fifty mules and ponies taken, besides an indefinite number killed and disabled. The amount of provisions and camp equipage must have comprised nearly all the enemy possessed, for teams have been constantly engaged in bringing into camp everything of any value to the troops, and much has been destroyed on the ground.

The casualties of the command amount to four killed, four severely wounded, three slightly wounded, and one missing, supposed to be killed or captured by the enemy. I enclose herewith a list of the above, and also field returns, exhibiting the strength of the troops engaged in the combat.

With regard to the officers and troops of my command, I have never seen a finer military spirit displayed generally; and if there has been any material difference in the services they have rendered, it must be measured chiefly by the opportunities they had for distinction.

Lieutenant-Colonel Cooke and Major Cady, the commanders of the mounted and foot forces, respectively carried out my instructions to them with signal alacrity, zeal, and intelligence.

The company commanders, whose position, either in the engagement or in the pursuit, brought them in closest contact with the enemy, were Captain Todd, of the 6th Infantry, Captain Steele and Lieutenant Robertson, of the 2nd Dragoons, and Captain Heth, 10th Infantry. Captain Howe and his company ('G', 4th Artillery) participated largely in the earlier part of the engagement, but for reasons stated in his commanding officer's report, he took no active part in the pursuit. Brevet Major Woods, Captain Wharton, and Lieutenant Patterson, of the 6th Infantry, with their companies, rendered effective service as reserves and supports, taking an active share in the combat when circumstances would permit.

Colonel Cooke notices the conduct of Lieutenants John Buford and Thomas J. Wright, Regimental Quartermaster and Adjutant of the 2nd Dragoons, in a flattering manner. Lieutenants Drum, Hudson, and Mendenhall, 4th Artillery; Lieutenants

Hight and Livingston, 2nd Dragoons, and Lieutenant Dudley, 10th Infantry, gave efficient aid to their company commanders. I should do injustice to Mr. Joseph Tesson, one of my guides, were I to omit a mention of his eminently valuable services in conducting the column of cavalry to its position in the rear of the Indian villages. To his skill as a guide, and his knowledge of the character and habits of the enemy, I ascribe much of the success gained in the engagement.

Mr. Carrey, also, chief of the guides, rendered good service in transmitting my orders.

The members of my personal staff rendered me most efficient service in the field. Major O.F. Winship, Assistant Adjutant-General and Chief of the Staff, and Lieutenant Polk, 2nd Infantry, my *aide-de-camp*, in conveying my orders to different portions of the command, discharged their duties with coolness, zeal, and energy. Assistant Surgeon Ridgeley, of the medical staff, was indefatigable in his attentions to the suffering wounded, both of our own troops and of the enemy. Lieutenant Warren, topographical engineer, was most actively engaged, previous to and during the combat, reconnoitring the country and the enemy, and has subsequently made a sketch of the former, which I enclose herewith.

Captain Van Vliet, assistant quartermaster, was charged with the protection of the train—a service for which his experience on the plains rendered him eminently qualified. Lieutenant Balch, of the Ordnance, was also left in charge of the stores of his department.

I enclose herewith several papers found in the baggage of the Indians, some of which are curiosities, and others may serve to show their disposition toward the whites. They were mostly taken, as their dates and marks will indicate, on the occasion of the massacre and plunder of the mail party in November last.

There are also in the possession of officers and others in camp the scalps of two white females, and remnants of the clothing, etc., carried off by the Indians in the Grattan massacre; all of which, in my judgment, sufficiently characterize the people I have had to deal with.

By this action of General Harney's this tribe was dispersed. Before proceeding farther with the history of our cavalry, it will be well to examine the different organisations of our own army, and explain to non-professional readers and beginners the difference between the regiments. We had now in the army (1855) dragoons, mounted riflemen, and cavalry. These names sound differently, and no doubt there were formerly nice shades of distinction; but, with us, that between dragoons and cavalry was only in *name*.

All cavalry in the United States service is light cavalry. Now the question will be asked what is the distinction between the light and heavy cavalry and the dragoons.

Heavy cavalry in the European Armies consists of large men in defensive armour, mounted on heavy, powerful horses. The power of this arm lies in the strength and breeding of the horses, and the courage and activity of the riders. The men wear helmets and *cuirasses*, and heavy equipments. The helmet is a piece of defensive armour or covering for the head, worn by nearly all of the cavalry regiments in Europe, and has been found, after ages of use, to be the only proper head-covering for a mounted man. Our own big, unwieldy uniform felt hat is nothing more or less than ridiculous, and our forage cap is little better.

The helmets worn by the soldiers of olden times were some of them models of beauty, strength, and grace. The helmet of the Romans was a head-piece of iron or brass, which descended behind as far as the shoulders, and left the face uncovered. Upon the top was the crest, in adorning which the soldiers took great pride. The usual ornament was horse-hair or feathers of divers colours. The helmets of the officers were sometimes very splendid, being adorned with gold and silver. A *dragon* was used as the crest of the helmet by the mounted soldiers in the Middle Ages, hence the name dragoon.

The *cuirass* is another piece of defensive armour, made of plate well hammered, serving to cover the body from neck to waist both before and behind, called breast and back plate. The *cuirassiers* of the Armies of Europe wear the *cuirass*. The helmets worn by the Russian soldiers are both serviceable and beautiful.

The heavy cavalry, then, consists of heavy men and heavy horses, who are used upon occasion to hurl down upon the enemy, and by their weight alone overpower them. It is questionable whether they are of much service, and no doubt we are as well off without them. They are incapable of doing the same duty that is required of the light cavalry, as even short marches break down both men and horses. They are more formidable in appearance than in reality.

Dragoons are next to be considered. They were originally organised to act either as cavalry or infantry skirmishers—a sort of hybrid corps to do duty on foot or on horseback; now they are simply a body of regular cavalry soldiers, in some countries divided into heavy and light dragoons.

All of the cavalry which has been organised in the United States is properly designated as light cavalry. The laws of Congress made two regiments of dragoons, one of mounted riflemen, and two of cavalry. It was no doubt intended to make the dragoons and cavalry all one arm, but a fault in the law, which was subsequently remedied, made it otherwise, and Jefferson Davis, who was Secretary of War, took advantage of it, and made two arms, thereby securing promotion for his favourites in the cavalry arm without reference to the dragoons. Army men will readily understand this distinction.

During the Mexican War the dragoons were armed with musketoons, which were carried on sling-belts except when marching, dragoon sabres of the Prussian pattern, and horse-pistols. This was unchanged for several years afterward. The Mounted Rifles were armed with percussion rifles and Colt's army revolvers—no sabres. The revolvers were supplied to all cavalry men as soon as was convenient. The cavalry regiments were armed with sabres, rifle-carbines, and Colt's navy revolvers.

Why they were not armed with army revolvers no person could ever give a good reason. The sabre in Indian fighting is simply a nuisance; they jingle abominably, and are of no earthly use. If a soldier gets close enough on an Indian to use a sabre, it is about an even thing as to which goes under first.

The trimming of the dragoon jackets after the close of the Mexican War was orange, and that of the Rifles green. The cavalry had, and still have, yellow. The dragoons and Rifles exulted in what was known as the "Albert hat," with orange and green pompons. The cavalry got—God knows where—the "cavalry hat," familiar to theatre-goers as that worn by Fra Diavolo. If the whole earth had been ransacked, it is difficult to tell where a more ungainly piece of furniture could have been found. It is now used by the whole army, being somewhat more unwieldy than the original pattern.

It seems to me that soldiers take delight in seeing into what ludicrous shapes they can get these hats, with a tassel hanging in front, on one side, or behind, and a black ostrich feather, which, after one or two wettings, has a most bedraggled and wilted appearance. The forage cap is a poor imitation of the French *kepis*, and seems with us to run mostly to visor. The old-fashioned dragoon cap was both graceful and soldierly.

The saddle used in the cavalry now is that known as the McClellan saddle, which was patented after his visit to Europe by General McClellan. The soldiers like it, as it is easy to ride on, and does not give a horse a sore back unless carelessly used. Men who ride saddles are generally the best judges of them, though heads of department sometimes think differently. It is fair, then, to say that the saddle, if it had a breast-strap, is a good one, as it has the verdict of the *men* in its favour. I do not like the bridle so well. The bit is ordinarily too powerful for the horse; it is made of poor steel, and the curb-chain is apt to straighten out upon pulling the reins. This could, no doubt, be remedied. I think, however, a decided improvement could be made in the choice of bits.

The swiftest horses are not always the best in cavalry. If all were equally fast, it would be very well; but, in making a charge upon any given point, a few horses will always come out ahead, and leave their companions far in the rear. Officers who insist upon their men preserving their lines in a charge, insist upon an impossibility.

Another subject has impressed itself strongly upon my mind, which is the fact that, in our regular service, the horses are *groomed too much*. I cannot say that this applies to the Volunteers. In my own experience, the fault with them lies the other way. What I mean is this, that in winter time, when the weather is cold, and the horses, as is almost always the case with us, are without suitable shelter, the grooming the horse one hour at daybreak, and one hour just before sunset, is absolutely hurtful.

Some cavalry officers, who have been taught certain rules, insist upon the men keeping at work steadily *one hour* on each horse, without any regard to time, place, circumstances, or anything else. Now, in the fine stables which the military of France and Great Britain have, it may do well to keep the horses looking sleek-coated, giving them each day gentle exercise; but with us, who have our poor animals trembling the great part of the winter from sheer cold, it is worse than nonsense to tear up their hides each day by means of the curry-comb and brush. The pores are left open, the skin is scratched, and the wretched animal stands crouched up all night, suffering from the effects of this well-meant, but ill-administered grooming.

The condition of our poor horses sometimes in winter is such as to make any heart susceptible of pity feel the most profound sorrow. But this I do not find fault with; in actual campaign both men and horses must suffer, but do not let us cavalry people make our only friends—our horses—suffer unnecessarily. British and French officers may think this singular advice, but they must recollect that their cavalry force is small compared with ours, and they have every convenience to make themselves and their horses comfortable good stables, plenty of forage, and nice roads to travel upon.

About marching, too, a few lines may not be amiss. In starting out after feeding, let the horses walk about one hour, when a halt of fifteen minutes ought to be sounded. Let the men close up, and then dismount. This eases the horse, gives him a chance to breathe a short time, and makes him feel better. When ready to start, tighten up the girths, which will be found to have slackened up, one or two holes. Do not let the saddle be loose on the back; it should sit snug; but, at the same time, caution all soldiers not to draw too tightly, as I have seen some dreadful sores made on horses' sides by the ring and strap which is used on the McClellan saddle, and which is borrowed from the Mexicans.

About riding I have to say that soldiers must learn to ride themselves, and *time alone will make good riders.* Some men never do know how to ride, and never learn. The sooner they are got rid of the better. Great, beefy creatures some of them are, who have no more elasticity than a dead animal, and who worry and fret their poor horses almost to madness. Our men are generally (I mean the Americans) natural riders, and soon become good horsemen. They quickly learn how to take care of horses.

This is particularly the case where the men become attached to their animals, and make pets of them. I have known many a soldier to sit up half the night in order to get a chance to steal a feed for his horse. This venial offense is forgiven generally by the officers. The quartermasters are the sufferers, but they always manage some way or other to keep even.

As to riders, the United States Cavalry, under the old system, had few superiors. The English, as a general thing, are most wretched riders, and it is no wonder that they are almost universally whipped whenever they go into battle. The "bumping" up and down on their saddles is not only excruciating to themselves, but ruinous to their unfortunate animals. Nolan, in his work on Cavalry, speaks in the most disparaging terms of the English cavalry, as does Lieutenant General

Sir Charles James Napier; and no doubt justly so, as it is hard to imagine a more helpless body of men than they are. Poor Nolan himself lost his life while charging at Balaklava, where the English horse was entirely cut to pieces by the Russians.

After a hard day's march, or, indeed, any march in hot weather, upon halting, the saddles should be removed, the saddle-blanket turned and left on the horse, strapped on by the surcingle. This will prevent saddle-boils. After the saddle is removed, nearly every horse wishes to roll. He should be allowed to do so, the man keeping hold of the halter-strap or lariat while he is rolling.

Ordinary marches for cavalry should not exceed eighteen miles a day. The horses should be watered once or twice on the march, if it is convenient, and should be allowed to drink as much water as they want, provided they are moved on after drinking, but on no account should they, after marching some distance, be allowed to drink and cool. If this is permitted, in nine cases out of ten the animals will be foundered. Officers should be continually on their guard watching recruits in this respect, as by its neglect many a fine animal has been ruined.

In cold weather care should be taken to see that the horses are well blanketed during the night, and, if necessary, men should be detailed to keep the blankets on, as horses are apt to rub or kick them off. No man can be a good cavalry officer unless he is continually on the alert looking out for the welfare of his horses. Cavalry soldiers generally do well enough for themselves, but cavalry horses must be looked after.

A march of a thousand miles is a better school for a recruit than all of the riding-halls ever built, and United States soldiers are *often* sent across the continent of North America merely as part of a summer campaign.

Horses' shoes should be inspected frequently, as, in spite of every care, shoes are sometimes left on too long, and sometimes they are knocked off, and the horse, on a rocky road, becomes lame at once. The Indians never shoe their horses; the hoofs of their animals become as hard nearly as flint They go over the rockiest roads with our cavalry chasing them, and as soon as the shoes of our horses are torn off by the rocks, they become disabled, and the Indians laugh at our efforts to overtake them.

The shoeing tools of the farrier should consist of a shoeing knife, a toe knife, a shoeing hammer, a clinching iron, a clinch-cutter, a pair of pincers, and a rasp. What is known as a buttress should never be used, nor ought a shoe to be put on while hot, any more than is sufficient to show that it is of the right shape. When starting on a march each horse ought to have two shoes at least fitted, so that the farrier will have nothing to do but nail them on in case any are lost while traveling. Altogether too little attention is paid to shoeing by cavalry officers. Whatever relates to the care and training of his horses is a part of his profession, and the smallest matter ought not to be neglected.

A good *rider* will always make a good *raider*.

As to the equipment, there is no doubt but there is now too much weight on the waist-belt. The sabre hangs on it, also the cartridge-box, with twenty or forty rounds in it, and the revolver. This is altogether too much, and breaks many a man down, causing diseases of various kinds, which are ruinous to cavalry men. Some system of shoulder-belts ought to be devised to lighten up the strain which now bears with so much weight and such ill effects upon a particular part of the body.

Our sabres are never really sharp, and good officers think there is no way of keeping them so as long as we continue to use the steel scabbard; but the question is, what are we going to get to replace it with? Nolan says the sabres used by the East India native cavalry are condemned English sword-blades, sharpened to the keenest edge, and kept in wooden scabbards. They are never drawn except in action, where, according to his account, they do dreadful execution.

Our revolvers, of Colt's pattern, cannot at present be much improved upon.

Sharp's carbines are the favourite cavalry carbines, though upon this subject there is a diversity of opinion, each commander having some pet arm which he thinks superior to any other. Our cavalry men ought to have good carbines, as our general officers employ them in every conceivable way; and it is really surprising how much, and how many different kinds of work they are called upon to perform. Some of our sapient political Brigadier-Generals can use up a cavalry regiment with a rapidity truly astonishing, and their ignorance is only exceeded by their conceit. In our rebellion, in many in stances, the less a man knew about military matters the better officer he was supposed to be.

Within the last eighteen months there has been a decided improvement in the carbines and accoutrements which have been issued to the cavalry. It is now conceded that the Spencer carbine, or rifle, is, by all odds, the best shooting weapon ever issued to mounted men; and the cartridge-box invented by Colonel Erastus Blakeslee, late of the 1st regiment of Connecticut Cavalry, leaves but little to be desired. This cartridge-box is carried by a belt over the right shoulder, thus relieving the strain on the abdomen. With it seven cartridges are loaded as quickly as one by the ordinary method, and it is more easily carried than any box in use.

CHAPTER 8

Colonel Sumner's Fight with the Cheyennes

The 1st regiment of Cavalry, under Colonel Sumner, was organised, as before stated, at Fort Leavenworth, Kansas, in 1855, and in the autumn of that year made an expedition out on the plains without any important results. The regiment wintered at Leavenworth, and subsequently took part in the Kansas difficulties, as did the 2nd Dragoons. This service was most distasteful to our officers, who were not politicians; but in every instance, I believe, they acquitted themselves creditably in trying to settle discordant factions, and earned the respect of all good men.

Upon the promotion of Sumner, Benjamin L. Beall became Lieutenant-Colonel of the 1st Dragoons, and Charles A. May major. May subsequently exchanged with Steen, and thus got back into his old regiment, the 2nd Dragoons. Major Winslow F. Sanderson, of the Mounted Rifles, died at Galveston on the 16th of September, 1853, when Captain John S. Simonson was promoted Major.

On the 27th of October, 1855, the 2nd Cavalry left Jefferson Barracks for Texas, under command of Colonel Albert Sidney Johnston, the whole ten companies being together, and numbering in all over seven hundred and fifty men, and eight hundred horses. The route lay through Missouri, in a south-westerly direction, across various streams, and over the Ozark Mountains. The regiment passed through Springfield and Neosho, down the boundary-line of Missouri to Maysville, in Arkansas, and thence off southwest again into the Indian Territory.

The Cherokee country was first visited, where the landscapes were indeed most beautiful. Wide, undulating prairies were seen, with groves of timber of the most magnificent proportions, and the blue outlines of the mountains far away in the distance. The streams of water were pure and sweet. In the latter part of November, the regiment reached Talequah, the capital of the Cherokee nation. Many houses in this place are well built. The Cherokees number some twenty thousand, and many of them have turned their attention to agricultural pursuits. Some of the farms were in the highest degree creditable. From Talequah the regiment marched to Fort Gibson.

Crossing the Neosho and Kansas Rivers, the land of the Creek Indians was reached, and many a grim old warrior watched its course as it passed along on its journey. The sight of the regiment was most imposing as it moved along over the hills and through the valleys. Each day gangs of wolves were seen trotting along parallel with the column, and herds of deer galloped off on the right and left.

On the 4th of December the regiment crossed the north fork of the Canadian River, and shortly after encamped near the Indian village of Mico, where there were some Florida Seminoles. The next day it forded the Canadian, which is skirted by some elegant timber. This was in the Creek nation. These Indians number about sixteen thousand. On the 7th of December the regiment encamped near a Choctaw village. These Indians number some twenty-seven thousand. Their land joins that of the Chickasaws, who numbered some five thousand five hundred.

After crossing two wretched streams, called the Middle Boggy and the Boggy, the regiment reached Fort Washita on the 12th of December, and on the 14th crossed Red River into Texas. The course of the troops was down through the "Upper Cross Timbers," which is a belt of woods composed of small oak and *mesquit* trees. The *mesquit* is the best wood for making fires of any in the world, and during the severe cold which prevailed was of great use. The "northers" were several of them very severe, and quite a number of horses and men lost their lives in consequence of being frost bitten.

Droves of antelope were seen along the route, and buffalo bones were strewed here and there. On one occasion one of the men killed a cougar, or South American lion, of quite formidable dimensions. The largest of these animals in Texas are in the jungles, near the southern Rio Grande, where they are called "*leones*," or lions, by the people.

After stopping a short time at Fort Belknap, four companies were sent down to the clear fork of the Brazos, some thirty miles distant, under Brevet Lieutenant Colonel Hardee, where there was a Comanche Indian reservation; and the other six, under Colonel Johnston, marched to Fort Mason, on the Llano River, or River of the Plains.

Captain Oakes, of this regiment, had a skirmish with the Indians in February on the Concho River, and Captain Brackett, of the same regiment, another on the 12th of March, 1856, on the Guadelupe. They were both minor affairs, but had a good effect in improving the men in riding and in soldiership.

In March, April, May, and June, 1856, the troops in Oregon had a number of severe conflicts in the mountains and valleys near Rogue River, in which they conducted themselves admirably, compelling the Indians to surrender, and terminating the war in Southern Oregon. Captain Andrew J. Smith's company, C, 1st Dragoons, particularly distinguished itself, and lost eleven men killed and eighteen wounded.

In April, 1856, a detachment of dragoons, under First Lieutenant Isaiah N. Moore, 1st Dragoons, had a skirmish with a band of Gila Apaches, near the Almaigre Mountains, in New Mexico. In the same month, some detachments of Rifles had a fight with a party of Lipans near the head of the Nueces River, Texas. The soldiers, under Captains Claiborne and Granger, of the Rifles, greatly exceeding the Indians in number, of course defeated them.

Captain Oakes, of the 2nd Cavalry, with a part of his company, had a skirmish on the Concho in May, 1856, and again on the Pecos in September. The losses to the Indians and our own troops were small, though the results to the frontier settlers were no doubt beneficial.

In August Captain George H. Stewart, of the 1st Cavalry, with Lieutenants Wheaton and McIntyre, of the same, and a detachment of cavalry men, routed a party of Cheyenne Indians near Fort Kearney, who had attacked a mail party. Several of the Indians were killed and wounded.

Captain Bradfute, with a part of his company of the 2nd Cavalry, fought and defeated a party of Comanches on the Concho River in November, 1856. In the same month, Second Lieutenant Horace Randall, 1st Dragoons, followed and dispersed a party of Gila Apaches.

In December, Lieutenants Witherell and Owens, of the 2nd Cavalry, with a detachment of men of that regiment, defeated a party of Indians near the Rio Grande, and drove them across into Mexico. Captain Johnson, with Lieutenant Porter and twenty-five men of his company, of the 2nd Cavalry, had a severe skirmish with the Indians near the head of the main Concho. In this sharp conflict Johnson lost four of his men. Thus, it will be seen that, although this was considered peaceful times, the cavalry soldiers had a fair share of work, and that work quite dangerous.

During the summer of 1856 the regiment of Mounted Riflemen was sent from Texas to New Mexico, leaving the 2nd Cavalry to guard Texas. The 2nd Dragoons and 1st Cavalry were in the Department of the West. Of the 1st Dragoons four companies were near Tucson, New Mexico, and the rest in California and Oregon.

During the year 1857 our cavalry had several very severe skirmishes with the Indians. It is hardly worthwhile to recount every one, as they were some of them of very little importance. Lieutenant Wood, with a party of the 2nd Cavalry, had a skirmish with the Indians on the Concho, in Texas, on the 13th of February, 1857. On the same day Sergeant McDonald, of the same regiment, had another near Camp Verde. In April, Lieutenant Jenifer had a fight with a party of Indians, his own force of the 2nd Cavalry being worsted by the superior number of the enemy. Jenifer retired without loss.

Lieutenant Baker, of the Rifles, fought and defeated a party of Indians near the *Ojo del Muerto*, in New Mexico, on the 11th of March, 1857. Captain Alfred Gibbs commanded a detachment of the same regiment, and was highly distinguished and severely wounded in a fight with the Mimbres Apaches in the same month.

Four companies of the 1st Dragoons, and three of the Mounted Rifles, in New Mexico, did good service against the Indians on an expedition from the depot on the Gila River. A band of Coyotero and Mogollon Apaches were signally defeated through the arrangements of Colonel Bonneville, commanding. This took place in June, 1857.

The cavalry officers who were distinguished in this affair were Captain Richard S. Ewell, Lieutenants Isaiah N. Moore, Alfred B. Chapman, and Benjamin F. Davis, of the 1st Dragoons, the latter of whom was wounded; and Captain Thomas Claiborne and Lieutenant John V. D. Dubois, of the Mounted Rifles.

In August, Captain Charles J. Whiting, of the 2nd Cavalry, with his company, followed and defeated a party of Indians in Texas, who had robbed a mail party. Sergeant Charles M. Patrick, of company I, 2nd Cavalry, also had a fight, and defeated the Indians on the 28th of September.

But the two fights of this year which were most important were those fought by Lieutenant Hood and Colonel Sumner.

Lieutenant John B. Hood (now lieutenant general in the rebel army), with twenty-five men of company G, 2nd Cavalry, left Fort Mason, Texas, on the 5th of July, and marched for the head of the Concho. Near the mouth of Kiowa Creek, he found a trail, which he followed until he came to a water-hole, near the head of Devil's River. Here he hurried on, though his horses were very much wearied, and trailed over the bluffs and mountains down the river, but keeping some three miles from it. Late in the afternoon of the 20th of July he left the trail, and went in toward the river to get water, as his men were very thirsty. About a mile from the trail, and two miles and a half from his party, on a ridge he discovered some horses and a large flag waving.

The orders in Texas at that time were to attack any Indians found away from the government reservations. He crossed over to the ridge without going to the water, and cautioned his men not to fire until he ordered it; his fighting force being seventeen men, the rest being with the pack-mules. He was ready to fight or talk. Hood's men advanced, when five of the Indians came forward with the flag, and when the soldiers were within about thirty paces they dropped the flag, set fire to a lot of rubbish they had collected, and about thirty rose up from among the "Spanish bayonets" within ten paces of the soldiers. Twelve had rifles, the rest bows and arrows; besides which, eight or ten, mounted on horseback, attacked with lances.

With a yell Hood's men went into them, and fought hand to hand, the Indians beating the soldiers back until Hood rallied them with their revolvers. When he commenced firing the Indians gave way; but when his shots were expended, he was obliged to fall back and leave the field. Of the number he took into the fight he lost six killed and disabled, and was himself wounded. This was a serious affair, and, though our men fought gallantly, the Indians gained a complete victory. Hood made his way to Camp Hudson, where he obtained supplies and help for his wounded men.

Colonel Sumner's fight is best given in his own words. In writing from the Headquarters Cheyenne Expedition, from near the site of Fort Atkinson, on the Arkansas River, he says:

On the 29th of July, while pursuing the Cheyennes down Solomon's fork of the Kansas, we suddenly came upon a large body of them, drawn up in battle array, with their left resting upon the stream and their right covered by a bluff. Their number has been variously estimated at from two hundred and fifty to five hundred. I think there were about three hundred. The cavalry was about three miles in advance of the infantry, and the six companies of the 1st Regiment of Cavalry were marching in three columns.

I immediately brought them into line, and, without halting, detached the two flank companies at a gallop to turn their flanks (a movement they were evidently preparing to make against our right), and we continued to march steadily upon them. The Indians were all mounted and well-armed; many of them had rifles and revolvers, and they stood, with remarkable boldness, until we charged and were nearly upon them, when they broke in all directions, and we pursued them seven miles. Their horses were fresh and very fleet, and it was impossible to overtake many of them.

There were but nine Indians killed in the pursuit, but there must have been a great number wounded. I had two men killed, and Lieutenant J. E. B. Stuart and eight men wounded, but it is believed they will all recover. All my officers and men behaved admirably. The next day I established a small fort near the battleground, and left my wounded there, in charge of a company of infantry, with two pieces of artillery, with orders to proceed to the wagon train, at the lower crossing of the south fork of the Platte, on the 20th of August, if I did not return before that time.

On the 31st of July I started again in pursuit, and at fourteen miles I came upon their principal town. The people had all fled; there were one hundred and seventy-one lodges standing, and about as many more that had been hastily taken down, and there was a large amount of Indian property of all kinds, of great value to them. I had everything destroyed, and continued the pursuit. I trailed them within forty miles of this place, when they scattered in all directions.

Sumner's pursuit of these Indians has been criticised somewhat by military men. He used only the sabre in pursuing the Indians, and it is maintained by some that, had he used the revolver instead, the loss of the enemy would have been much greater. My own opinion is that, in this case, the revolver would have been the better weapon.

The condition of affairs in Kansas was still most vexatious. To maintain the supremacy of the law, and to sustain the regularly constituted authorities of the government, the soldiers were compelled to take the field against those whom it was their habit to regard not only with feelings of kindness, but with protective care. Forbearance tempered with firmness, and directed by a sound judgment, enabled them to check civil strife, and restore order and tranquillity without shedding blood.

On account of the very earnest representations of the Governor of Kansas, calling for aid from the troops, Sumner's command was brought in from the plains; and that engaged under Lieutenant-Colonel Joe Johnston, of the 1st Cavalry, which was marking the southern boundary of Kansas, was also brought in. But, by careful management, the troops had no trouble with the citizens.

The Territory of Utah, peopled almost exclusively by the religious sect known as the Mormons, now commenced making trouble, or rather they had been engaged in it for years past, and had on many occasions set the authority of the United States at defiance. They had substituted for the laws of the land a theocracy, having for its head an individual who claimed to be a prophet of God.

It was impossible to let this state of things continue, though it was the desire of the federal government to prevent a collision, if possible, with the Mormon people. It was thought best to send out with the newly-appointed civil officers a military force which should be sufficient for their protection, and to act, in case of necessity, as a *posse comitatus* in enforcing obedience to the laws.

Brevet Brigadier-General Harney was selected by the War Department as the head of the Utah Army, and had his headquarters at Fort Leavenworth, where his troops assembled.

Whether right or wrong in this matter, Brigham Young published one of the most remarkable proclamations ever issued to a people, and one which contained truths which could not be controverted.

General Harney did not go on to Utah, but left the whole affair in the hands of Colonel E. B. Alexander, of the 10th Infantry, who was without any orders of any kind. His command consisted of the 5th and 10th Infantry, and Phelps's Light Artillery Battery. The Dragoons intended for the expedition were kept back by the folly of the Governor of Kansas, and Alexander's command was left without a mounted force; but the colonel, by the most energetic efforts, saved the trains which reached him, though two of them were burned. It was now late in the season, the snows were whitening the hills and valleys, and want was apprehended. At a late hour, Colonel Albert Sidney Johnston, of the 2nd Cavalry, who was in Texas, was ordered to Washington, and was there ordered to take command of the "Utah Expedition."

It was now November, and Colonel Alexander had concentrated his force at the Black Hills. On the 6th of that month, Johnston having arrived, he determined to winter in the neighbourhood of Fort Bridger. The day was dreadfully cold, and that night more than five hundred animals perished; their frozen bodies were seen next morning around the camp, reminding the beholders of the terrible retreat of the French from Moscow.

The dragoons started late in the season, as the Governor of Kansas would not part with them before, and the march was one of severe hardships. When they reached the Rocky Mountains, the snow lay from one to three feet on the loftier ridges which they were obliged to cross. Nearly a third of the horses died of cold, hunger, and fatigue; and when, on the 20th of November, Lieutenant-Colonel Cooke reached the camp, his command was entirely incapacitated from active service.

The 2nd Dragoons was afterward sent out on Henry's Fork, to guard the animals belonging to the expedition, during the winter of 1857-58. The command suffered dreadfully for want of salt during that winter, but finally all things were bettered, and with the return of spring the soldiers were once more made comfortable. This account of the Utah Expedition is given as a part of the history of the Cavalry, and, though the campaign was a bloodless one, it is undoubtedly true that on no other expedition did our mounted men ever suffer so much.

In the spring of 1858, the Mormons deserted the City of the Great Salt Lake and fled to the mountains; and their hatred toward the United States on account of this religious persecution, as they considered it, was of the most bitter character. In the history of the Jews writhing under the Spanish Inquisition, of the Albigenses hunted through Languedoc, a record of similar bitterness may be found, but its parallel does not exist outside the annals of religious persecution.

The entrance of the army into Salt Lake City was one of the most remarkable scenes in American history. All day long the troops marched through the long streets. The only sounds which broke the stillness of the scene was the music of the military bands and the dull clanking of the baggage wagons as they rolled along. The streets and houses were deserted. The stillness was so profound that, during the intervals of the columns, the gurgling of the creek which runs through the city could be distinctly heard by the few who were passing silently along. It was like the city of the dead, so quiet was it.

During the winter, Captain Marcy, of the 5th Infantry, had been sent to the settlements in New Mexico for supplies—salt in particular—and, upon his return, had been accompanied by a detachment of the Mounted Rifle Regiment, under Colonel Loring, who had been promoted colonel upon the promotion of Persifer F. Smith to the grade of Brigadier-General, on the 30th of December, 1856. George B. Crittenden then became Lieutenant-Colonel, and Charles F. Ruff Major.

The order of march from Fort Bridger was as follows:

Brevet Colonel C. F. Smith's battalion;
10th Infantry, and Phelps's Battery;
5th Infantry, and Reno's Battery;
Loring's battalion of Mounted Riflemen;
3rd Infantry;
6th Infantry;
Volunteers;
2nd Dragoons.

The 2nd Regiment of Cavalry received orders to march to Utah, and concentrated on the Brazos River, near Fort Belknap, in the summer of 1858, but the order was countermanded, and the regiment was again scattered over Texas.

The Mormons promised to obey the laws, a camp was established thirty-six miles from Salt Lake City, and thus ended the widely-known Utah Expedition. For his conduct on this expedition, Colonel Johnston was made a brevet Brigadier-General.

Brigadier-General Persifer F. Smith died at Fort Leavenworth in the month of May, 1858. On the 14th of June, Colonel Harney, who was a brevet Brigadier-General, was appointed to fill the vacancy. P. St. George Cooke then became Colonel of the 2nd Dragoons, Marshal S. Howe Lieutenant-Colonel, and Lawrence P. Graham Junior-Major.

CHAPTER 9

Indian Skirmishes in 1858

During the year 1858, the Indians in Oregon, New Mexico, and Texas were very troublesome, and several mounted officers and men fell while maintaining the honour of our flag on distant and obscure fields. It is wonderful the amount of labour done by the mounted regiments, and the number of conflicts they had with the Indians.

In May of this year occurred one of the most sad events that ever befell our cavalry. The Indians of Oregon had broken the terms of the peace, and had murdered some white men. Lieutenant-Colonel Steptoe was sent out to try and see what could be done. He had with him three companies of the 1st Dragoons, and company E, 9th Infantry—in all, five company officers and one hundred and fifty-two enlisted men. Hearing that the hostile Pelouses were near Al-pon-on-we, in the Nez Perces land, he moved to that point, and was ferried across Snake River by a Nez Perces chief. The enemy fled north, and he followed leisurely on the road to Colville.

On Sunday morning, the 16th of May, he found his command suddenly surrounded by ten or twelve hundred Indians, of various tribes Spokanes, Pelouses, Coeur d'Alenes Yakimas, and some others all armed, painted, and defiant. He moved slowly on until just about to enter a ravine, when, seeing it was the intention of the Indians to attack him in that place, he turned aside and encamped. The Indians moved up alongside, the whole wild and frenzied mass yelling and taunting the soldiers in every way.

The Indians now wished to parley. Steptoe gave them the opportunity, when they inquired why he was invading their country. He told them he was not doing so, but was on his way to Colville, and wished, if possible, to keep peace. The Indians appeared to be satisfied, but would not give him boats with which to cross the Spokane River. He therefore concluded to retrace his steps, and the next morning turned back toward the post.

He had not marched more than three miles, when the Indians, who had gathered on the hills adjoining the line of march, began an attack on the rear guard, and immediately the fight became general. The soldiers were obliged to defend the pack-train while in motion in a country peculiarly adapted to Indian warfare. They had but a small supply of ammunition, and, becoming excited, fired in the wildest manner.

They did, however, sustain the reputation of the army for gallantry, and fought for some hours, charging repeatedly with determination and success. The difficult and dangerous duty of flanking the column was assigned to Brevet Captain Oliver H. P. Taylor and Lieutenant William R. Gaston, of the 1st Dragoons, to both of whom it proved fatal.

Gaston was killed about twelve o'clock, when his company gave way before overwhelming numbers. About half an hour afterward Captain Taylor was brought in mortally wounded.

Upon this, Steptoe took possession of a neighbouring height and halted. The fight still continued, the enemy occupying the neighbouring hills and picking off our men. The number of wounded continued to increase, and it was evident the Indians intended to attempt to carry the hill by assault. The loss of their officers and comrades began to tell on the spirits of the men; they were becoming discouraged; added to this was the fact that their ammunition was nearly exhausted, and two companies were armed with musketoons, which, in their present condition, were of no service whatever.

It was plain the enemy would give them no rest during the night, and, after a consultation with his officers, Steptoe determined to make a forced march for Snake River, eighty-five miles distant, and secure the canoes in advance of the Indians, who had already threatened to do so in regard to them.

Accordingly, about ten o'clock at night, the command started, and, after a most fatiguing march, crossed Snake River in safety. This was a most deplorable affair, but no one was to blame. Our men fought the best they could, but were overpowered by superior numbers. The loss to the Indians was not ascertained, though several were known to have been killed, but they gained a decided advantage, and it made them more arrogant than ever.

It was determined immediately to punish the Indians, and a force was fitted out, under command of Colonel George Wright, of the 9th

INDIAN FIGHT, BATTLE OF FOUR LAKES

Regiment of Infantry. A work was thrown up at the junction of the Snake and Tucanon Rivers, called Fort Taylor, after which the troops crossed the former stream. This was on the 26th of August.

On the 1st of September a fight took place, which is known as the "Battle of the Four Lakes." I give the following graphic description of the fight, written by Lieutenant Kip, of the artillery. He says;

> My place, as adjutant of the artillery battalion, was of course with Captain Keyes. We rode to the top of the hill, when the whole scene lay before us like a splendid panorama. Below us lay 'four lakes'—a large one at the foot of the barren hill on which we were, and just beyond it three smaller ones—surrounded by rugged rocks, and almost entirely fringed with pines. Between these lakes, and beyond them to the northwest, stretched out a plain for miles, terminated by bare grassy hills, one succeeding another as far as the eye could reach. In the far distance was dimly seen a line of mountains covered with the black pine.
>
> On the plain below us we saw the enemy. Every spot seemed alive with the wild warriors we had come so far to meet. They were in the pines on the edge of the lakes, in the ravines and gullies, on the opposite hillsides, and swarming on the plain. They seemed to cover the country for some two miles. Mounted on their fleet, hardy horses, the crowds swayed back and forth, brandishing their weapons, shouting their war-cries, and keeping up a song of defiance.
>
> Most of them were armed with Hudson Bay muskets, while others had bows and arrows and lances. They were in all the bravery of their war array, gaudily painted, and decorated with their wild trappings—their plumes fluttered above them, while below, skins and trinkets, and all kinds of fantastic embellishments, flaunted in the sunshine. Their horses, too, were arrayed in the most glaring finery. Some were even painted, and with colours to form the greatest contrast the white being smeared with crimson in fantastic figures, and the dark-coloured streaked with white clay. Beads and fringes of gaudy colours were hanging from their bridles, while the plumes of eagles' feathers, interwoven with the mane and tail, fluttered as the breeze swept over them, and completed their wild, fantastic appearance.
>
> *By heavens! it was a glorious sight to see*

The gay array of their wild chivalry.

But we had no time for mere admiration, for other work was at hand. Orders were at once issued for the artillery and infantry to be deployed as skirmishers, and advance down the hill, driving the Indians before them from their coverts until they reached the plain, where the dragoons could act against them. At the same time, Lieutenant White, with the howitzer battery, supported by company A, under Lieutenant Tyler, and the Rifles, was sent to the right to drive them out of the woods. The latter met with a vigorous resistance; but a few discharges of the howitzer, with their spirited attack, soon dislodged the enemy, and compelled them to take refuge on the hills.

In the meanwhile, the companies moved down the hill with all the precision of a parade, and, as we rode along the line, it was pleasant to see the enthusiasm of the men to get within reach of the enemy. As soon as they were within some six hundred yards they opened their fire, and delivered it steadily as they advanced. Our soldiers aimed regularly, though it was no easy task to hit their shifting marks. The Indians acted as skirmishers, advancing rapidly and delivering their fire, and then retreating again with a quickness and irregularity which rendered it difficult to reach them. They were wheeling and dashing about, always on the run, apparently each fighting on his own account. But Minie-balls and long-range rifles were things with which now, for the first time, they were to be made acquainted. As the line advanced, first we saw one Indian reel in his saddle and fall then—two or three—then half a dozen. Then some, horses would dash madly forward, showing that the balls were telling upon them. The instant, however, that the braves fell, they were seized by their companions and dragged to the rear, to be borne off. We saw one Indian leading off a horse with two of his dead companions tied on it.

But in a few minutes, as the line drew nearer, the fire became too heavy, and the whole array broke and fled toward the plain. This was the chance for which the dragoons had been impatiently waiting. As the line advanced, they had followed on behind it, leading their horses. Now the order was given to mount, and they rode through the company intervals to the front. In an instant was heard the voice of Major Grier ringing over the plain, as he shouted, Charge the rascals! and on the dragoons went at headlong speed. Taylor's and Gaston's companies were there, burning for revenge, and soon they were on them.

We saw the flash of their sabres as they cut them down. Lieutenant Davidson shot one warrior from his saddle as they charged up, and Lieutenant Gregg clove the skull of another. Yells, and shrieks, and uplifted hands were of no avail, as they rode over them. A number were left dead upon the ground, when once more the crowd broke and dashed forward to the hills. It was a race for life, as the flying warriors streamed out of the glens and ravines, and over the open plain, and took refuge in the clumps of woods or on the rising ground.

Here they were secure from the dragoons. Had the latter been well mounted they would have made a terrible slaughter. But their horses were too much worn out to allow them to reach the main body. For twenty-eight days they had been on their march, their horses saddled all day and engaged in constant scouting, at night picketed, with only a little grass after camping. They were obliged, therefore, to halt when they reached the hill-side, their horses being entirely blown.

Then the line of foot once more passed them and advanced, renewing their fire, and driving the Indians over the hills for about two miles. As we ascended, the men were so totally exhausted that many had fallen out of the ranks, and Captain Keyes was obliged to order a short halt to let them come up. When a portion had joined, we resumed our march.

The enemy was completely routed, and retreated precipitately. The loss to Wright's command was trifling, and the Indians are supposed to have lost seventeen killed and between forty and fifty wounded.

Colonel Wright, in his report, mentions the gallant conduct of the cavalry officers with him. They were, Brevet-Major Grier, Lieutenants Henry B. Davidson, William D. Pender, and David McM. Gregg. The latter, with Assistant Surgeon John F. Randolph, was with Steptoe at the time of his fight. Randolph behaved admirably, and was thanked by the commanding officer.

Again, the enemy was met on the Spokan Plains, and here, too, they were again defeated; the dragoons here, as before, doing their whole duty. Finding that they had mistaken the strength of the whites, the Indians sued for peace, which was granted them, and they were glad to remain quiet. The blood of Taylor and Gaston was avenged!

The grain which the Indians had collected was destroyed; but the most severe blow was given to them in the destruction of their horses, a large number of them having been captured. Without horses these Indians were powerless.

Brevet Captain Oliver H. Perry Taylor, who was killed, was a native of Rhode Island, and, after graduating at West Point, joined the 1st Dragoons in July, 1846. He was breveted First Lieutenant at Embudo and Taos, and Captain at Santa Cruz de los Resales. He was a fine man, and by his amiable character had won many friends.

Second Lieutenant William F. Gaston was from North Carolina. He graduated at West Point in July, 1856, and became a Lieutenant in the 1st Dragoons in November. His classmates, who knew him, entertained a high respect for him. He had often expressed a wish to die in battle, and the wish was gratified.

In the month of September, Brevet Major Earl Van Dorn, with four companies of the 2nd Cavalry, left the clear fork of the Brazos River on an extended scout after Indians. He travelled to Otter Creek, where he built a stockade enclosure for the protection of his supplies, and, leaving a small party of infantry to guard it, pushed on toward the Antelope Hills. He had moved but a short distance, when his spies came in, and informed him that they had found a large Comanche camp, near the Witchita village, about ninety miles due east from the depot.

Upon the receipt of this information, he had all the stores, draught-mules, and extra horses moved at once into the defensive enclosure, and marched for that point with the cavalry and Indian allies. After making a forced march of ninety odd miles in thirty-eight hours, during the latter part of which the men were continuously in the saddle for sixteen and a half hours, including the charge and pursuit, they arrived at the village on the morning of the 1st instant.

He had been in hopes to reach a point in close proximity to the enemy before daylight, and had made dispositions for an attack based on information received from the spies; but, as daybreak came upon them when they were yet four or five miles off, he found the information incorrect.

He formed his companies in four columns, with intervals of one hundred yards, and then moved on, giving orders to the captains to deploy and charge whenever they came in sight of the village. After marching in this way for some time, the charge was sounded on the left, and in a moment the soldiers swarmed down into the enemy's camp in gallant style, and soon found themselves warmly met by the Indians, who defended their camp with obstinacy.

There being many ravines near the camp, it was an hour and a half before the Indians were entirely beaten out of it, during which time there were many hand to hand encounters, both by officers and men. The friendly Indians meantime had been stampeding the animals of the Comanches, and ran off the whole *caballada*. Van Dorn gained a complete victory, the Indians leaving between seventy and eighty dead on the field. But our own loss was serious; and Second Lieutenant Cornelius Van Camp, of the 2nd Cavalry, a young officer of much promise, was killed on the field, with several of the men. Major Van Dorn was severely wounded, together with a number of the soldiers. This was, perhaps, the most complete victory ever achieved over the Comanches; indeed, the commanding general of the department said, in his general order upon the subject, that it was "a victory more decisive and complete than any recorded in the history of Indian warfare."

The officers engaged were Major Van Dorn, Captains Charles J. Whiting, Nathan G. Evans, and Richard W. Johnson; Lieutenants Charles W. Phifer, Cornelius Van Camp, James E. Harrison, A. Parker Porter, and James W. Major, all of the 2nd Cavalry.

This, with the fights in Oregon, were the most important fought during the year; but there were others, which, in justice to those engaged, I will give in the order in which they occurred. The facts are gathered mainly from Lieutenant General Scott's Order, No. 22, for the year 1858.

In May, the northern column of the Gila Expedition, under Colonel Loring, of the Mounted Rifles, after a difficult pursuit, overtook a party of Mogollon Indians in the mountains, and, after a spirited skirmish, defeated them. Among the killed was a notorious Mogollon chief named Cuchillo Negro. The families of the Indians were taken prisoners, their camp equipage captured, and a flock of about a thousand sheep taken.

Second Lieutenant James B. Witherell, of the 2nd Cavalry, with a small detachment from that regiment, came up with a party of Indians (who had robbed the mail party of a number of mules) near the head waters of the Nueces (Texas) in November, 1858. A short and severe contest took place; the Indians were routed and defeated. Lieutenant Witherell and three of the soldiers were wounded. In their flight the Indians made their first march of ninety miles without stopping.

Lieutenant William W. Averell, and a detachment of Mounted Rifles, captured a party of Indians near Fort Craig, New Mexico. They attempted to escape, when the lieutenant and his men fired upon them, killing all of them. They had been committing various depredations, and merited their fate.

Sergeant McDonald, of the 2nd Cavalry, had a fight with a party of Indians near the Llano River, in Texas, killing some of them, and having three of his own men wounded.

In August, Captain McLane, with a party of Mounted Rifles, and a body of guides and spies, was attacked by a large force of Navajo Indians near Bear Spring, New Mexico. This was an unequal contest, highly creditable to Captain McLane, who was severely wounded, and he succeeded in beating the Indians, with considerable loss.

In New Mexico, the Mounted Rifles, under Lieutenant-Colonel Miles, fought the Indians on several occasions during the autumn of 1858; Captains Elliott and Hatch, Lieutenants Lane and Averell, particularly distinguished themselves.

It may be well to mention that the camels which were purchased by the government were sent to Camp Verde, in Texas, where they were for a time in charge of a cavalry company. At that place they increased in numbers very considerably, a portion having been sent across to California with Mr. Beale. There is no doubt about the fact that they will do well in this country, though our people as yet do not understand loading and packing them; but, as we gain knowledge upon this subject, we may yet render these animals in America very useful. The rebellion has retarded progress in many ways, and at its close, if there are any camels left, they may yet be successfully experimented with.

The few times they were sent out on the sterile plains of Western Texas they did well, and those who had them in charge spoke highly of their capacity. The Bedouins of the desert have many absurd ideas about them, which it will do well for us to discard, if we intend to make use of them here. They are not very handsome animals, and I do not think cavalry men would readily take a liking to them. The deserts of America exhibit nearly the same features as the well-known desert districts on the Libyan and Arabian sides of the Nile valley, and we may yet see a dromedary corps fitted out for that region, though the time appears now to be far distant.

The year 1859 was not an eventful one for the cavalry, although one or two fights occurred which were of some importance. The regiments remained in their former positions, with the exception of five

CAMELS IN TEXAS

companies of the 1st Cavalry, which were sent to the Department of Texas. It seems almost too monotonous to continue to describe the skirmishes which our cavalry troops had from time to time, but I see no help for it, and must record events as they happened. To say that the mounted force was at peace would be to say what was not so, although the country itself might have been.

The life of the cavalryman on the frontier was one of extreme hardship, and officers grew prematurely old while undergoing the privations incident thereto. There seemed no prospect of a better condition of things. Their lives were spent among the wildest scenes, and, as a class, this served to purify them, and they were honest, upright, and charitable. Their leaves of absence from duty were few, and at long intervals; and many people who, in the commencement of the rebellion, welcomed their coming as one of the greatest blessings to the Union cause, had, while they were stationed on the frontiers, let no opportunity escape of disparaging them, or the noble little army to which they belonged.

But that school made them true soldiers, than whom there are no better on earth.

In October, 1858, the Regiment of Mounted Rifles in New Mexico had several conflicts with the Indians, in which they were almost uniformly successful. In these, Captains McLane, Lindsay, Washington L. Elliott, Duncan, and Morris, and Lieutenants Howland, Averell, and Lane were much distinguished. These fights were some of them severe, and the Rifles lost a number of men killed and wounded.

In February, Lieutenant David S. Stanley, of the 1st Cavalry, with some men of his regiment, after an exciting chase, killed several Comanches who had been robbing near Fort Arbuckle.

In May, Captain Albert G. Brackett, with Lieutenant Wesley Owens, and his company of the 2nd Cavalry, made a scout down the great Comanche trail a long distance, met a party of Indians and defeated them, and returned by way of Presidio del Norte, in the Mexican State of Chihuahua, to the American side of the Rio Grande.

In August, Lieutenant Ebenezer Gay, with company G, 2nd Dragoons, had a severe fight with the Indians in Utah, and defeated them most signally. Gay had several men wounded, and killed quite a number of the enemy.

But the main fight of this year was again fought by Van Dorn, with a command of the 2nd Cavalry, against the Comanches, in Texas, who are among the best riders in the world. Their horsemanship is truly remarkable. In this fight, both Captain E. Kirby Smith and Lieutenant Fitzhugh Lee, of the 2nd Cavalry, were wounded. They have since become widely known as leaders in the ranks of the rebels. The fight of Van Dorn took place in the valley of the Nescutunga; but I can do no better than give his somewhat flowery account of the position and of the fight. He says:

On the 12th of May, the second day after leaving the Cimarron, the column descended into the valley of the Nescutunga, a beautiful stream—direct tributary of the Arkansas—whose sweet waters and green sloping banks, shaded by groves of the thickest foliage, were especially inviting to me, just emerging from a desert, as they were, no doubt, at all times to the Comanches. Here was found the remains of a camp of several hundred, probably as many as a thousand Indians, which had not been abandoned more than ten or twelve days.

I accordingly halted, and ordered out my Indian spies, who returned about dark with the intelligence that there was a large, fresh trail going north, about four miles down the valley. I put the column on this trail the next morning and followed it. There was an incessant fall of rain during the march, accompanied by a cold north wind, which, though it increased the probabilities of our success, made the ground extremely heavy, slippery, and leg-wearying to the horses and pack-mules. After following the trail, therefore, until about two o'clock, I halted to rest and to graze them, intending to move on later in the evening.

Our bivouac fires had not been kindled long before an alarm was given by a sentinel of the picket guard, who reported that he had seen two Comanches peering over the crest of a neighbouring hill into camp. I immediately detached Lieutenant W. B. Royall, with thirty men, to ascertain the truth of the report, and to see if he could discover any sign of the enemy's presence in our vicinity. In a short time, a messenger from the lieutenant dashed into camp, and reported to me that there was a large party of Comanches in a ravine about three miles off; that Lieutenant Royall was endeavouring to separate them and their horses; that he would try and keep them at bay until I could bring up my command.

I ordered to horse sounded, the guard to be left in charge of pack-mules, and then mounting, proceeded at a gallop to the scene. Upon my arrival, I found Lieutenant Royall, with his detachment mounted, near the ravine, holding the Comanches in check in their camp, from whom he had very adroitly driven off their horses, for which great credit is due him. The position taken by the Indians I found to be a remarkably strong one for defence, being in a deep ravine, densely covered with a stunted growth of timber and brambles, through which a small stream, with abrupt banks, meandered from bluff to bluff on either side. It was impossible to penetrate this jungle but slowly; and it was equally impossible to get a glimpse of the concealed enemy until within a few yards of him, or until the flight of his arrow, which seemed to come from the ground, indicated his locality. It was necessary to use caution. I accordingly dismounted some riflemen and felt for his position. In doing this, the skirmishers, who entered above into the ravine, and some farther down, under Captain E. K. Smith, got on opposite sides of the ravine, and were endangering each other's lives by a cross fire. I immediately sounded the rally, and had the companies reformed. Mounted troops were then placed on the crest of the hills above the ravine, and at the outlet below, and dismounted skirmishers sent in above to sweep the ravine through.

A small party, under Lieutenants Lee and Harrison, first entered, and gallantly charged through on the left side, finding the Indians in the creek and behind a breastwork of logs, from which nothing could be seen of them but their heads and shoulders as they raised up to fire. Lieutenants Eagle and Cosby were then ordered in with parts of companies A 7 and H, accompanied by Lieutenants Lee, Harrison, and Kimmel, with detachments of their companies, then by detachments from the other companies, 'B,' 'C,' 'F,' and 'G,' led by their officers, and soon the engagement became general, as the enemy's position was better ascertained. It was soon over.

The Comanches fought without giving or asking quarter until there was not one left to bend a bow, and would have won the admiration of every brave soldier of the command but for the intrusive reflection that they were the murderers of the wives and children of our frontiersmen, and the most wretched of thieves.

The result of this engagement has already been given you in the short report of the affair written on the ground immediately after it occurred. A too high meed of praise for gallantry and unflinching courage cannot be awarded to the officers and men who have achieved this success over so desperate and skilful a foe. Although superior in numbers to the Indians, it nevertheless required the coolest and most undaunted in dividual bravery to advance upon the danger that presented itself in this fearful ravine—a danger as imminent as it was unseen—without a single one of those immediate incentives to chivalric deeds—the open field, the charge, the shout of defiance, the gallant overthrow of an enemy by a comrade, the clank, clash, and glitter of steel—without one of these, the troops of this command moved, as it were, into darkness, and, with a courage that challenged admiration, *felt* for the danger they were called upon to encounter.

Nothing gives me greater pleasure than in thus being able to call the attention of the commanding general to their gallantry, and in testifying to their good behaviour throughout the expedition. To the officers with me I am not only indebted for the most hearty assistance in every military duty, but also, without exception, for their conspicuous gallantry and energy in achieving the successes it has been my good fortune to report to the department. They were, Lieutenant Fitzhugh Lee, adjutant to the expedition; Surgeon James Simons, and Assistant Surgeon W. H. Babcock, M.D., on the staff; and Captain E. K. Smith, and Lieutenants W. B. Royall, R. N Eagle, G. B. Cosby, J. B. Witherell, J. E. Harrison, and M. M. Kimmel, 2nd Cavalry, in command of the troops. Surgeon Simons and Assistant-Surgeon Babcock were assiduous in their attentions to the wounded, not only of the officers and men of the command, but also of the Indians who were taken prisoners.

In this fight First Sergeant John W. Spangler, of company H, 2nd Cavalry, was wounded, and was afterward promoted to a second lieutenancy in another regiment.

CHAPTER 10

Skirmishes with Indians in 1859 and 1860

During the summer of 1859, General Twiggs, then commanding the department of Texas, had stripped the Rio Grande frontier of all its troops. Thus Brownsville, Ringgold Barracks, and Laredo, on the American side of that stream, were left without garrisons, and, being on the borders of Mexico, where there is always a bad population, trouble occurred, as every thinking man knew it would. Why Twiggs pursued this policy is not known, but difficulties took place soon enough, and the blame of the whole affair may be properly laid at his door.

The troops were moved into the interior of Texas, and up on the El Paso Road. A Mexican, named Cortinas, thinking he had been wronged by certain citizens of Brownsville, crossed from the Mexican side of the Rio Grande, in the autumn of 1859, with a body of armed men, and committed various depredations, killing several citizens of Brownsville.

Immediately the whole frontier was in a blaze of excitement, and Twiggs was called upon to assist the unarmed settlers. There had been wrong on both sides, American as well as Mexican, but that gave the latter no right to invade our soil. This was done, however, by irresponsible parties, and the Mexican authorities at Matamoros, opposite Brownsville, disclaimed all participation in the affair. I believe this was truly the case, and have no doubt but the Mexican citizens of the better class were as much opposed to the robber band of Cortinas as the Americans themselves.

Twiggs, seeing that he had committed a grave error, immediately assembled a force, and sent it with all dispatch to Brownsville, under command of Major Heintzelman, United States Army. There was but one mounted company which could be readily detached; this was Captain George Stoneman's, of the 2nd Cavalry, which was sent immediately from Fort Clark. On the 14th of December, 1859, Heintzelman attacked the enemy, who had blockaded the main road not far from Brownsville, and, after a sharp fight, drove them off. His force consisted of Stoneman's company, three companies of Texas Rangers, and three companies of artillery, serving as infantry, with two 24-pounder howitzers.

Major Heintzelman followed them up, and again met them at Ringgold Barracks with the same force. Here a severe fight took place, and the enemy, under Cortinas, retreated across the Rio Grande into Mexico. From that side he continued to harass our people for some time. The closing scenes of this affair I will give as soon as I have given an account of several fights which occurred in different portions of the country between our cavalry and the Indians.

In November, 1859, Major Shepherd had a fight in New Mexico with a band of Tunicha Navajo Indians, in which they were defeated as usual. Lieutenants Du Bois and Claflin, of the Mounted Rifles, accompanied the command, and behaved well. Lieutenant McNeill, of the Mounted Rifles, had another fight on the 3rd of December near Fort Buchanan; and Sergeant McCabe, of the same regiment, another on the 4th of the same month, both of which were creditable.

Captain McLane, with Lieutenant Cressey and forty men of the Mounted Rifles, had a most successful affair on the 5th of February, 1860. On the 8th of the same month Sergeant McQuade also successfully fought the Indians; and on the same day, though in another locality, Lieutenant-Colonel Andrew Porter, of the same regiment, again defeated them. The losses to our men were considerable; and on the 13th of October, 1860, Captain George McLane, who had met the Indians so often and who had behaved so well, was killed in an action with the Navajos in their country. He was from Maryland, had served with credit at Contreras and Churubusco, and was breveted Captain for gallantry at Chapultepec.

Major Sedgwick, of the 1st Cavalry, had a fight near the Upper Arkansas with a band of Kiowas, in which Lieutenant George D. Bayard, of the same regiment, was severely wounded. This occurred on the 11th of July, 1860.

In Texas, Sergeant Patrick Collins, of the 2nd Cavalry, fought and defeated a party of Comanches on the 14th of December, 1859. Lieutenant Fitzhugh Lee defeated another party on the 15th of January,

1860. First Sergeant Chapman, of the same regiment, another on the 24th of January; Sergeant Craig, of the same regiment, another on the 27th of January; and Captain Richard W. Johnson, same regiment, another party on the 30th of the same month. All of these were minor affairs, but still very creditable to those engaged.

Major George H. Thomas, of the 2nd Cavalry, was severely wounded by the Indians in August, 1860. He was accompanied by Lieutenant William W. Lowe, of the same regiment, who took care of him, and brought in the command after the major was disabled.

Captain Samuel D. Sturgis, with six companies of the 1st Cavalry, had the most important Indian fight of the year at Solomon's Fork of the Arkansas River, where he defeated a large band of Comanches. This occurred on the 3rd of September. The officers who accompanied him, all of whom distinguished themselves, were Assistant Surgeon Charles T. Alexander; Captains Beall, McIntosh, and Carr; and Lieutenants Stockton, Riddick, Church, Ingraham, Lomax, Fish, and Andrew Jackson, junior.

First Sergeant Feilner, of the 1st Dragoons, had a severe fight with the Indians in California, in which he signally distinguished himself, in May, 1860. Major Enoch Steen, with Captain Andrew J. Smith's command, had several skirmishes with the Indians in Oregon in May and June, and almost always succeeded in worsting them. He was accompanied by Lieutenants Johnson, Fender, Gregg, and Wheeler, of the same regiment.

This ended the fighting of the cavalry with the Indians for the present, as they were soon called to new fields.

To return to the Cortinas difficulties. General Twiggs left Texas on a furlough in 1860, and soon afterward Lieutenant-Colonel Robert E. Lee, of the 2nd Cavalry, was placed in command of that department. In March of that year, he started from San Antonio to visit the Rio Grande, taking as his escort Captain Brackett's company of the 2nd Cavalry from Camp Verde. At Eagle Pass he took another company of the 2nd Cavalry, which was stationed there under Lieutenant Eagle. He marched to Laredo, and thence to Ringgold Barracks (Rio Grande City). After stopping a day or two, he pushed forward to Edinburgh, opposite Reynosa. He learned while at Ringgold that Stoneman and Ford had crossed into Mexico, where they had had another fight.

Colonel Lee's arrival at Edinburgh, opposite Reynosa, was most opportune, as the Mexican soldiers had on the morning of the day before (April 6th, 1860) fired into Major Ford's Texas Rangers from across the Rio Grande. The fire was returned, and two Mexicans were severely wounded. This state of things, amounting almost to actual war between the two nations, Colonel Lee took immediate measures to suppress by sending Captain Brackett, with a white flag, as bearer of a peace message to the authorities of Reynosa. Before his arrival all communication had ceased.

The captain was ordered to inquire into the cause of the firing across the river, and to direct some of Cortinas's men, who were known to be in that town, to be delivered up to the Americans. All of the streets of Reynosa were barricaded, and loaded cannon were planted in front of the House of Justice. Four companies of Mexicans were under arms in the *Plaza*, and they expected a re-enforcement of cavalry from Camargo, and infantry from Matamoros the same day. To Colonel Lee's letter they replied that none of Cortinas's men were in town, and that he had fled into the interior.

Upon receiving this reply, Lee went to Brownsville, and, crossing over to Matamoros, had a consultation with General Garcia, the Mexican commander. With him he arranged a plan for capturing the outlaw Cortinas. In April, Garcia sent out a body of Mexican soldiers, who fell in with the main party of Cortinas's men near the Rancho de Santa Cruz, in the Mexican State of Tamaulipas. A fierce skirmish ensued, and Florencio Fernandez, one of Cortinas's leaders, was shot, and afterward hung. Francisco Cisneros was taken prisoner and carried to Matamoros, and the band of Cortinas was entirely dispersed. He escaped, and it was years before he again appeared on the stage.

Two companies of cavalry were retained on the Rio Grande, and two were sent to the interior of Texas to guard the frontier settlers. Meantime General Twiggs had returned to Texas, where his public career was about to close in the most dishonourable manner. He who had been lauded as one of the leaders of American soldiery was guilty of a treason blacker than that which shrouds the name of Benedict Arnold. True to his instincts, he betrayed his master for gold. He is well styled "Twiggs the Traitor." How a man who had occupied his position, and had received so many favours from the federal government, could have acted in the manner he did is a mystery, and will ever remain so.

The Act of Secession was passed by the Convention of Texas after that of South Carolina, and Twiggs gave his aid to everything that was done by that body. Some good men in the Northern States have always said they did not understand why the soldiery of Texas should have delivered up their horses, etc., to the Texans. The answer is this: If they had had a true and reliable commanding officer, they no doubt could have made their way to the Red River, and thus have made their escape; but, unfortunately, their general was a most villainous traitor, and against this the best efforts of men in inferior grades availed nothing. Twiggs had scattered the troops far and wide; he had decreased the amount of their transportation and supplies; and against this no man or set of men could do anything. The depot at San Antonio was given up to McCulloch and his minions, and several men who had fattened at government expense joined in the conspiracy.

Twiggs was dismissed, and the old man's grey hairs bowed with infamy. Waite took command, but it was too late, and all this just and good man could do amounted to nothing. The 2nd Cavalry, which for years past had protected the frontier settlers, was about to be driven out of the country, and its chief officers joined with alacrity the Southern cause. One of the most painful pictures of this dreary scene was the return of Van Dorn with commissions from his master, Jeff. Davis, to such officers as would join the rebel cause. Thank heaven, he gained none, and left camp thoroughly dispirited. He had joined the secession cause at once, and had boasted that he could take the regiment with him; but he discovered his error, and went away a sadder though not a better man.

The regiment assembled at Green Lake, thirty miles from the Gulf coast, and thence six companies left in March for "the States." They marched to Indianola, the officers who were true having abandoned their property, which they had been years in accumulating, and there, taking steamships, left the inhospitable shores. It was a dreary scene, and one which called up many bitter reproaches against the Texans. The best years of many of the officers and men had been given to Texas, to shield her frontier settlements from the wrath of the Indian warriors. Some were suffering from wounds received in that service, and all felt the gloom which must pervade the earth on the last day.

Discarded by those who ought to have been their friends by all laws of justice and right, they turned their faces sorrowfully toward the North. The dearly-loved plains were left behind, the bright skies and balmy atmosphere were changed for the cool breezes of Northern climes, and all the grounds hallowed by the blood of comrades were left in possession of those who had polluted our flag and set at naught our glorious Union. Rejected by those who ought to have loved them—borne down by those who ought to have cherished them, they still clung to the dearly-loved symbol of all that is dear to liberty and the human race on this continent. May they receive their reward!

The six companies which left first embarked on ship-board at Indianola, and went thence to Florida, thence to Cuba, and thence to New York City, where, stopping only one night, they went to Carlisle Barracks, in Pennsylvania. Two companies were sent to Washington, and the other four, under Major Thomas, followed overland in a few days. Palmer, Stoneman, Brackett, Jenifer, Chambliss, Harrison, and Kimmel, came out first, with six companies, and were followed by Whiting, Johnson, Lowe, and Porter, with the other four. After refitting, the latter four joined the army under General Patterson.

Never before, since the dawn of the Republic, had a body of United States Cavalry been in the harbour of New York, and the appearance of the men and officers gave rise to many singular remarks from the money-loving people of that city.

Many cavalry officers had by this time resigned, others were on the point of doing so, and all good fellowship and confidence in one another had disappeared. Sumter fell before the cowardly fire of the South Carolinians, who had arrayed an army of fifteen thousand men against a brave little band of ninety United States soldiers, and the rebellion was begun in earnest. Without waiting for Congress to assemble, President Lincoln ordered the regular army to be increased, and called out a body of volunteers.

By this order, another regular cavalry regiment, the 3rd, was added to the army.

David Hunter was appointed colonel. He was a native of the District of Columbia, had graduated at West Point, served sometime in the 1st Infantry, and was appointed Captain in the 1st Regiment of Dragoons in March, 1833; he resigned in July, 1836, and was reappointed from Illinois, as paymaster, in March, 1842. He was serving in that grade when appointed colonel, on the 14th of May, 1861. Hunter is one of the most amiable and upright of men; he is a good soldier, and has won a high reputation for daring and skill, which is justly his due.

William H. Emory, who had just resigned from the 1st Cavalry, was appointed Lieutenant-Colonel.

Edward H. Wright, of Maryland, a citizen, was appointed senior major. He served some time on the staff of the general-in-chief, and resigned in 1863. The next major was James H. Carlton, then Captain in the 1st Dragoons. He had served with credit in the Mexican War, and was breveted Major for gallantry at Buena Vista. The junior Major was Lawrence A. Williams, who was promoted from a Captaincy in the 10th Infantry.

Lieutenant-Colonel Joseph E. Johnston, of the 1st Cavalry, was promoted Quarter-Master General, and shortly afterward resigned. Of the colonels of the five old cavalry regiments four had resigned, *viz.*, Fauntleroy, of the 1st Dragoons, Loring, of the Mounted Riflemen, Robert E. Lee, of the 1st Cavalry, and Albert Sidney Johnston, of the 2nd Cavalry. All of them joined the rebels.

Colonel Sumner, of the 1st Cavalry, had been promoted Brigadier-General on the 16th of March, 1861 (in place of Twiggs, dismissed), and Lieutenant-Colonel Robert E. Lee had been promoted in his place. The sad record given above was increased by the resignation of several other cavalry field-officers. They were Brevet Colonel May; Lieut. Cols. Crittenden, Emory, and Hardee: Majors Van Dorn, Kirby Smith, and Sibley—all of whom, except May and Emory, have attained high rank in the South.

When our army crossed the Potomac River from Washington, in May, 1861, there were but three companies of cavalry with it. One, under Major Stoneman, went to Alexandria; another, under Captain Brackett, to Arlington; and the third, under Lieutenant Tompkins, went across the Chain Bridge, and was stationed at Fort Corcoran. They all belonged to the 2nd Regiment, and continued to occupy these positions until our forces moved on to Bull Run.

Lieutenant Tompkins, with his company, made a night march to Fairfax Court-house, where he had a spirited skirmish with the enemy, and, it being the first cavalry fight which occurred in the Eastern States, he gained a good deal of credit. It was a daring feat, and was well executed.

It seems strange now to look back to that period and see what a prejudice there was against the raising of any more cavalry. It was considered, and is; in fact, an expensive arm of the service; but this gave those in power no *right* to ignore it altogether, and a severe lesson which they and the country received a few days afterward taught them that they must have cavalry, and plenty of it.

When the army left Arlington Heights and thereabouts, it had seven companies of cavalry and no more. People years hence will hardly believe this, but it is, nevertheless, strictly true. There were two companies of the 1st Regiment, four of the 2nd, and one company of the 2nd Dragoons, under Major Palmer. Two companies of the 2nd Cavalry were left in Washington.

Lieutenant Tompkins, at the head of Company B, U.S. Dragoons, charging into town at Fairfax Court House

Upon reaching Blackburn's Ford, on the 18th of July, 1861, Major Palmer detached two companies of the 2nd Cavalry, under Captain Brackett, to go forward with Brigadier-General Tyler and assist him in making a reconnaissance. Tyler had some infantry with him, who were thrown out on the right and left of the road as skirmishers. Upon nearing Bull Run, the enemy was discovered in small numbers on this side of that stream, and as our infantry advanced, they retired.

Tyler halted upon the crest of a hill which overlooks the valley of Bull Run, and, by the aid of glasses, discovered a considerable force of cavalry on the other side of the stream well to the left, and perhaps two miles distant. Not being able as yet to ascertain anything positive as to the position or strength of the enemy, Tyler sent back an order to have two twenty-pounder rifled guns brought up, under Lieutenant Benjamin. They were placed in battery on the right of the road, and opened fire upon the cavalry, which was seen on the distant hills.

After firing six or seven shots, the enemy blazed away with a battery which was directly in front, and, after one or two rounds, ceased firing. Tyler then ordered a section of Ayres's Battery forward (it having come up in the meantime), supported by the cavalry. Ayres went forward himself with two twelve-pounder howitzers, and Brackett's squadron accompanied him. After getting into the timber, and very close to the enemy, Ayres opened fire, and the banks of the Run on the other side being lined with troops, their loss was considerable.

The artillery was plied until the ammunition was expended, when Ayres and the cavalry moved back again to the top of the hill. During this time the enemy had kept up a fierce fire of artillery and small-arms, by which several of the artillery and cavalry men and horses were killed and wounded. Lieutenant Loraine, of the artillery, was severely wounded in the foot. Upon reaching the crest of the hill the remaining pieces of Ayres's Battery commenced firing, and continued until sunset.

What General Tyler's object was has never been entirely clear. He knew as much about the enemy's strength after firing fifteen minutes as he did after firing three hours; and, as it was only intended that he should feel the enemy, he ought to have ceased firing long before he did. Beauregard's report of the fight is simply ridiculous. He tries to make out a great battle and a great victory, when in truth it was neither. Ayres's fighting in the woods was bloody, and that is pretty much all there was of it; but it is fair to say that Richardson and his Michigan men fought most gallantly, and were well sustained by the Massachu-

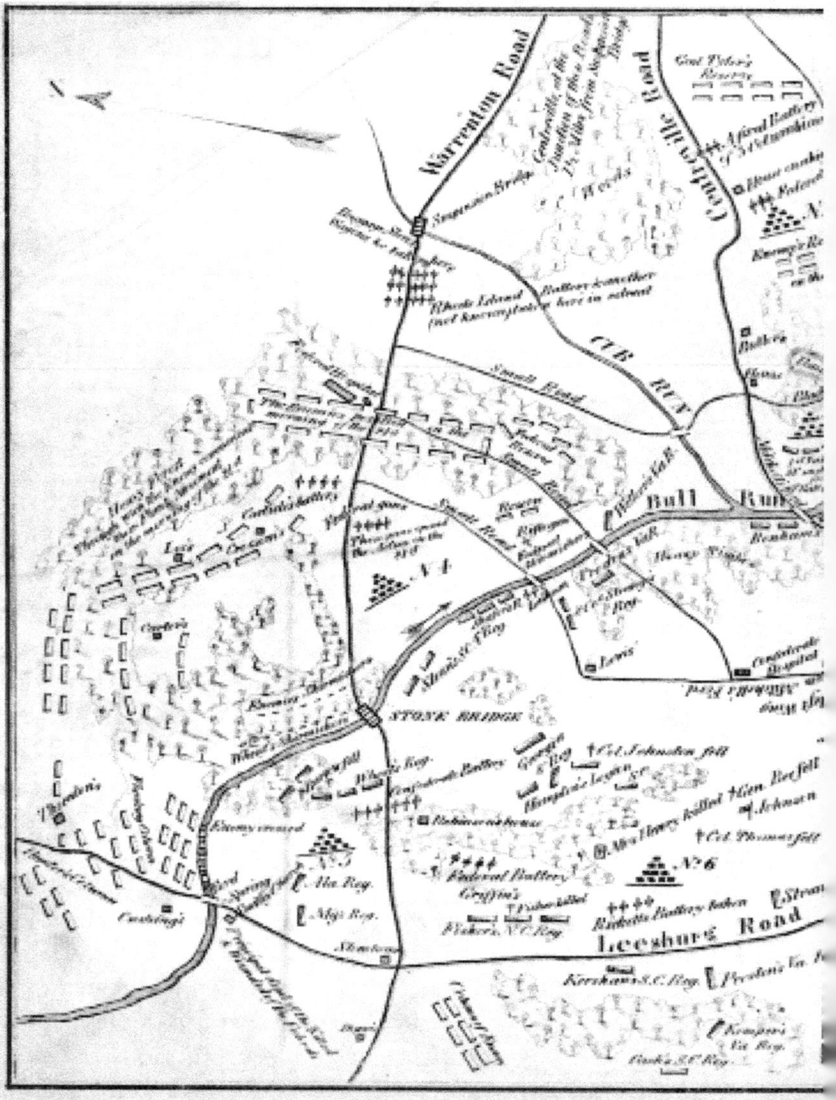
Warrenton Road
Centreville Road
Bull Run
STONE BRIDGE
Leesburg Road
N° 6
Ala. Reg.
Miss. Reg.
Kershaw's S.C. Reg.
Woods

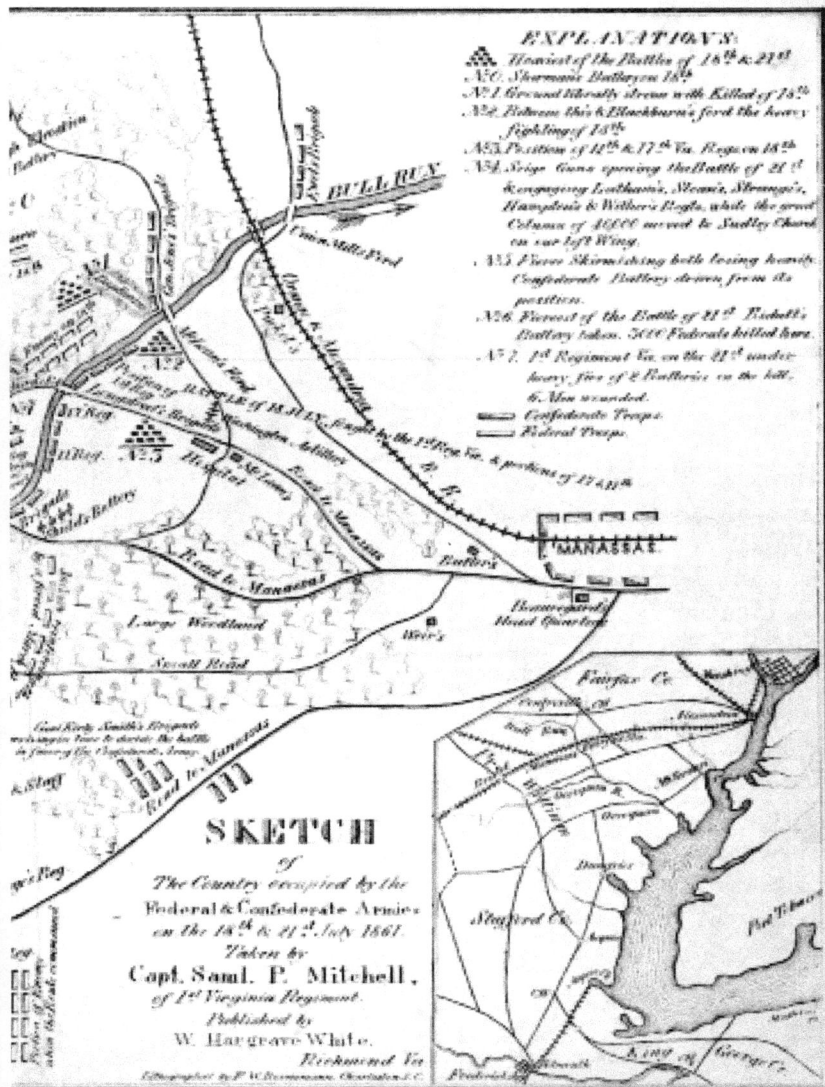

EXPLANATIONS.

Heaviest of the Battles of 18th & 21st.
N.O. Sherman's Battery on 18th
N.º 1 Ground literally strewn with Killed of 18th
N.º.2. Between this & Blackburn's ford the heavy
fighting of 18th
N.º.3. Position of 12th & 17th Va. Reg.on 18th
N.º.4. Seige Guns opening the Battle of 21st
Kemper's, Latham's, Sloan's, Strange's,
Hampton's & Walker's Regts. while the great
Column of 45000 moved to Sudley Church
on our left Wing.
N.º.5. Fierce Skirmishing both losing heavily.
Confederate Battery driven from its
position.
N.º.6. Fiercest of the Battle of 21st Ricketts'
Battery taken. 500 Federals killed here.
N.º.7. 1st Regiment Va. on the 21st under
heavy fire of 8 Batteries on the hill.
6 Men wounded.

Confederate Troops.
Federal Troops.

BULL RUN

MANASSAS.

Beauregard's
Head Quarters.

Butler's

Weir's

Road to Manassas

Large Woodland

Small Road

Road to Manassas

SKETCH
of
The Country occupied by the
Federal & Confederate Armies
on the 18th & 21st July 1861.
Taken by
Capt. Saml. P. Mitchell,
of 1st Virginia Regiment.
Published by
W. Hargrave White.
Richmond Va

Fairfax Co.

Stafford Co.

King George Co.

Fredericksbg.

setts men, who on this occasion evinced the most determined pluck.

Brackett's cavalrymen behaved well, and Lieutenant Drummond, of the 2nd, and Spangler and McClellan, of the 3rd, who were with him, manifested the greatest coolness and bravery.

About dusk the different corps returned to Centreville, and there passed the night. The cavalry rejoined Palmer, and, on the morning of the 19th, Brackett's company was detailed as General McDowell's escort. Captain Lowe's company, of the 2nd Cavalry, was sent to Colonel Heintzelman, commanding a division; Captain Armstrong's company, of the 2nd Dragoons, to Colonel Hunter, also commanding a division; and the remaining four companies, under Major Palmer, were attached to Colonel Andrew Porter's brigade, of Hunter's division.

The army lay in and about Centreville until about two o'clock on the morning of the 21st of July, 1861, when all of the command moved toward Bull Run, with the exception of Blenker's brigade, which remained at Centreville, and was never within five miles of the field; and Richardson's brigade still occupied a position in front of Blackburn's Ford.

Hunter's division led the way, followed by Heintzelman's. On the road leading to the Stone Bridge, down which Tyler's men had gone, the two divisions first named turned to the right through a new road which had been cut, and McDowell, with his staff, halted near a black smith's shop, where our troops left the main road. It was now past daylight, and the morning rapidly wore away.

McDowell was anxious and uneasy, and, after waiting a suitable length of time, kept saying, "Why don't Hunter commence? what can be delaying him?" In the meantime a heavy rifled thirty-pounder, which Tyler had taken with him down to the Stone Bridge, commenced firing, in order to attract the attention of the enemy. Hunter met with many obstacles; his march was necessarily slow; when at last McDowell, losing patience, started on with his escort to see what detained him. McDowell passed the divisions of Heintzelman and Hunter, and, after crossing Bull Run, was the first man, with his escort, on the field of Manassas.

"There is the enemy," said he, as a regiment of rebel troops moved out on the plain in splendid order, and poured into his staff and escort two or three rounds of musketry, which knocked the dust about the horses, and wounded some of them. At this moment Burnside's brave fellows from Rhode Island, being the leading brigade of Hunter's division, came on the field, and, forming in fine order, went steadily at their work. This had been going on but a short time when Colonel Hunter, of the 3rd Cavalry, commanding division, was severely wounded, and was carried off the field.

Palmer, with the cavalry, moved well over to the right, leaving Brackett's and Armstrong's companies in a skirt of timber, which protected them from the enemy's cannon-balls, though they were in direct range, and the shot tore through the trees and knocked up the dirt about them in the most approved style. The fighting was now going on in earnest, and the enemy was being steadily driven back. Some regiments did not move up as promptly as they ought to have done, they being three months men, and their term of service having expired on the day of the battle; but, as a general thing, they did well for troops who were then for the first time under fire.

All of the cavalry was now concentrated on the right, where by their steadiness they did much toward giving confidence to the raw troops who surrounded them. They were kept in front of the enemy's fire, and showed their training by behaving in the most cool and determined manner. The cannon-shot and shells of the enemy fell among them, killing and wounding several men and horses; but they kept their places, though unable to return the fire, in a position which was calculated to test the nerves of any man.

A lull succeeded, and the enemy appeared to be giving way; but the re-enforcements of the rebels arrived, under Kirby Smith, and made a most vigorous onslaught on our men. The volunteers retired. Their officers again coaxed them to reform, and again they moved up to the murderous work; the whole hill-side appeared a blazing sheet of fire, and the shot from the Washington Battery, which was behind the Confederate line, dropped their shells thick and fast among our men. It is a question whether the same number of any troops, however good, could have carried that hill against the overpowering numbers of the enemy. Our men were forced to give way, and retired sullenly from the field.

Away to the rear there was a scene of dreadful confusion, though the soldiers, who had fought most valiantly, did not partake of the panic. They were broken, it is true, but still their spirits were good, and they had met with obstacles which it was impossible to overcome. As the infantry left, the cavalry was ordered to form in line across the field, to cause the enemy to think that our army was still in good condition. This manoeuvre had the desired effect, and the enemy halted in the pursuit.

The cavalry waited until the infantry had cleared the field, when they were ordered to leave. Below Sudley's Church they halted, and dismounted. A body of Confederate cavalry then came down, but halted in sight of our men. Heintzelman and Porter were with the rear of the infantry column, the former being wounded, and as soon as the rebel horsemen halted, they ordered two of Arnold's pieces to be unlimbered and loaded with canister. This was thrown with tremendous effect among the rebel horsemen, and they galloped off most furiously. It was the last that was seen of them on that portion of the field of Manassas.

Keeping in rear of the infantry column for miles, the cavalry marched slowly along. Our army had been beaten, but the men who fought on the right had not lost their honour. It was a sorrowful sight, but enough, and more than enough has been said about that retreat.

Upon reaching Centreville it was dark, and the cavalry returned to their old quarters in a field which they had occupied before the battle. Here they unsaddled, and fed their horses with such stuff as the men could get, and then, using the saddles for pillows, the men went to sleep. All were tired. A streaming multitude was passing along the road nearby, but still the men slept until aroused about midnight, and ordered to saddle up and march to Arlington.

They obeyed quietly, and the next day resumed their old places on the hill-sides.

The cavalry officers who were at Bull Run were Colonel Hunter (wounded); Major Palmer; Captains Brackett, Lowe, Colburn, Armstrong, and Harrison; Lieutenants Kimmel, Sweet, Tompkins, Holloway, Drummond, Gordon, Leib, Custer, L'Hommedieu, Walker, McCormick, Spangler, McClellan, and McQuade, the latter of whom died of his wounds at Richmond, Virginia.

Lieutenant David S. Gordon was taken prisoner by the enemy, as was Assistant-Surgeon Charles C. Grey, who was serving with the cavalry, and who staid back with the wounded from his high sense of duty.

Shortly after this battle, Congress, which was then in session, authorised the raising of five hundred thousand volunteers. On the 3rd of August, the dragoons, mounted riflemen, and cavalry were all organised into one arm, to be called cavalry. In consequence of this, the 1st Dragoons became the 1st Cavalry; the 2nd Dragoons became the 2nd Cavalry; the Mounted Riflemen became the 3rd Cavalry; the 1st Cavalry became the 4th Cavalry; the 2nd Cavalry became the 5th

Cavalry; the 3rd Cavalry became the 6th Cavalry,

This changing the names of the old regiments had a bad effect, because by it they lost the honour which was attached to their old names, and which they had been years in gaining. While these events were transpiring in the Eastern States, the cavalry in Missouri was doing well, and a detachment of Captain Stanley's company of the 4th Cavalry, at Dug Spring, made a most brilliant and successful charge upon a large body of rebels, and completely dispersed them. In this affair Lieutenant Sullivan was severely wounded.

CHAPTER 11

Cavalry Operations on the Peninsula

At the Battle of Wilson's Creek, in Missouri, fought August 10th, 1861, several cavalry officers gained much distinction; and after the death of General Lyon, Major Sturgis, of the 4th Regiment, took command of the United States troops. Captain Granger behaved most gallantly, as did Captain Carr and Lieutenants Dubois, Sokalski, and Canfield.

Dubois and Canfield served with the artillery during the fight, and did much damage to the enemy. The Union troops fell back to Springfield, and thence to points nearer St. Louis. There were other cavalry operations in Missouri during the autumn of 1861 which were of considerable importance, and added much to the good reputation of those concerned. It must be borne in mind that the enthusiasm, for volunteering in the States had reached a high pitch, and government, waking from its misconceived dreams of needing no cavalry, was daily adding new regiments to its forces; but it required time to arm and drill them, and many were sent into the field very poorly supplied.

At Lexington, Missouri, the 1st Illinois Cavalry, under Colonel Marshall, after sustaining a siege of several days with other troops, under Colonel Mulligan, was forced to surrender to the superior numbers of the enemy, and to the fact that they were cut off from the water by the Confederates. The behaviour of these men was good, and, though poorly armed, they fought as well as could have been expected of them. There was no chance for anything like cavalry operations, and they were herded together within an enclosure with the other troops until forced to surrender. Lieutenant-Colonel Day, of the 1st Illinois Cavalry, was severely wounded, with several other officers and men.

This occurred on the 20th of September, 1861.

In October a fight occurred at Fredericktown, Missouri, where a portion of the 1st Indiana Cavalry, under Colonel Baker, made a most brilliant charge upon the enemy, and routed them; but, in so doing, two of Indiana's worthy sons were slain. They were Major Gavitt and Captain Highman. Gavitt headed the charge, and the brave Indianians followed. It was daring, perhaps rash, but it was successful, and the regiment gained much credit. These two officers were the only ones killed during the battle.

Meantime General Fremont's army was making its way toward the western portion of Missouri, he taking with him Major Zagonyi's battalion of cavalry as his bodyguard.

When near Springfield, the major formed the design of taking the town, though his command numbered not more than one hundred and sixty men.

On the 25th of October, having formed his men near where he knew the enemy was posted, he gave the order to advance. With a shout the men obeyed, and pressing their horses into a gallop, they turned a corner of the road which brought them in sight of the enemy. There was no confusion, and the men are said to have behaved admirably. The enemy was drawn up in line of battle near some woods, their rear being protected by underbrush, which the cavalry could not enter.

Here the rebels waited steadily until our men reached the foot of the hill, when they poured in a volley, which luckily passed over the heads of our cavalrymen. Zagonyi pushed forward up the hill, and threw his men with terrible effect upon the rebels, who broke and ran in all directions, seeking the cover of the wood.

The cavalry of the enemy also gave way before the impetuosity of the charge, and the Union men chased them far away through the streets of Springfield. The fright of the enemy is said to have been of the most appalling character. Their numbers are given as amounting to *twenty-two hundred*. This seems almost incredible, but it is vouched for by good authority. There can be no doubt but it was a most splendid charge of cavalry, and entitles those engaged in it to much credit.

Zagonyi took possession of the town, hoisted the Union flag upon the Court-house, and at nightfall left to join the main army, his force not being strong enough to run the risk of a night attack. His loss was sixteen killed and twenty-five wounded. Among the wounded were Lieutenants Westerborg, Vansteenkiste, Kennedy, and Goff.

Many may pronounce this rash. No doubt it was so; but, *without some little recklessness, cavalry can never accomplish anything*. Upon Fre-

CAVALRY ENGAGEMENT IN THE PENINSULA CAMPAIGN

mont's return to St. Louis this cavalry was disbanded, as it did not wish to serve under any other commander.

In 1861 the Army Regulations were revised, and the following excellent rules with regard to the cavalry service were embodied in them. The Regulations say:

That cavalry and infantry do not march together, unless the proximity of the enemy makes it necessary.

In cavalry marches, when distant from the enemy, each regiment, and, if possible, each squadron, forms a separate column, in order to keep up the same gait from front to rear, and to trot, when desirable, on good ground. In such cases the cavalry may leave camp later, and can give more rest to the horses, and more attention to the shoeing and harness. Horses are not bridled until the time to start.

The cavalry should be distributed in echelon, on the wings and at the centre, on favourable ground.

When it is necessary to dismount cavalry and send them to the trenches, they should be employed as near their camp as possible, and posted between the detachments of infantry.

Men belonging to the cavalry may, in assaults, be employed in carrying fascines and other materials to fill ditches and make passages.

The general officers of cavalry are more particularly employed in the service of posts and detachments placed in observation to protect the siege. They and the field officers of this arm are employed in the command of escorts to convoys of whatever arms the escorts may be composed. When these duties are not sufficient to employ them, they take their share of the duty of the trenches.

Mixed brigades are sometimes formed of infantry and light cavalry, especially for the advanced guards.

The light cavalry is employed as flankers and partisans, and generally for all service out of the line.

Heavy cavalry belongs to the reserve, and is covered, when necessary, in marches, camps, or bivouacs, by light troops, or infantry of the line.

The arrangement of the troops on parade and in order of battle is, 1st, the light infantry; 2nd, infantry of the line; 3rd, light cavalry; 4th, cavalry of the line; 5th, heavy cavalry.

In the cavalry, each troop moves a little in rear of the point at which its horses are to be secured, and forms in on a rank; the men then dismount; a detail is made to hold the horses; the rest stack their arms and fix the picket rope. After the horses are attended to, the tents are pitched, and each horseman places his carbine at the side from the weather, and hangs his sabre and bridle on it.

Cavalry patrols should examine the country to a greater distance than infantry, and report to the infantry guard everything they observe. The morning patrols and scouts do not return until broad daylight; and when they return, the night sentinels are withdrawn, and the posts for the day resumed.

The horses of cavalry guards are watered or fed by detachments, during which the rest are ready to mount.

In the cavalry, dismounted men are employed in preference on the police guard. The mounted men on guard are sent in succession, a part at a time, to groom their horses. The advanced post is always formed of mounted men.

In each company a corporal has charge of the stable-guard. His tour begins at retreat, and ends at morning stable-call. The stable-guard is large enough to relieve the men on post every two hours. They sleep in their tents, and are called by the corporal when wanted. At retreat he closes the streets of the camp with cords, or uses other precautions to prevent the escape of loose horses.

In the cavalry, horses are packed for all mounted service.

In the cavalry, dismounted men, and those whose horses are not in order, are preferred for the detail for dismounted service. Those who are mounted are never employed on those services if the number of the other class are sufficient.

Every non-commissioned officer and soldier in the cavalry detailed for dismounted service must, before he marches, take to the first sergeant of the troop, or sergeant of his squad, his horse equipments and his valise ready packed. In case of alarm, the first sergeant sees that the horses of these men are equipped and led to the rendezvous.

Cavalry is employed in escorts chiefly to reconnoitre; the proportion is larger as the country is more open.

On the 12th day of November, 1861, Colonel Philip St. George

Cooke, of the 2nd Cavalry, was promoted Brigadier-General, and Lieutenant-Colonel Thomas J. Wood was promoted Colonel in his place. On the 17th of July, 1852, the whole cavalry was organised into regiments of twelve companies each, and three majors were allowed. This placed them on the same footing as the 6th Regiment, which already had three majors and twelve companies. By this arrangement, Captain Brackett became Major of the 1st, Whiting of the 2nd, Newby of the 3rd, Johnson of the 4th, and Carr of the 5th Cavalry.

The year 1862 tended to develop the cavalry resources of our country, and many new regiments were formed. The different states seemed to vie with each other which should send the greatest number of regiments into the field; the expense connected with the maintenance of this force caused some opposition to it on the part of those in power, but its good services were seen and appreciated, and it soon became a favourite.

The first skirmish of the year of any note was at Silver Creek, in Missouri, on the 8th of January, where Majors Torrence and Hubbard, with portions of the 1st Iowa and 1st Missouri Cavalry, defeated and dispersed a considerable force of the enemy. This was followed on the 18th of the same month by the Federal success at Mill Springs, Kentucky, where Major-General George H. Thomas, Colonel of the 5th United States Cavalry, gained the first substantial Union victory over the rebels during the war.

In this action Colonel Wolford's 1st Kentucky Cavalry bore an honourable part, and the only commissioned officer killed during the action belonged to his regiment. This was First Lieutenant Richard Miller.

At the skirmish at Sugar Creek, in Missouri, on the 17th of February, the Missouri Cavalry routed the rebels, who were opposing the advance of General Curtis's army, after a brisk fight. Major Bowen and Captain Switzler, of that corps, were wounded, as was Major McKinney, Assistant Adjutant General to General Curtis.

At the Battle of Pea Ridge, Arkansas, fought March 6th, 7th, and 8th, 1862, the wooded nature of the country rendered cavalry movements difficult; the loss of the 3rd Illinois, the 1st Missouri, and the 3rd Iowa was, nevertheless, quite heavy. Colonel C. A. Ellis, of the 1st Missouri Cavalry, Lieutenant-Colonel H. H. Trimble, 3rd Iowa Cavalry, and Colonel Eugene A. Carr, of the 3rd Illinois Cavalry, were wounded. The latter commanded one of the divisions of Curtis's army during the fight. Bowen's Missouri Cavalry battalion also did good service in

5TH UNITED STATES CAVALRY IN THE CIVIL WAR

this battle, as did the 4th, 5th, and 6th Missouri Cavalry Regiments.

It is impossible at this time to give the particulars of every skirmish in which the Union Cavalry has been engaged during this war, as they are almost without number; and many of the accounts given in the papers are unsatisfactory, they being greatly exaggerated and the details incorrect.

In Virginia our cavalry was engaged early in the season, and on the 7th of March, Capt. J. P. Wison, of Colonel Friedman's regiment, was wounded in a skirmish near Fairfax Court-house. In the same month, Lieutenant Hidden, of the Union Cavalry, was killed by the enemy near the same place.

In New Mexico the Texans attempted to invade the country, and at the Battle of Valverde, February 21st, 1862, met with partial success. In this fight, Captain Alexander McRae, of the 3rd regiment United States Cavalry, was killed while gallantly defending himself against the rebels. Shortly after this, Major Duncan, of the same regiment, was severely wounded at Galisteo, in that territory. The Texans were driven out with great loss, though not until another fight had occurred at Apache Canon, March 27th, in which First Lieutenant Peter McGrath, of the 6th Cavalry, was mortally wounded, and died on the 1st of May.

At the Battle of Winchester, Virginia, fought on the 23rd of March, the Michigan Cavalry, under Colonel Broadhead, participated, and rendered efficient service; and upon taking Island No. 10, in the Mississippi, in April, 1862, the 2nd Iowa Cavalry was instrumental in taking many prisoners and capturing much property belonging to the rebels, who had reached the main land.

At the Battle of Pittsburg Landing, or Shiloh, fought on the 6th and 7th of April, our cavalry was unable to accomplish much, though it was under fire a long time, and lost several men. The cavalry at that action consisted of the 4th and 11th Regiments from Illinois, and the 5th Ohio. On the 17th of the month, General Andrew J. Smith, chief of cavalry upon General Halleck's staff, led a force of mounted men out on the upper road leading from Pittsburg Landing to Corinth, Mississippi. This consisted of the 2nd Indiana, two Illinois, two Kentucky, and two Ohio cavalry regiments.

After marching some distance, they came upon the outposts of the enemy, and soon encountered a heavy force. After a skirmish unimportant, so far as fighting is concerned, the force returned to the Landing; but Smith ascertained that the enemy had fallen back on

Corinth, and had commenced fortifying that place.

On the 18th of April, Falmouth, opposite Fredericksburg, Virginia, was occupied by the forces of the United States. The advance was disputed by the enemy, who were finally driven across the Rappahannock, though not until they had killed five and wounded seventeen of our cavalrymen. Lieutenant Decker, of the Ira Harris New York Cavalry, was killed. In the afternoon of that day our troops received the surrender of Fredericksburg.

Cavalry Operations on the Peninsula.

The cavalry which was sent to the peninsula of Virginia, in March and April, 1862, was under the direction of General Stoneman, Chief of Cavalry of General McClellan's army, and consisted of the following organisations:

Cavalry Reserve, Brigadier-General P. St. G. Cooke.
Emory's Brigade.—5th United States Cavalry, 6th United States Cavalry, 6th Pennsylvania Cavalry.
Blake's Brigade. 1st United States Cavalry, 8th Pennsylvania Cavalry, Barker's squadron of Illinois Cavalry.

Belonging to General Sumner's Second Corps.
8th Illinois Cavalry, Colonel Farnsworth; one squadron 6th New York Cavalry.

Belonging to General Hemtzelman's Third Corps.
3rd Pennsylvania Cavalry, Colonel Averill; Provost Guard, the 2nd regiment United States Cavalry.

At General McClellan's Headquarters.
Two companies 4th United States Cavalry, and one company Oneida (N.Y.) Cavalry.

McClellan had moved out from Washington across the Potomac with his army, and afterward marched to Manassas; here changing his plan of operations, he moved down on the Peninsula and commenced the siege of Yorktown. The cavalry was employed during the siege in doing picket duty, and was kept busy until the morning of the 4th of May, when General McClellan was made aware that the enemy had abandoned their works at Yorktown and were retreating toward Williamsburg.

He immediately ordered General Stoneman to follow with four batteries of horse artillery and all the available cavalry force. Stoneman accordingly moved out with the 1st and 6th United States Cavalry, the 3rd Pennsylvania, 8th Illinois, and Barker's squadron of Illinois Cavalry, and the four horse-artillery batteries, and met with but little opposition until he arrived in front of the enemy's works about Williamsburg.

At a point about eight miles from York-town, in accordance with McClellan's instructions, he detached General Emory, with Benson's Battery, Averill's 3rd Pennsylvania Cavalry, and Barker's squadron, to gain the Lee's Mill Road and endeavour to cut off the portion of the enemy's rear guard which had taken that route. General Emory had some sharp skirmishes with a regiment of cavalry and a battery, under the rebel General Stuart, and drove them in the direction of Lee's Mill, but they escaped by a circuitous route along the bank of James River.

The position in which General Stoneman encountered the enemy is about four miles in extent, the right resting on College Creek, and the left on Queen's Creek, nearly three fourths of its front being covered by tributaries of those two creeks, upon which, there are ponds. The ground between the heads of the tributary streams is a cultivated plain, across which a line of detached works had been constructed, consisting of Fort Magruder, a large work, in the centre, with a bastion front, and twelve other redoubts for field-guns.

General Stoneman debouched from the woods with his advance guard, consisting of a part of the 1st United States Cavalry and one section of Gibson's Battery, under the command of General Cooke, and the enemy immediately opened on him with several field-pieces from Fort Magruder, having the correct range, and doing some execution. Gibson's Battery was brought into position as rapidly as the deep mud would permit, and returned the fire, while the 6th United States Cavalry was sent to feel the enemy's left.

This regiment passed one redoubt, which it found unoccupied, and appeared in the rear of the second, when a strong cavalry force, with infantry and artillery, came down upon it, whereupon the regiment was withdrawn. The rear squadron, under command of Captain William P. Saunders, repelled a charge of the enemy's cavalry in the most gallant manner.

In the meantime, the enemy was being re-enforced with infantry; and the artillery fire becoming very hot, General Stoneman, having no infantry to carry the works, ordered the withdrawal of the battery. The enemy attempted to prevent the movement, but their charges were met by the 1st United States Cavalry, under command of Lieutenant Colonel William N. Grier, and they were driven back, losing several officers and one stand of colours. General Stoneman then took up a defensive position a short distance in rear of the first, to await the arrival of the infantry.

The cavalry remained in this position until evening, when the infantry came up, and the next day was fought the Battle of Williamsburg. The town was taken on the 5th, and Colonel Averill was sent forward at once with a strong cavalry force to endeavour to overtake the enemy's rear guard. He found several guns abandoned, and picked up a large number of stragglers, but the condition of the roads and the state of his supplies forced him to return after advancing a few miles. In this battle Lieutenant-Colonel Grier, of the 1st Cavalry, and Lieutenant Curwen B. McClellan, of the 6th Cavalry, were wounded, the latter severely.

A very dashing and successful reconnaissance was made near New Bridge, Virginia, on the 24th of May, by Lieutenant Bowen, Topographical Engineers, escorted by the 4th Michigan Volunteers, under Colonel Woodbury, and a squadron of the 2nd United States Cavalry, under Captain George A. Gordon. Our troops encountered a Louisiana regiment, and, with little loss, drove it back upon its brigade, killing a large number and capturing several prisoners. Great credit is due to the staff officers, as well as to Colonel Woodbury, Captain Gordon, and their commands, for their conduct on this occasion.

At the Battle of Hanover Court-house, May 27th, Captain James E. Harrison, of the 5th United States Cavalry, with a single company, brought in as prisoners two entire companies of rebel infantry, with their arms and ammunition. A part of the 6th Pennsylvania Cavalry (Rush's Lancers) also captured an entire company with their arms.

On the 28th, a party under Major Williams, 6th United States Cavalry, destroyed the common road bridges over the Pamunkey, and the Virginia Central Railroad bridge over the South Anna, On the 29th he destroyed the Fredericksburg and Richmond Railroad bridge over the South Anna, and the turnpike bridge over that stream. On the same day, and mainly to cover the movement of Major Williams, General Emory moved a column of cavalry toward Ashland from Hanover Court-house.

The advance of this column, under Captain William P. Chambliss, 5th United States Cavalry, entered Ashland, driving out a party of the enemy, destroyed the railroad bridge over Stony Creek, and broke up the railroad and telegraph. General Stoneman on the same day moved

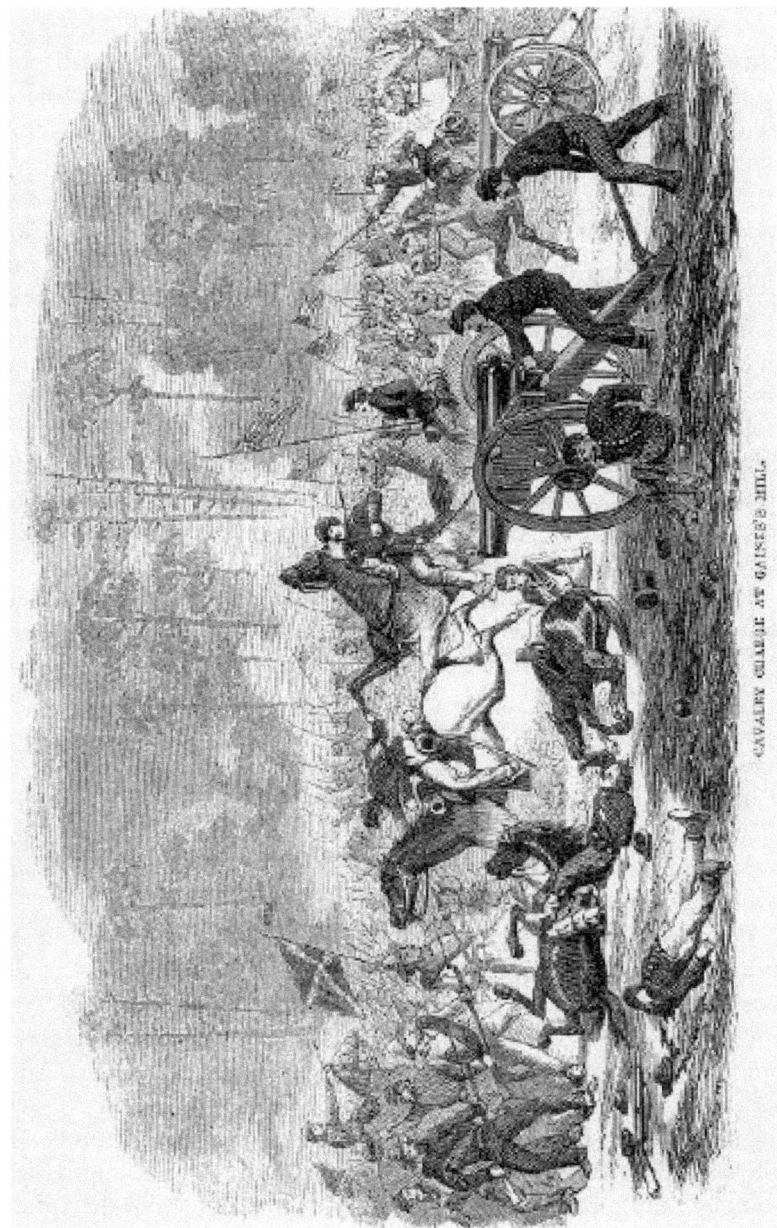

CAVALRY CHARGE AT GAINES'S MILL.

on Ashland by Leach's Station, covering well the movements of the other columns.

On the 13th of June two squadrons of the 5th United States Cavalry, under command of Captain William B. Royall, stationed near Hanover Old Church, were attacked and overpowered by a force of the enemy's cavalry, numbering about fifteen hundred men, with four guns. In this affair Captain Royall was very severely wounded.

At the Battle of Gaines's Mill, June 27th, 1862, two squadrons of the 1st Regular Cavalry, five companies of the 5th United States Cavalry, and three squadrons of the 6th Pennsylvania Cavalry were under command of General P. St. George Cooke. They were ordered to make, and did make, a most unfortunate charge, in which First Lieutenant John J. Sweet, 5th United States Cavalry, was killed, and First Lieutenant Robert Allen, junior, 1st United States Cavalry, was mortally wounded.

The loss to the cavalry in the "Seven Days' Battles," from June 26th to July 1st, 1863, was nineteen killed, sixty wounded, and ninety-seven missing, making a total of one hundred and seventy-six. Captain Chambliss was among the severely wounded.

On the 30th of August the command of the army in the field passed from the hands of General McClellan to those of Major-General John Pope.

On the 8th of May four companies of the 7th Illinois Cavalry, under command of Major Applington, when reconnoitring within a mile and a half of Corinth, Mississippi, discovered two rebel regiments of infantry in position on both sides of the road. Major Applington gallantly charged upon them, but fell pierced by a ball through the brain. Four of his men were wounded. The rebels lost thirty killed and wounded, and four prisoners.

Colonel Philip H. Sheridan, of the Second Michigan Cavalry, in command of a body of Union troops, had a spirited action with the enemy at Booneville, Mississippi, on the 1st of July, 1862. The enemy consisted of parts of eight regiments of cavalry, numbering about four thousand seven hundred men, under General Chalmers. After skirmishing with them for some time, Sheridan succeeded in getting a portion of his men in their rear, when they retreated, and were followed some distance. The loss to Sheridan was forty-one killed, wounded, and missing, while that of the enemy was about the same.

CHAPTER 12

The Cavalry under General Pope

On the 5th of May, Brigadier-General Dumont fought and defeated a considerable body of rebels at Lebanon, Tennessee. He says,
in his dispatch:

I surprised and attacked the enemy, under Colonels Morgan
and Wood, this morning at four o'clock at this place, and, after
a hard-fought battle of one and a half hours, and a running fight
of eighteen miles in pursuit, achieved a complete and substantial
victory. My force was about six hundred, composed of detachments from Colonel Wynkoop's 7th Pennsylvania, Colonel G.
Clay Smith's 5th, and Colonel Wolford's 1st Kentucky Cavalry;
that of the enemy, as stated by himself, upward of eight hundred. Besides which, the disloyal inhabitants not in the army
opened a murderous fire on our soldiers from their houses, and
kept it up until all the organised forces of the enemy had fled,
or were slain or captured.

The forces on either side were exclusively mounted. I captured
say one hundred and fifty prisoners, among whom is Lieutenant-Colonel R C. Wood, three captains, four lieutenants, and
upward of one hundred and fifty horses, and one hundred
stand of arms. Our killed will not exceed six, and our wounded
twenty-five. Among the latter are Colonels G. Clay Smith and
Frank Wolford, the former in the leg, the latter in the abdomen.
We lost no prisoners except Major Givan, 7th Pennsylvania
Cavalry, who fell into the hands of the enemy during the street
fight by mistaking them for our troops.

In this affair intrepidity and personal daring were conspicuous
throughout.

While General Pope's command was at Farmington, Mississippi, on the 9th of May, the 2nd Regiment of Iowa Cavalry, under command of Lieutenant-Colonel Edward Hatch, made a most wild and reckless charge upon the enemy by order of Brigadier-General E. A. Paine. The regiment fell upon the rebels with their sabres, and did some execution, but were forced to retire with a loss of about fifty officers and men killed and wounded.

This was the main event of the battle, and General Pope withdrew his forces to the north side of a creek, as Major-General Halleck, who was commander-in-chief, did not at that time wish to bring on a general engagement with the enemy.

This regiment, with a battalion of the 2nd Michigan Cavalry, under command of Colonel W. L. Elliott, 2nd Iowa Cavalry, made a successful expedition on the 28th of May in rear of Corinth, where a large quantity of stores belonging to the enemy were destroyed, and the track of the Mobile and Ohio Railroad was torn up in many places. He burned several cars containing small arms, and destroyed three pieces of artillery.

After the Battle of Pea Ridge, General Curtis marched through Arkansas to Batesville, and was there joined by Brigadier-General Steele's division, which had marched through from Pilot Knob, Missouri, *via* Pittman's Ferry, Pocahontas, and Jacksonport. Colonel Albert GL Brackett, with the 9th Regiment of Illinois Cavalry, was left at the junction of the Black and White Rivers, opposite Jacksonport, Arkansas, with orders to patrol the country and keep it in order.

On the 12th of June he sent a train of wagons across Black River for the purpose of obtaining forage for his horses, and sent a battalion of his regiment, under Major Humphrey, to guard it. When about four miles below Jacksonport, the train was attacked by a large body of rebels, commanded by the notorious Hooker. Major Humphrey lost several of his men wounded, and, halting his train near the Waddell Farm, sent back for re-enforcements. In a short time, Colonel Brackett arrived, bringing with him two more companies of his regiment; also, two small howitzers, and two companies of Bowen's Missouri Cavalry Battalion.

Leaving one company to guard the train, and placing the two howitzers in the road, guarded by the Missouri Cavalry, under Captain Williams and Lieutenant Ballou, he formed the Illinois Cavalry in line of battle in a cottonfield. While these preparations were going on, the rebels, who were in line in front, were indulging in various playful epithets regarding the Union troops, and occasionally sending a shot over to remind us that they "still lived."

Everything being in readiness, Colonel Brackett sent a couple of shells from the howitzers over toward them, and at the same time the Illinoisans galloped into them with drawn sabres. The result may be easily imagined. Hooker's troops put spurs to their horses, and did some of that lofty running which is peculiar to Butternut horsemen. They were chased through fields and woods to Village Creek, which the rebels cleared at once, and sought safety in the dark cypress swamps.

During the fight the cotton-gin was fired, as well as the store-house, in which there was an immense number of cotton bales, and they were soon destroyed. In the morning this was one of the finest plantations in Arkansas; at evening it was a mass of ruins. The loss to the 9th Illinois Cavalry was twelve wounded and one taken prisoner by the enemy. The rebels lost twenty-eight killed, wounded, and prisoners. The train was saved, and was carried back to camp filled with rebel produce.

Shortly after this event, the Army of Arkansas, under Major-General Curtis, left Batesville on its way to the Mississippi River, whither it had become necessary for him to move in order to obtain supplies. He had a fine army, the cavalry portion of which was made up of the following regiments, *viz.*: 1st Indiana Cavalry, Colonel Conrad Baker; 3rd Illinois Cavalry, Colonel Eugene A. Carr; 5th Illinois Cavalry, Colonel J. Hall Wilson; 9th Illinois Cavalry, Colonel Albert G. Brackett; 13th Illinois Cavalry, Colonel Joseph W. Bell; 1st Missouri Cavalry, Colonel C. A. Ellis; 4th Missouri Cavalry, Colonel George E. Waring, Jr.; 5th Missouri Cavalry, Colonel Joseph Nemitt; Missouri Cavalry Battalion, Major William D. Bowen; 2nd Wisconsin Cavalry, Colonel C. C. Washburne; 3rd Iowa Cavalry, Colonel Cyrus Bussey; 4th Iowa Cavalry, Colonel Asbury B. Porter; 5th Kansas Cavalry, Colonel Powell Clayton.

It required an immense deal of forage to do the animals of these regiments, besides those of the artillery and the heavy baggage-train; and in a new country like Arkansas, where only a small portion of the land is under cultivation, this was difficult to obtain; consequently, on the march, the horses suffered terribly.

Curtis's army moved down from Batesville, and crossed White River on a pontoon bridge. He halted a short time in Jacksonport, expecting the arrival of steamboats from the Mississippi River *via* the White River, as Memphis had fallen into our hands, and the navigation of the Mississippi was unimpeded as low down as the mouth of White River, or even to Vicksburg. While the troops were encamped along Village Creek, foraging parties were frequently sent out to bring in food for the animals.

On the 27th of June a large train was sent out by the quartermaster, guarded by a portion of the 3rd Iowa Cavalry and a company of infantry. At the same time, the train of the 9th Illinois Cavalry was sent out, guarded by a battalion of that regiment under Major Wallis. In the afternoon the quartermaster's train was attacked about four miles out, and a lieutenant and three men of the 3rd Iowa Cavalry were killed outright. A portion of the wagons came hurrying back to camp, bringing in some wounded men, when General Steele, who was in command of the division, ordered Colonel Bussey to go to the relief of his men, and ordered Colonel Brackett to bring his train in.

As soon as the horses could be saddled, Colonel Brackett, with Major Humphrey's battalion of his regiment, started out, and soon overtook his train coming in, safely guarded by Major Wallis. Sending the train on to camp, he ordered Wallis to follow with his battalion, and pressed on to the scene of the fight. Upon arriving there, he found the 3rd Iowa Cavalry in the road, halted near the quartermaster's train, and passing them, made some inquiries as to the direction the rebels had taken after the attack.

He learned that they had disappeared in the woods nearby from an infantry lieutenant who was standing with his men drawn up in line in rear of the train. Moving on to Stewart's plantation, he learned from "a reliable contraband" that Colonel Matlock, with a mixed command of Arkansas and Texas troops, had disappeared in the timber shortly after killing the Iowa men. Pressing the negro into service as a guide, Colonel Brackett moved on, determined to test the muscle of the trans-Mississippi chivalry. He left the clearing and marched along a road which was, even in daylight, dark and gloomy, from the deep shadows of the trees, and had not gone far before his curiosity was gratified.

Captain Knight, with his company, was in advance, and by his side was riding an Arkansas Union guide, named William McCulloch, and in front of these was the negro, leading the way. Suddenly, at a turn of the road, as he was marching along, he met the rebels face to face, and not ten steps from him. Both parties immediately fired, as their pistols were ready, and the two leading rebels fell dead from their horses, and the brave Captain Knight was shot through the body, and also fell from his horse. The negro disappeared, and it is even now a question as to what became of him; he disappeared instantly, as thoroughly as if he had been swept off the face of the earth.

The rebels turned and ran, jumping off their horses in the wildest manner, and betaking themselves to a strong position on the road, to the right and left of which there was an impassable cypress swamp, and in front a dense undergrowth. Knight's company halted a moment, and then poured a deadly fire into the rebels, who returned it in good faith, and soon the place became as warm as need be. It was sundown when the fight commenced, and it continued until it was too dark to see anything except the spiteful flashes of the enemy's guns.

Seven companies of the 9th Illinois Cavalry were engaged, averaging thirty men, making a total of two hundred and ten; in a half hour's time thirty-three of this number were killed and wounded, being about one sixth of the whole number engaged. For cavalry this did very well. The colonel tried to force the rebels out with the sabre, but the brush in front was so thick the horses could make no headway through it.

As darkness came on, the enemy retreated. Colonel Brackett, Major Wallis, Captain Knight, and Adjutant Blackburn, were among the wounded, and the regiment presented a sad sight as it again reached the main road, where the gallant lieutenant, with his infantry men, were still staying, hoping to be of some benefit to their friends who were fighting. Whoever he was, he certainly was a brave man, and his company appeared to be equally so. Every officer and man who was engaged in this fight behaved admirably; they were Majors Wallis and Humphrey; Captains Gifford, Knight, Cameron, Blakemore, and Booth; Adjutant Stevenson and Battalion Adjutant Blackburn; Lieutenants Harrington, Shear, Ellsworth, Bayley, and Shattuck. The loss to the rebels was over fifty killed and wounded.

After getting in the main road at Stewart's plantation, the wounded and dead men were carried along on horses. The regiment had proceeded but a short distance on its way back to camp when it was met by Brigadier-General Benton, who had started out, on hearing the firing, with his whole brigade to assist the Illinoisans. It was very dark by this time, and farther operations were impossible. The next morning, however, Benton went on, and buried the dead rebels, who were found lying in the timber.

General Curtis's army moved on toward the Mississippi River; and, after crossing the Cache River, a portion of it, consisting of the 33rd Illinois Infantry, 11th Wisconsin Infantry, and the 1st Indiana Cavalry, had a very spirited battle with the rebels. It was on the 7th of July, when Colonel Charles E. Hovey, of the 33rd Illinois, commanding his own and Colonel Harris's 11th Wisconsin Volunteers, was suddenly attacked by a large force of Arkansas and Texas troops, under General Albert Rust.

Hovey drew up his command along a rail fence, and as the rebels came up, he delivered his fire coolly and with deadly certainty among them. In a short time, the 1st Indiana Cavalry rode up in fine style, under command of Lieutenant-Colonel Wood, and immediately charged upon the rebels with their sabres, at the same time letting them have the benefit of two small rifled pieces which belonged to that regiment. For a few minutes the rebels stood this, but it was too much, and, after three desperate charges, they broke and left the field.

Our men followed, and slaughtered them in a most dreadful manner, one hundred and eleven dead rebels being left on the ground. The chase continued several miles. In this fight, Captain William W. Sloan, of the 1st Indiana Cavalry, was killed, and Major Clendenning and ten men of that regiment were wounded. The regiment acquitted itself with great credit.

After this time the rebels kept at a respectful distance, trying to damage the country as much as possible by filling up the wells with rails and dead horses, so as to prevent our people getting water, on which account both men and animals suffered intensely. Finally, however, Curtis reached the Mississippi, and the appearance of the river was greeted with cheers by our wayworn soldiers.

A fight occurred near Fort Donelson, Tennessee, on the 26th of August, 1862, between the 5th Regiment of Iowa Cavalry, under command of Colonel William W. Lowe, and a regiment of rebels, commanded by Colonel Woodward, which resulted in the defeat of the latter, with the loss of several men and their artillery. Lowe had two men killed and eighteen wounded; among the latter was Lieutenant Summers, who received a mortal wound. The bearing of the cavalry was without a fault.

Colonel Lowe, in command of portions of the 5th Iowa Cavalry and the 71st Ohio, 11th Illinois and 13th Wisconsin Infantry, recaptured the town of Clarksville, Tennessee, from the rebels, on the 8th of September, after a well-fought affair, in which the enemy lost seventeen killed and fifty wounded. Lowe took about fifty horses, and a number of arms, etc., from the rebels. The colonel is an experienced officer, and for a long time commanded Forts Henry and Hieman, where he conducted affairs skilfully, and with credit to himself and to those under his command.

By making a forced march of twenty miles, a body of cavalry, consisting of the 7th Pennsylvania, under Wynkoop, and the 5th Kentucky Regiment, under command of Colonel Haggard, came upon a body of rebel cavalry, under command of General Adams, near Jasper, Tennessee, on the 3rd of June, when a fierce skirmish ensued, in which the rebels were put to flight with considerable loss. General Neagly, in his report of the affair, speaks highly of the conduct of the officers commanding the regiments, and also of Lieutenants Wharton, Funk, Sypher, and Nell. Major Adams, a brother of the rebel general, was wounded and taken prisoner.

On the 18th of July, near Memphis, Missouri, Major John Y. Clopper, in command of a detachment of Merrill's Horse, about three hundred strong, and a detachment of Major Rogers's battalion of the 11th Regiment of Cavalry, Missouri State Militia, numbering about one hundred, attacked the combined guerrilla bands of Porter and Dunn, and, after a severely-contested fight, entirely routed them. The rebels left twenty-three of their number lying dead on the field. The loss to Major Clopper's command was considerable.

In writing of General McClellan's operations on the Peninsula, I had failed to mention that on the 7th of August a skirmish occurred near Malvern Hill, Virginia, in which Lieutenant-Colonel Gamble, of the 8th Regiment of Illinois Cavalry, was wounded, together with several of his men. The enemy on this occasion lost about fifty killed and wounded, and fifty taken prisoners.

Major-General John Pope was assigned to the command of the Army of Virginia on the 26th day of June, 1862. In his report he says the cavalry numbered about five thousand, but most of it was badly mounted and armed, and in poor condition for service. Soon after taking command, Brigadier-General John P. Hatch was relieved from the command of the cavalry of General Banks's corps, and Brigadier-General John Buford was sent to Banks, to act as his Chief of Cavalry. Brigadier-General John Buford and George D. Bayard were General Pope's Cavalry Commanders, although Brigadier-General Benjamin S. Roberts was his Chief of Cavalry.

Buford and Bayard were both excellent officers, and both had seen considerable service. Their cavalry was kept busily employed in making reconnoissances, and on duty of like character; and it was not until the close of the Battle of Cedar Mountain, on the 9th of August, that they had an opportunity of doing much damage to the enemy. They hung round the rear of the retreating rebel army, and, before they could reach the Rapidan, had captured many stragglers.

Pope sent a cavalry expedition to Louisa Court-house on the 16th of August, which captured the rebel General J. E. B. Stuart's adjutant general (who had in his possession some very valuable papers), and came very near capturing Stuart himself.

During the Battles of Groveton, August 29th, and Bull Run, August 30th, the cavalry was kept continually on the move, and became completely broken down. Pope, in his report, says:

> On the morning of the 30th, as may be supposed, our troops, who had been so continually marching and fighting for so many days, were in a state of great exhaustion. They had had little to eat for two days previous, and artillery and cavalry horses had been in harness and saddled continuously for ten days, and had had no forage for two days previous. It may easily be imagined how little these troops, after such severe labours, and after undergoing such hardship and privation, were in condition for active and efficient service.

At the Battle of Chantilly, on the 1st of September, our mounted men could be of little service, as, according to the report of Generals Buford and Bayard, there were not five horses to the company that could be found to trot. It was impossible, therefore, to cover the front of the army or to make reconnoissances, as is usual and necessary in the presence of an enemy.

Pope's shattered legions finally found safety in the entrenchments opposite Washington, and he was shortly after relieved from the command at his own request. In his report Pope says:

> Generals Bayard and Buford commanded all of the cavalry belonging to the Army of Virginia. Their duties were peculiarly arduous and hazardous; and it is not too much to say that throughout the operations, from the first to the last day of the campaign, scarce a day passed that these officers did not render services which entitle them to the gratitude of the government. When the rebel army, under General Lee, invaded Maryland, Major-General McClellan again took command of the United States Army. At the Battle of South Mountain, September 14th, 1862, our cavalry force consisted of one division, under command of Brigadier-General Alfred Pleasanton. This division was kept in hand until evening, when, finding the enemy's line had given way, our mounted men were pressed forward, and over

taking their cavalry at Boonesboro, made a dashing charge, killing and wounding a number, and capturing two hundred and fifty prisoners and two guns.

At the terrible Battle of Antietam, fought on the 17th of September, 1862, the cavalry took very little part, as it could not be advantageously used on that dreadful day, which was purely a contest between the infantry and artillery of both armies. Pleasanton's men were held in reserve near a bridge over Antietam Creek, and lost but few of their number. Lee's army withdrew during the night, and soon made its way back into Virginia. In this battle, Col. John Sedgwick, of the 4th U. S. Cavalry, was very severely wounded. He was Major-General of Volunteers at the time, and commanded a corps. Colonel J. H. Childs, of the 4th Penn. Cavalry, was killed in this battle.

While the fight was going on at South Mountain, Maryland, on the 14th of September, Harper's Ferry, Virginia, which was not more than ten miles distant, was closely besieged by a large rebel force, under command of Stonewall Jackson. It became evident that Colonel Miles, the Union commander, was about to surrender the place, which the cavalry portion of the troops would not submit to. Lieutenant-Colonel Hasbrouck Davis, in command of his own regiment, the 12th Illinois Cavalry, the 8th New York, the 1st Maryland, and the 1st Rhode Island Cavalry, in all about two thousand men, cut their way through the enemy's lines on the night of the 14th, and, after a series of thrilling adventures, made their escape.

Not only did the cavalry do this, but they captured the wagon-train belonging to the rebel General Longstreet, with over a hundred prisoners, and carried them in safety to Greencastle, Pennsylvania. This was one of the most heroic feats of the war, and alone would shed a lustre upon the cavalry service. On the following day every other portion of the command, numbering 11,583, surrendered to the rebels!

At the Battle of Iuka, Mississippi, September 19th, our cavalry behaved admirably. In his congratulatory order to his army, Major-General Rosecrans says:

To Colonel Mizner, Chief of the Cavalry Division, and to the officers and men of his command, the general commanding here publicly tenders his acknowledgments. For courage, efficiency, and for incessant and successful combats, he does not believe they have any superiors. In our advance on Iuka, and during the action, they ably performed their duty. Colonel Hatch fought and whipped the rebels at Peyton's Mills on the 19th, pursued the retreating rebel column on the 20th, harassed their rear, and captured a large number of arms. During the action, five privates of the 3rd Michigan Cavalry beyond our extreme right opened fire, captured a rebel stand of colours, a captain and lieutenant, sent in the colours that night, alone held their prisoners during the night, and brought them in next morning.

Again, at Corinth, on the 3rd and 4th of October, General Rosecrans found that his cavalry did good service, and for it he thanked the commanders in general orders. After the fighting the mounted men followed the enemy more than sixty miles.

On the 8th of October the Battle of Perryville, Kentucky, was fought by the United States forces, under Major General Buell, against the rebels. In this action the cavalry was under command of Brigadier-General Gay. A battalion of the 2nd Michigan Cavalry, under Colonel A. P. Campbell, and a portion of the 9th Pennsylvania Cavalry, under Colonel James, bore a conspicuous part Captain Jared W. Jenkins, of the 1st Kentucky Cavalry, was killed in this battle.

During the summer of 1862, in addition to the fights already mentioned as having occurred in Missouri, there were several others of considerable importance. At Independence, Missouri, on the morning of the 11th of August, an attack was made by the rebel forces under Colonel J. H. Hughes, and, after a severe fight, they were driven off with considerable loss. The Union troops be longed to the 7th Missouri Cavalry Volunteers, and a battalion of the Missouri State Militia. Our loss was twenty-six killed and thirty wounded; among the latter were Lieutenants Vance and Pence, both of the 7th Missouri Volunteer Cavalry.

Again, on the 9th of August, a portion of Merrill's Horse, the 9th Missouri State Militia, and two companies of the 7th Missouri State Militia, under Colonel Guitar, attacked the rebel camp of Colonel Poindexter at Compton's Ferry, Missouri, and, after a brisk skirmish, entirely routed the enemy. Our loss was trifling; theirs was considerable.

At Lone Jack, Missouri, on the morning of the 16th of August, the rebels, under Colonel Coffee, attacked about six hundred State Militia, under Major Foster, defeating him, and capturing two pieces of artillery. The loss on each side was about fifty killed and from seventy-five to one hundred wounded; among the latter was Major Foster.

August 21st was the day on which a fight occurred near Gallatin,

Tennessee, between the Union Cavalry, under Brigadier-General R. W. Johnson, and the rebel General John Morgan. The Union Cavalry numbered six hundred and forty, taken from the 2nd Indiana, Lieutenant Colonel Stewart; 4th Kentucky, Captain Chilson; 5th Kentucky, Major Winfrey; and 7th Pennsylvania, Colonel Wynkoop. Our men were defeated, and the conduct of many of them, according to General Johnson's report, was anything but creditable. Johnson himself was taken prisoner, with about seventy-five men. Thirty of his men were killed and fifty wounded; among the former was Adjutant Wynkoop, a brave and gallant officer.

On the 30th of August a fight occurred near Bolivar, Tennessee, between a body of Union troops and the rebels. Our soldiers were forced to retire after a lengthy engagement. The cavalry on our side consisted of four companies of the 2nd Illinois regiment, under Lieutenant-Colonel Hogg, and two companies of the 11th Illinois Regiment, under Major Puterbaugh. In this affair Lieutenant Colonel Hogg was killed.

In October, General Pleasanton, with a cavalry force, crossed the Potomac, and made a daring reconnaissance as far as Martinsburg, driving the rebel cavalry, under Wade Hampton, before him, and obtaining all the information he desired. The enemy had declared that they wished to fall in with Pleasanton's men; but upon the approach of the Union troops, they thought better of the matter, and placed themselves beyond the reach of harm. Our cavalry was seven hundred strong, consisting of the 8th Illinois, and portions of the 8th Pennsylvania and 3rd Indiana.

On the 10th of October, a body of United States troops, commanded by Lieutenant-Colonel Boyle, of the 9th Regiment Kentucky Cavalry, completely surprised a detachment of rebel troops belonging to General Bragg's army, and captured sixteen hundred prisoners. This was a most successful affair, and reflects great credit upon the Union troops engaged.

The next day a fight occurred near Helena, Arkansas, between a detachment of the 4th Iowa Cavalry, under Major Rector, and a superior force of Texas Rangers, under Lieutenant-Colonel Giddings; the latter were routed, and nine of them, including Giddings, were captured. The Iowa men lost three killed and nine wounded.

While this was going on in the West, three hundred horsemen, commanded by Colonel McReynolds, of the 1st New York Cavalry, fell upon the camp of the rebel Colonel Imboden, at Cacapon Bridge, seventeen miles from Winchester, Virginia, and captured "a major, lieutenant, twenty-five privates, a large number of horses and mules, one thousand blankets, a quantity of ammunition, brass cannon, wagons, fire-arms, clothing, and Colonel Imboden's private papers."

CHAPTER 13

Cavalry at Prairie Grove

When the rebel Stuart invaded Pennsylvania, General Pleasanton, with a United States cavalry force, was sent to oppose him. On the morning, according to the official account, of October 11th, he received orders to start with his command, and was soon *en route* for Hagerstown, arriving there about eleven o'clock. Here, learning the rebels were moving in the direction of Mercersburg, he started for Clear Spring in hopes to intercept them. He had proceeded only five miles when he received a dispatch from headquarters ordering him to halt.

At half past one o'clock p.m. he was ordered to march to Mechanicstown *via* Cavetown and Harrison's Gap. He sent patrols to Emmittsburg and Gettysburg to obtain information of the enemy, and reached Mechanicstown about eight o'clock in the evening. At half past twelve o'clock a.m. he sent scouts in the direction of Middleburg, who reported that the rebel cavalry under Stuart had passed through Middletown, five miles to the east of Mechanicstown, one hour before that time, taking a private road to Woodsborough, and thence to Liberty, *en route* to the mouth of the Monocacy.

General Pleasanton started for this point by way of Frederick City, passing through the latter place at five o'clock Sunday morning. He reached the Monocacy at eight o'clock a.m., and found four or five hundred infantry guarding the canal aqueduct and the roads to the ferries. They told him that they had neither seen nor heard of the rebel cavalry. He crossed the Monocacy, with portions of the 8th Illinois and the 3rd Indiana Cavalry, and two guns of Pennington's Battery, and sent forward a company on the Barnesville Road to reconnoitre, while the main column moved in the direction of Poolesville.

The advanced squadron had not passed more than one and a half miles from the ferry before they discovered a body of cavalry approaching, dressed in the uniform of United States soldiers. The officers in command of the squadron made signals in a friendly manner, which were returned by the parties, who approached to within a short distance of each other, when the officer commanding the opposite party ordered his men to charge.

Skirmishing took place. The enemy brought up a superior force, and opened a couple of guns, which obliged our men to retire. The two guns of Pennington's Battery were brought into position, and opened with a brisk fire, which checked the enemy's advance. At this time Pleasanton's command was not more than four hundred strong; four small companies of infantry were then taken to support the guns. Skirmishing took place until the remainder of Pennington's guns came up, and they soon drove off the enemy's guns.

It was then discovered that the enemy had two guns in position at White's Ford on this side, and one gun on the other side of the river. Pleasanton then took all the infantry at the mouth of the Monocacy, with the exception of two companies, and made a general advance. The enemy then retreated toward White's Ferry, keeping up a rapid fire all the time. Pennington's horses gave out, and the men were obliged to push the cannon up the hills.

The enemy, owing to this delay, effected a crossing over the river. This was half past one o'clock p.m. He then received information from Colonel Ward, of General Stoneman's division, that a brigade of infantry, and a regiment of cavalry, and a section of artillery were in the neighbourhood. He sent word to the general that the enemy had escaped. This was the first intimation he had of troops being in that vicinity.

General Pleasanton succeeded in driving the rebels from the mouth of the Monocacy to White's Ford, a distance of three miles. The general was of the impression that, had White's Ford been occupied by any force of ours previous to the occupation of it by the enemy, the capture of Stuart's forces would have been certain; but with Pleasanton's small force, which did not exceed one fourth of that of the enemy, it was not practicable for him to occupy that ford while the enemy was in his front. Thus ended the daring raid of the rebel cavalry under Stuart into Pennsylvania.

They escaped, carrying off considerable plunder, and doing much damage. It was not the fault of Pleasanton, however, as he travelled ninety miles in twenty-four hours, with the rain pouring down upon his men; and had he had a sufficient force with him, there is little doubt but Stuart, with his Virginia and South Carolina chivalry, would have been captured. The rebels passed completely around the army of General McClellan.

On the 13th of October, the 6th Regiment of Cavalry, Missouri State Militia, under Colonel Catherwood, returned to Sedalia, after a very successful scout after guerrillas, in which they dispersed several small bands, killed several, and took Colonel William H. McCown, of the rebel army, prisoner.

A fight took place near Lexington, Kentucky, on the 17th of October, between about four hundred Union Cavalry, under Major Charles B. Seidel, of the 3rd Ohio Cavalry, and a large rebel force, under General John Morgan. The Union troops behaved well, but were forced to retreat before superior numbers, losing four killed, twenty-four wounded, and a large number of prisoners. On the next day, near the same place, Morgan attacked a detachment of the 4th Ohio Cavalry, under Captain Robey, and captured the whole Union force. In this affair, as in the one before alluded to, our people behaved well, but their small numbers could do nothing with Morgan's men, who amounted to three thousand cavalry men, with six pieces of artillery. Afterward the rebel chief entered Lexington, and passed through without stopping, and moved off in the direction of Versailles.

Two skirmishes occurred in Missouri on the same day, October 20th, in different portions of the state. Major Woodson, of the 10th Cavalry, Missouri State Militia, near the Auxvois River attacked a party of guerrillas, killing and wounding several, capturing their arms, ammunition, horses, etc., and completely dispersing them. Lieutenant-Colonel James Stuart, with a portion of the 10th Illinois Cavalry, attacked about two hundred rebels near Marshfield, Missouri, completely routing and disorganising them, and capturing twenty-seven of them.

A skirmish occurred at Woodville, Tennessee, on the 21st of October, when Major John J. Mudd, 2nd Illinois Cavalry, completely routed a party of guerrillas, and captured forty of them. On the following day, Major B. F. Lazear, leading a Union force, attacked and routed a party of rebels near Van Buren, Arkansas, with considerable loss to them.

Colonel Edward M. McCook, of the 2nd Indiana Cavalry, encountered several bands of Morgan's guerrillas near Big Hill, Kentucky, on the 23rd of October, killing four or five of them and destroying several wagons partly loaded. From there he went to Richmond, and captured and paroled some two hundred sick and wounded rebels who had been left behind.

General Herron, with the 1st Iowa Cavalry, the 7th Missouri State Militia Cavalry, and a portion of the 1st Missouri Volunteer Cavalry, attacked a force of Texas Rangers, under Colonel Craven, near Cross Hollows and Fayetteville, Arkansas, on the 28th of October. The Union soldiers made a tedious night march, and, falling upon the enemy with great vigour, routed them, capturing all of their camp equipage and killing some six or eight of them. The Union loss was one killed and four wounded.

On the 3rd of November, Captain Flint, of the 1st Vermont Cavalry, with eighty men of his company, doing picket duty near New Baltimore, Virginia, was attacked by about one hundred and fifty rebel cavalry. The brave Vermonters drove the rebels off with considerable loss, and then returned to their post, which they held.

On the 8th of November, Colonel Lee, of the 7th Kansas Cavalry, with about fifteen hundred Union Cavalry defeated a party of rebels near Hudsonville, Mississippi, killing sixteen and capturing one hundred and seventy-five of them, together with one hundred horses and a large number of fire-arms.

A portion of the last-named regiment, with a detachment of the 2nd Illinois Cavalry, under Major John J. Mudd, 2nd Illinois Cavalry, attacked a body of rebels on the 12th of November near Lamar, Mississippi, utterly routing them with great loss.

The 3rd New York Cavalry, under Lieutenant-Colonel Mix, attacked a North Carolina infantry regiment, supported by some North Carolina cavalry, at Cove Creek, North Carolina, on the 18th of November, and, after a spirited fight, the North Carolina troops were put to flight, losing a portion of their arms and equipments.

At the fight at Cane Hill, Arkansas, November 28th, between the Union forces under General Blunt and the rebels under General Marmaduke, the 6th Regiment of Kansas Cavalry behaved well, and charged upon the enemy's artillery with sabres. Owing to the position of the artillery the charge was unsuccessful, though the men engaged, led on by Colonel Judson, Lieutenant-Colonel Jewett, and Major Campbell, did everything in their power to carry it; but they were forced back, and, under cover of the night, the enemy escaped. Lieutenant Colonel Jewett was killed, and Lieutenant J. A. Johnson, of the same regiment, was very severely wounded. In this action, the 2nd Kansas Cavalry, under Colonel Cloud, also participated.

An expedition to Yellville, Arkansas, under command of Colonel

Dudley Wickersham, of the 10th Illinois Cavalry, returned to General Herron's camp on the 30th of November. The troops engaged were the 10th Illinois Cavalry, the 3rd Wisconsin Cavalry, Colonel William A. Barstow, and the 1st Iowa Cavalry, Colonel Anderson. The expedition was successful, and succeeded in destroying portions of the rebel saltpetre-works, several storehouses, and about five hundred small-arms.

Several skirmishes occurred in the neighbourhood of Oxford, Mississippi, between Hatch's brigade and the rebel forces in December; and, on the 4th of the month, that brigade, with one commanded by Colonel Lee, attacked the rebels at Water Valley, Mississippi, in which the latter were routed, leaving three hundred and fifty prisoners in the hands of the Union soldiers.

Brigadier-General C. C. Washburne led an expedition, composed of portions of several cavalry regiments, from Helena, Arkansas, across the river into the State of Mississippi during the latter part of November and first part of December. He had two skirmishes with the enemy, in both of which he was successful, and accomplished the main object of his expedition, which was to give the leaders of the rebel forces an idea that his force was the advance-guard of a large Union army sent in to cut off the retreat of General Price and his rebels from their position. Price believed it, and left accordingly. Washburne had his force divided into two brigades, as follows, *viz*:

First Brigade, Colonel J. Hall Wilson, 5th Illinois Cavalry, commanding.

	Commander.	No. of men.
1st Indiana Cavalry	Captain Walker	300
9th Illinois "	Major Burgh	150
3rd Iowa "	Major Scott	188
4th Iowa "	Captain Perkins	200
5th Illinois "	Major Seeley	212

Second Brigade, Colonel Thomas Stevens, 2nd Wisconsin Cavalry, commanding.

6th Missouri Cavalry	Major Hawkins	150
5th Kansas "	Lieut.-Col. Jenkins	208
10th Illinois "	Captain Anderson	92
3rd Illinois "	Lieut.-Col. Ruggles	200
2nd Wisconsin "	Lieut.-Col. Sterling	225

On the 5th of December a severe fight occurred between our cavalry and a large rebel force near Coffeeville, Mississippi. The Union troops, over two thousand in number, under command of Colonel T. Lyle Dickey, of the 4th Illinois Cavalry, Chief of Cavalry on General Grant's staff, had been driving the enemy before them for some distance, when they were suddenly checked by coming upon a large force of rebel infantry and a battery of artillery, which had been concealed by them until our people approached very near.

Colonel Dickey's force was in three brigades, the first commanded by Colonel Lee, of the 7th Kansas Cavalry, the second commanded by Colonel Hatch, of the 2nd Iowa Cavalry, and the third commanded by Colonel Mizner, of the 3rd Michigan Cavalry. The enemy outnumbering our forces so greatly, it was found necessary to give way, and Colonel Dickey ordered his men to fall back. Our forces retired in good order, but were annoyed by the enemy's fire, who followed closely, and killed and wounded many of our men.

After the enemy had followed our troops three miles, they desisted and returned to Coffeeville, the Union soldiers continuing their retreat toward Oxford, Mississippi. This was a most unfortunate affair for the Union forces, though they had conducted themselves well, and had done everything that brave troops could do. Colonels Dickey, Lee, and Mizner; Lieutenant-Colonels Prince and McCullough; Majors Coon, Love, and Rickards, and those under them were everywhere exposed to the most galling fire, and personally directed the movements of their commands.

One of Colonel Lee's best officers was killed, and five officers of the 2nd Iowa Cavalry were wounded. Lieutenant-Colonel William McCullough, of the 4th Illinois Cavalry, a brave and daring officer, was killed at the head of his column, having been shot through the breast. The losses to the United States troops were as follows, *viz.*:

	Killed.	Wounded.	Missing.
4th Illinois Cavalry,	1	13	3
7th " "	3	11	20
3rd Michigan "	2	1	0
2nd Iowa "	1	21	4
7th Kansas "	3	8	8
	—	—	—
Total	10	54	35 = 99

The rebel cavalry and infantry were commanded by General Van

Dorn, whose whole force was estimated at near five thousand men.

Captain George D. Bayard, of the 4th United States Cavalry, Brigadier-General of Volunteers, died December 14th, 1862, of wounds received at the Battle of Fredericksburg.

At the Battle of Prairie Grove, Arkansas, fought December 7th by Brigadier-Generals Blunt and Herron, against the combined rebel forces of Hindman, Marmaduke, Parsons, and Frost, the cavalry rendered most efficient service, as is proved by the reports of the Union commanders.

The cavalry regiments which participated were the 10th Illinois, Colonel Wickersham; a battalion of the 1st Missouri, under Major Hubbard; the 7th Missouri Cavalry Volunteers, Colonel Dan. Huston, Jr.; the 8th Missouri, Colonel Geiger; the 1st Iowa, Colonel Anderson; the 3rd Wisconsin, Colonel William A. Barstow and Major Calkins; the 2nd Kansas, Lieutenant-Colonel Bassett; and a portion of the 1st Arkansas Union Cavalry.

During the battle, Colonel Dan. Huston, Jr., of the 7th Missouri Cavalry, commanded the 2nd Division of Herron's forces, and Colonel Wickersham commanded the greater portion of the cavalry. The loss to the mounted men was severe. Lieutenant-Colonel Bassett, of the 2nd Kansas, was killed, and Captain A. P. Russell, of the same regiment, was mortally wounded. Major Hubbard, of the 1st Missouri, was taken prisoner.

Others, equally worthy and meritorious, were lost, but where all behaved so well it is idle to make distinctions. The result of this hard and well-fought battle was the retreat of the rebel forces who had started out to invade Missouri. Our loss was so severe that the enemy could not be followed closely, and they made good their escape. Their loss was very heavy.

On the 12th of December, Brigadier-General D. S. Stanley, with a strong force of Union Cavalry, marched from Nashville to Franklin, Tennessee, where he destroyed a great deal of rebel property and captured a few prisoners.

On the 18th of the same month, Lexington, Kentucky, was occupied by a large force of rebels under General Forrest. Before capturing the town, the rebels encountered the 11th Regiment of Illinois Cavalry, under Colonel R. G. Ingorsell, who, after a stout resistance, were forced to leave the field.

Before this, however, and on the 16th of December, one of the most successful expeditions occurred which has taken place during the war. It was near New Haven, Kentucky, while Buell's army was falling back toward Louisville. The Union force consisted of seven hundred men, under Lieutenant-Colonel Stewart, of the 2nd Indiana Cavalry, as follows: two hundred and fifty from the 1st Kentucky, two hundred from the 3rd Kentucky, and two hundred and fifty from the 2nd Indiana Cavalry. With this command, Stewart determined to capture the whole rebel force, which was known to be nearby.

As the enemy was on the alert, and using the utmost vigilance to prevent surprise, the most difficult part was to capture the pickets, so as not to give the alarm. Lieutenant Coppage and Sergeant Humphrey, with twelve men, were sent forward to attempt this part, and most adroitly and gallantly did they execute it. Sergeant Humphrey and one other went before some fifty yards, with instructions that if there were only two men on picket to dash up to them, and, presenting arms, demand an immediate and silent surrender; but, in case there were several on picket, they were to make signal to those in rear, who were to dash forward at full speed and overpower them, or give chase, and the whole column would charge after them.

The advance two came upon the first picket of two men, and, by a rapid dash, captured them without firing a gun or giving any alarm. The second picket was taken in the same way, with like success, and they now learned that there was a third picket of fifteen near the bridge over the Rolling Fork. The first twelve were now sent forward, and a company detailed to advance closely behind to sustain them. By another brilliant dash these also were captured, and no gun fired to alarm the camp, now about a mile distant. The rest of the command was now brought up, and forming four abreast, they dashed across the bridge at full speed, passed through the town of New Haven into the woods beyond, where the enemy's camp was situated.

The sun was just rising as they entered the camp, shouting wildly and carrying terror to the hearts of the bewildered rebels, who were completely surprised. The colonel commanding the rebels roused up, and, rubbing his eyes, could scarcely understand what had happened. Stewart, with his long hair, came riding forward, and lifting his broad-brimmed black hat from his head, said to him, in tones which at least the "secesh" Colonel Crawford never has forgotten, "Behold the conquering hero comes."

Crawford immediately surrendered, and his quaking and panic-stricken followers were only too glad to be allowed to do the same. It proved that Stewart had captured the whole of the 3rd Regiment of

Georgia Cavalry, a portion of the Kentucky rebel cavalry, and some Texas Rangers, without even firing a gun. With his game thus quietly and easily bagged, Lieutenant Colonel Stewart, with his men, returned to camp, and continued on his way toward Louisville.

General Van Dorn attacked and captured the town of Holly Springs, Mississippi, on the 20th of December. The attack was sudden and overpowering, and the garrison was speedily captured. Six companies of the 2nd Illinois Cavalry, under the brave Major Mudd, refused to surrender, and cut their way through the ranks of the enemy and escaped. A more brave and gallant action has not been done during this war, as the command was completely surrounded, and had been called upon to surrender by a force of not less than eight thousand men. Van Dorn destroyed an immense amount of United States property in this affair, and his treatment to the sick in hospital is said to have been barbarous in the extreme.

Colonel Spears, with a portion of the 11th Pennsylvania Cavalry, had a spirited engagement at Joiner's Bridge, four miles above Franklin, on the Blackwater River, Virginia, on the 24th of December, with a rebel cavalry detachment, supported by a body of infantry. The Pennsylvanians routed the rebels completely, dispersing them and capturing several of their number.

On the 26th of December, Major Stivers, of the 14th Kentucky Cavalry, with one hundred and fifty men, attacked a large party of guerrillas in Powell County, Kentucky, capturing several, and completely dispersing the remainder, who outnumbered the Union men, but who could not stand up against them. The next day, Major Foley, commanding about two hundred and fifty men of the 6th and 10th Kentucky Cavalry, surprised a camp of rebels in Campbell County, Tennessee, numbering three hundred and fifty. Of this number the Union troops claimed that they killed thirty, wounded one hundred and seventy-six, and captured fifty-one, without the loss of a man!

All of their camp equipage was burned, eighty horses and a large amount of arms captured. This statement is made in accordance with General Wright's dispatch. Such amazing disparity of loss is almost incredible. I had failed to mention that a daring reconnaissance was made by a portion of General Sigel's command, under General Stahel, who met and attacked the enemy at Snicker's Ferry on the 28th of November. Colonel Di Cesnola, of the 4th New York Cavalry, Colonel Wyndham, 1st New Jersey Cavalry, with portions of their own regiments and of the 2nd Pennsylvania, 9th New York, and 1st

Michigan Cavalry, behaved well; and, as Sigel says, " Our men charged splendidly whenever they met the enemy, and used their swords, no fire-arms being brought into use."

Forty of the enemy, belonging to the 3rd, 7th, and 12th Virginia Rebel Regiments, were captured, with their horses and arms, fifty were killed and wounded, and two colours taken. Our loss was fifteen killed and wounded. Lieutenants John T. Rutherford and N. Herrick, of the 9th New York Cavalry, and Lieutenant Marvine, of the 1st Michigan Cavalry, were among the wounded. The conduct of Major Knox, Captain Coffin, and Lieutenant Herrick is highly spoken of by their commanding officer.

When Morgan made his raid into Kentucky in December, the 12th Kentucky Cavalry, under Colonel Shanks, and the 4th and 5th Regiments Indiana Cavalry, under Colonel Gray, harassed his march very much, and near Munfordville had three quite spirited engagements. The officers above mentioned, with Captains Dickey and Twyman, rendered valuable services, and were highly spoken of. Our soldiers captured a considerable number of the rebels with very small loss to themselves. Captain Dickey commanded a portion of the 2nd Michigan Cavalry in these skirmishes.

THE CAVALRY AT MURFREESBOROUGH.

At the Battle of Murfreesborough, on Stone's River, fought on the 31st of December, 1862, and the 1st of January, 1863, the cavalry of General Rosecrans's army, commanded by Brigadier-General David S. Stanley, Chief of Cavalry, rendered important service. The first brigade was commanded by Colonel Minty, of the 4th Michigan Cavalry, and the 2nd by Colonel Lewis Zahn, of the 3rd Ohio Cavalry. The reserve cavalry, consisting of the 15th Pennsylvania (Anderson Cavalry), 1st Middle Tennessee, 2nd East Tennessee, and four companies of the 3rd Indiana Regiments, was commanded by Stanley in person.

On the 28th there was some little skirmishing, and on the 29th of December the reserve cavalry under Stanley encountered the cavalry of the enemy in strong force at Wilkinson's Cross Roads. Our cavalry drove them rapidly across Overall's Creek, and within one half mile of the enemy's line of battle. The 15th Pennsylvania behaved most gallantly, pushing at full charge upon the enemy for six miles. Unfortunately, they advanced too far, and fell upon two regiments of rebel infantry in ambush, and, after a gallant struggle, were compelled to re tire, with the loss of Majors Rosengarten and Ward, and six men killed, and five men desperately wounded.

On the 30th the entire cavalry force was engaged in guarding the flanks of our army in position, and nothing of importance was done. At half past nine o'clock on the 31st Stanley was ordered to hasten to the right of our infantry line, which was giving way. Galloping on at the head of the first brigade, he found, upon his arrival there, that order had been restored, and halted his men in a piece of woods. In this position our cavalry was attacked about four o'clock p.m. by a long line of foot skirmishers.

With Colonel Minty in command of the 4th Michigan and 7th Pennsylvania Cavalry, Stanley held the enemy at bay for half an hour, when, seeing he was likely to be outflanked, he ordered his men to retire to an open field. The enemy followed, when Stanley, being joined by the 15th Pennsylvania, 3rd Kentucky, and 1st Tennessee Cavalry Regiments, he dashed against the enemy, and routed them from this part of the field.

In the meantime, the 1st, 2nd, and 3rd Ohio and 2nd East Tennessee Regiments, forming the second brigade under Colonel Zahn, had occupied the extreme right of our line of battle, and when the infantry gave way early on the morning of the 31st, they were for a time nearly cut off from the main body of our forces by the rebel troops, which had been hurled against our line. They were forced to give way before overwhelming numbers for some distance, when, being rallied, they in turn were thrown against the enemy amid a fierce cannonade, and checked the advance of the rebels.

In this charge the gallant Colonel Milliken and Second Lieutenant Condit, of the 1st Ohio Cavalry, were killed outright, and Adjutant Scott, of the same regiment, was severely wounded. Before this, Major Moore, of the 1st Ohio Cavalry, had been killed, the first shell from the enemy having, by its explosion, mortally wounded him, and he expired soon afterward. Several skirmishes occurred during the day, in which the second brigade behaved well.

On the 1st of January, 1863, the enemy showed a line of skirmishers in the woods to our front, and soon after brought a six-gun battery to bear upon our cavalry. As our men could not reach the enemy's skirmishers nor reply to his artillery, Stanley ordered the cavalry to fall back. A part of Zahn's brigade marched this day to Nashville to protect our trains. While on his way, a little below Lavergne he was attacked by Wheeler's cavalry brigade, which he twice repulsed, killing several of them, and saved all of the train but one or two wagons, which were broken down during the excitement.

The 4th Regiment of United States Cavalry, commanded by Captain Elmer Otis, was also present during the battle, acting independently. It made a splendid charge upon the enemy on the morning of the 31st, in which over a hundred prisoners were taken, and two companies of our own men in their hands were released. In this charge, Captain Eli Long led his company with the greatest gallantry, and was wounded by a ball through his left arm. Lieutenants Mauck, Kelly, Lee, and Healy, could not have done better. Sergeant Major John Gr. Webster behaved gallantly, taking a lieutenant mounted on a fine mare.

Colonel John Kennett, of the 4th Ohio Cavalry, was present, commanding the division under General Stanley, and accompanied Minty's brigade most of the time during the battle.

Our cavalry engaged was as follows:

4th Regiment, United States Cavalry, Captain Elmer Otis, acting independently.

First Brigade, Colonel Robert H. G. Minty, commanding.
7th Pennsylvania Cavalry, Major John E. Wynkoop.
3rd Kentucky Cavalry, Colonel Eli H. Murray.
4th Michigan Cavalry, Lieut.-Colonel W. H. Dickinson.
One company of the 2nd Indiana Cavalry.

Second Brigade, Colonel Lewis Zahn, commanding.
1st Ohio Cavalry, Major James Laughlin.
3rd Ohio Cavalry, Lieutenant-Colonel D. A. Murray.
4th Ohio Cavalry, Major J. L. Pugh.

Reserve.
1st Middle Tennessee Cavalry, Colonel W. B. Stokes.
2nd East Tennessee Cavalry, Adjutant William S. Hall.
15th Pennsylvania Cavalry, Colonel William J. Palmer.
Four companies 3rd Indiana Cavalry, Major E. Klein.

The loss to the cavalry was two hundred and seventy-eight killed, wounded, and missing.

The following is a list of the officers killed and wounded, *viz.*:

Killed.—Colonel Minor Milliken, 1st Ohio Cavalry Volunteers; Major D. A. B. Moore, 1st Ohio Cavalry Volunteers; Major Adolph G. Rosengarten, 15th Pennsylvania Cavalry Volunteers; Major Frank B. Ward, 15th Pennsylvania Cavalry Volunteers; Captain Miller R. McCulloch, company G, 2nd Kentucky Cavalry; Captain Morris, company L, 2nd East Tennessee Cavalry; Lieutenant T. L. Condit, company

L, 1st Ohio Cavalry Volunteers.

Wounded.—Captain Eli Long, 4th Regiment United States Regular Cavalry; Captain John M. Thomas, company I, 3rd Kentucky Cavalry; Captain Wortham, company C, 1st Tennessee Cavalry; Adjutant William H. Scott, 1st Ohio Cavalry Volunteers; Lieutenant Thomas V. Mitchell, company H, 4th Michigan Cavalry.

Brigadier-General Stanley, in his official report, notices the gallant conduct of Colonels Kennett, Minty, Murray, and Zahn; Majors Kline, Ward, Rosengarten, and Wynkoop; and of Captain Otis.

Major-General Rosecrans in his report, says:

> Brigadier General Stanley, in command of our ten regiments of cavalry, fought the enemy's forty regiments of cavalry and held them at bay, and beat them whenever he could meet them.

Six companies of the 2nd Kentucky Cavalry, under command of Major Thomas I. Nicholas, served in General Rousseau's division during the battle, doing good service. They were ordered down to watch and defend the fords on Stone's River, near Rousseau's left and rear. The cavalry of the enemy several times, in force, attempted to cross at these fords, but Nicholas very gallantly repulsed them with loss, and they did not cross the river.

Captain McCulloch, of this regiment, serving on the staff of Brigadier-General Jefferson C. Davis, was killed. He was a fine officer, and his loss was much regretted.

The 2nd and 3rd of January the cavalry was engaged in watching the flanks of our position. Upon the 4th it became evident that the enemy had fled. The cavalry was collected and moved to the fords of Stone's River, and upon the 5th entered Murfreesborough. From the 26th of December till the 4th of January the saddles were only taken off to groom, and were immediately replaced.

The rebel General John Morgan made an attack upon the Union garrison of Lebanon, Kentucky, on the 1st of January, 1863, and, after a brisk fight, was driven off. Ninety of his followers were taken prisoners and several were killed. He also lost his caissons and ammunition wagons. This victory over the rebels was rendered sad by the death of Colonel D. J. Halisy, of the 6th Regiment of Kentucky Cavalry, who was killed on the field. He was a brave and daring officer, and his loss was a severe one.

General Marmaduke, at the head of a horde of rebels, penetrated into the State of Missouri, and on the 8th of January made an attack upon the town of Springfield. Our first line which opposed him was made up of the 3rd Missouri State Militia Cavalry, under command of Colonel Walter King, the 4th Missouri State Militia Cavalry, under Colonel George H. Hall, and a battalion of the 14th Missouri State Militia Cavalry, under Lieutenant-Colonel Pounds. This line was driven back gradually, the 3rd and 4th Regiments behaving admirably, but the battalion of the 14th breaking in confusion.

Brigadier-General Egbert B. Brown, the Commander of the Union troops, was present, and directed all the movements of our troops until he was stricken down by a rifle-ball, which shattered his right arm, and he was carried from the field. At the edge of the town the cavalry halted, and being joined by the infantry and artillery and the battalion of the 14th, which had been rallied, they fought the enemy until nightfall, when darkness put an end to the action. Our troops prepared to renew it in the morning, but under cover of the night the rebels withdrew. Our loss was one hundred and sixty-two killed, wounded, and missing, while that of the enemy was equal, if not greater.

Brigadier-General Fitz Henry Warren, in command at Houston, Missouri, hearing of the attack upon Springfield, sent the greater portion of his command on the road thither to re-enforce General Brown. While on the march, and when near Hartsville, Missouri, these troops met the enemy under Marmaduke, who was falling back from Springfield after his unsuccessful assault upon that place. The advance of the enemy came suddenly upon our troops, who had barely time to form line of battle, early on the morning of the 11th of January.

At their first fire, Captain Bradway, of the 3rd Missouri Cavalry, and two of his men, were killed. After skirmishing a short time, the enemy fell back to their main line, which was formed near the town of Hartsville, and soon the action became general. The fight continued until night, when the enemy commenced retreating toward Arkansas, and our people, being too weak to follow, fell back toward. Houston. The 3rd Iowa Cavalry and the 3rd Missouri Cavalry Volunteers were the only mounted troops of ours in the fight. Lieutenant John D. Brown and three men of the former regiment were taken prisoners by the enemy.

In General Warren's official report, he speaks in the highest terms of Captain Black, commanding the 3rd Missouri Cavalry, and of Captain Lemon, of the same regiment. In this fight the rebel Brigadier-General Emmett McDonald, of St. Louis, Missouri, was killed, together with Colonels Porter, Thompson, and Hinkle.

CHAPTER 14

Cavalry Fight at Kelly's Ford

The third battalion of the 5th Pennsylvania Cavalry, commanded by Major William Gr. McCandless, made a reconnaissance in the direction of Barnesville, Virginia, on the 19th of January, 1863, thoroughly scouting all the roads branching from the Richmond and Williamsburg Turnpike. Two companies were off on the by roads, and two were left on the main pike under command of Captain Cameron. The captain sent eighteen men forward as an advance-guard, under Lieutenant Vezin, and the lieutenant sent Sergeant Anderson, with six of these men, about two hundred yards in advance of his party. The squadron marched in this way until within about a mile of "Burnt Ordinary," when there rode out in front of the six men under Sergeant Anderson about seventy rebels, who formed line across the road.

Seeing this, the sergeant turned, and was surprised to find his retreat cut off by another party of twenty rebels, who had formed line across the road in his rear. The sergeant and his men made a dash at those in rear, and all were captured except the sergeant, who cut through the line, and succeeded in reaching Lieutenant Vezin with his twelve men. Vezin immediately gave orders to "draw sabres," and, dashing forward, put the enemy to flight and recaptured all but one of his men. This was a daring feat, with scarce a parallel in the war. He captured four rebel soldiers and five horses fully equipped. Thirteen men and one officer put to flight near a hundred rebels drawn up in line of battle!

Colonel S. H. Mix, of the 3rd New York Cavalry, engaged in several expeditions with his regiment during the month of January, in which he captured several prisoners and obtained some valuable information. On the 25th of the month a battalion of this regiment captured a rebel picket near Newbern, North Carolina, and took nine rebels prisoners, with their horses and arms.

During the same month, a party of cavalry from the 10th Illinois and 1st Arkansas Cavalry, under Lieutenant-Colonel Stewart, captured a steamboat near Van Buren, Arkansas, and about three hundred prisoners.

Colonel Conner, with the 2nd Regiment of California Cavalry Volunteers, had a severe fight with the Indians on Bear River, in Washington Territory, on the 29th of January. The Indians were well posted in a strong position, and, after a fight of three hours, were forced to retreat with great loss. The conduct of Colonel Conner and Majors McGarry and Gallagher is highly spoken of. Lieutenant Chase was killed, Major Gallagher, Captain McClean, and Lieutenant Barry were wounded. The loss to the whites was fourteen killed and forty-nine wounded.

A severe hand to hand sabre fight took place in the vicinity of Rover, Tennessee, January 31st, between a body of Union Cavalry, under Colonel Kennett, and a body of rebels, which, terminated in the complete rout of the latter, with a loss of twelve killed on the field, about the same number wounded, and three hundred taken prisoners.

Colonel Stokes's 5th Regiment of Union Tennessee Cavalry dashed upon a camp of rebels near Middletown, Tennessee, and, by a brilliant sabre charge, captured about one hundred prisoners, with all their camp equipage, etc. Major Douglass and all of his officers were taken.

On the 7th of February, a deserter from the rebels came into camp at Yorktown, Virginia, and said that there were twenty-five more deserters who were anxious to come into the Union lines, but were afraid they would be fired upon. Colonel Lewis, of the 5th Pennsylvania Cavalry, sent out a squadron of his regiment to escort them in. When about five miles from camp, they were fired upon by a party of rebels who were secreted along the sides of the road, and twenty Union saddles were emptied in an instant.

At this time a rebel cavalry party was seen coming down the road in front, when our cavalry put spurs to their horses and dashed toward them. They had gone but a short distance, when horses and men commenced falling and rolling over one another in the wildest confusion. The rebels had stretched telegraph wires across the road from tree to tree on either side, and as the cavalry came along, they tripped and fell, doing much damage. In this condition the rebel troops fired into our men, killing a lieutenant and mortally wounding a captain. One captain and one lieutenant were taken prisoners, and thirty-five of our men were missing, and were either killed or taken prisoners. This was a most disastrous affair, but showed great ingenuity on the part of the rebels who planned it.

On the 14th of February, a squadron of the 5th Michigan Cavalry was surprised by the enemy at Anandale, Virginia, and were forced to retreat with a loss of fifteen killed and missing, and several wounded.

Lieutenant-Colonel Wood, with a portion of the 1st Indiana Cavalry, surprised a party of rebels near Yazoo Pass, Mississippi, February 19th, killing nine and capturing fifteen. The next day, near the same place, the 5th Illinois Cavalry had another skirmish with the enemy, who lost six killed and twenty-six captured.

Major Mudd, of the 2nd Illinois Cavalry, was killed in a skirmish which took place near Greenville, Mississippi, on the 23rd of February. He was a gallant officer, and behaved very well at the time Holly Springs was captured by Van Dorn, he refusing to surrender, and making his escape with the greater portion of his regiment.

On the 25th of February, a cavalry scout of the enemy attacked our pickets on the Strasburg Road, Virginia, and, after capturing twelve of our men and wounding two more, retired. A force of five hundred men from the 1st New York and 13th Pennsylvania Cavalry was sent out on the 26th in pursuit, and beyond Strasburg recaptured our men and took some prisoners. While the Union Cavalry was resting in the road, they were suddenly charged upon by a superior force of rebel cavalry, thrown in confusion, and, after a weak resistance, retreated, losing about two hundred men in killed and missing.

A skirmish took place about fifteen miles from Newbern, North Carolina, on the 27th of February, between a detachment of the 3rd New York Cavalry, under command of Captain Jacobs, and a strong party of rebel infantry. The cavalry dashed suddenly upon the rebels, killed several, and captured forty-eight, including a commissioned officer.

On the 1st of March a fight occurred near Bradyville, Tennessee, between a cavalry force under General Stanley and the rebels under Colonel Basil Duke. Stanley's force consisted of the 3rd Ohio, Colonel J. W. Paramore, 4th Ohio, Colonel Eli Long, and a part of the 1st Tennessee Cavalry, under Major Murphy, in all about seven hundred men. For fifteen or twenty minutes the rebels made a stubborn resistance, until our flanking detachments arrived in position and opened an enfilading fire upon both flanks of the rebel line. They immediately gave way in confusion, when our men charged gallantly among them with sabres and pistols, cut down a number as they ran, and drove them in utter rout a distance of three miles.

Five dead rebels were found on the field, from thirty to forty were wounded, and nearly a hundred prisoners were left in our hands. Among the latter were eight commissioned officers, including the adjutant of the 2nd Kentucky (rebel) Cavalry. On our side, Captain Rifenberick, of the 4th, and Lieutenant Hall, of the 3rd Ohio, were wounded; two privates were killed and four wounded.

The 1st Regiment of East Tennessee Cavalry captured seventy-two rebels and killed twelve at Chapel Hill, Tennessee, on the 3rd of March. Majors Macy and Burkhart were in command of the Union troops.

A detachment of United States troops, belonging to the 6th and 7th Illinois Cavalry, attacked the camp of the rebel Colonel Richardson, near Covington, Tennessee, on the 9th of March, killed twenty-five of them, took some prisoners, and burned the camp and garrison equipage. In the headlong stampede of the remaining rebels, they came near rushing into the hands of the 4th Illinois and 2nd Iowa Regiments, who were also out after them.

CAVALRY FIGHT AT KELLY'S FORD

A cavalry action took place at Kelly's Ford, Virginia, on the 17th of March, 1863, between the Union forces under General Averill and the rebels commanded by J. E. B. Stuart and Fitzhugh Lee. The United States force consisted of the 1st and 5th Regiments of United States Regular Cavalry, under Captain Reno; 1st Massachusetts Cavalry, Lieutenant-Colonel Curtis; 3rd, 4th, and 16th Pennsylvania, under Colonel John B. McIntosh; 1st Rhode Island, 4th New York, and 6th Ohio, Colonel Duffie; and the 6th New York flying battery of six guns. On riding down to the ford on the morning of the 17th at daylight, to cross over, the enemy were found to be in strong force on the opposite side, having posted numerous pickets, and constructed a formidable abattis along the bank.

A detachment of the 4th New York charged down into the stream, and attempted to force a passage, but were met and repulsed by a strong force of the enemy. Rallying, they dashed into the river, and were again repulsed. A third attempt proved no more successful. At this juncture, Lieutenant Brown, followed by a squadron of the 1st Rhode Island, plunged boldly in, cut their way through the abattis, and, charging up the acclivity, routed the enemy. The whole force then

BATTLE OF KELLY'S FORD.

crossed over and formed line of battle. This was about half past seven in the morning. At the ford twenty-four prisoners were captured.

As the men moved forward up the acclivity, the rebels, who in the meantime had rallied, charged upon us, when the 1st Rhode Island met them with a counter charge and put them to flight. The second time, the rebels once more attempting to rally, the 5th United States Cavalry seized the opportunity, dashed at them, and they again broke and ran wildly. The 3rd Pennsylvania Cavalry, posted to the right, likewise charged upon the force opposed to them most successfully. The 16th Pennsylvania, still farther to the right, did splendid execution, many of the rebels being dismounted. Our artillery, in the meantime, kept playing on the fleeing rebels and quickening their speed. Our line now moved forward about a mile and a half from the river; as it moved, our men kept charging, forming, and taking prisoners, until the outskirts of a wood were reached.

Here Averill again arranged his regiments in line of battle, keeping the 1st Regiment of United States Cavalry in reserve. Our men moved through the woods steadily and rapidly, firing as they went. Another open space was reached, and found to be full of skirmishers. The firing now became very brisk, the enemy for the first time opening on us with artillery, of which they had twelve pieces. Their solid shot and shell fell thick and fast among our men, but they pressed on, inspired by the success already won, and led forward by their officers.

After so many brilliant and profitable dashes on our part, the rebels thought it well to attempt again something in that line themselves, and charged. They ran against the 3rd Pennsylvania Cavalry, which broke them instantly. From the time of crossing the river there had been many personal encounters; single horsemen dashed at each other at full speed, cutting away with their sabres until one or the other was disabled. The wounds received by both friend and foe in these single combats were frightful in the extreme.

Our men continued to drive the rebels, they skirmishing and using their artillery as they retreated. The Union soldiers had now been fighting several hours, but, regardless of themselves, pursued their mission of keeping the rebels traveling, and did it most effectually. In this way Averill chased the enemy six miles, and until he came upon a line of rifle-pits which were filled with rebel infantry. Seeing that he could not move them, he determined to retire, as his artillery ammunition was expended, and he could do no farther good.

Detachments of cavalry were deployed in front of the artillery, and the whole force commenced its return march, Captain Reno, with a portion of the regular cavalry, covering the rear. Captain Sandford, with three squadrons of the 1st U. States Cavalry, assisted by Lieutenants Hunt and Bigelow, did good service supporting the battery. On the return, at one time this command was in danger of being annihilated. The men were stationed to the left of the battery, within easy supporting distance, ready to charge upon the rebels should they attempt to take it.

No sooner, however, had our guns ceased firing for want of ammunition, than the rebels turned their fire upon the supporting cavalry, keeping it up for a long period, and making sad havoc among the horses. The cavalry could not leave their positions, for the guns would have been lost. They succeeded in bringing all the pieces away, notwithstanding many of the horses were shot. At sundown General Averill retired to the north bank of the river.

The following officers were killed and wounded:

Lieutenant Cook, 1st Rhode Island, killed; Lieutenant Dimmock, 4th New York, mortally wounded; Major Chamberlain, chief of staff, wounded; Lieutenant Bowditch, 1st Massachusetts, severely wounded; Major Farrington, 1st Rhode Island, wounded; Captain Weichel, 3rd Pennsylvania, wounded; Lieutenant Wolfe, 6th Ohio, wounded; Captain McBride, 6th Pennsylvania, wounded; Lieutenant Thompson, 1st Rhode Island, wounded.

Our total loss did not exceed fifty in killed and wounded, while that of the enemy was considerably greater. Major Breckinridge, of the 1st Virginia (rebel) Cavalry, and about fifty men, were captured.

This was purely a cavalry fight, and reflects credit upon the actors.

A force of national cavalry, under the command of Colonel R. H. G. Minty, of the 4th Michigan Cavalry, returned to Murfreesborough, Tennessee, on the 14th of March, after a successful reconnaissance of eleven days duration in the enemy's country, during which time he dispersed several bands of guerrillas, captured fifty prisoners, a number of wagons and mules, and obtained much valuable information concerning the rebels.

On the 18th of March, a portion of the First Louisiana National Cavalry, under Captain Perkins, followed a party of rebel cavalry some distance inside the rebel lines near Brashear City, Louisiana, when, coming upon an additional force of cavalry, he was obliged to retreat, but was closely followed, and kept up the fight for several miles. The loss on each side amounted to four or five killed and as many wounded.

Brentwood, Tennessee, was captured and sacked by the rebels, under Generals Wheeler, Forrest, and Armstrong, on the 25th of March, 1863. After the capture, the rebel forces were pursued by a body of national troops, under General Green Clay Smith, consisting of portions of the 9th Pennsylvania, 4th and 6th Kentucky, and 2nd Michigan Cavalry Regiments, numbering about five hundred and fifty men. After a pursuit of nine miles, General Smith came upon the enemy drawn up in line of battle, and, ordering his troops into line, he gave directions for the men to "go in," and at it they went with their Colt's revolving rifles and Burnside carbines.

The enemy could not stand the firing, and broke their line, commencing a disorderly retreat, and abandoning the plunder which they had taken at Brentwood. They were driven six miles, when, coming to a cross road, a large body of rebel cavalry was seen advancing on it toward our troops. This was more than our people could stand, when, in turn, they commenced retreating before the enemy. In good order they moved off, turning frequently upon the rebels, and delivering some fires which made them fairly reel.

The 2nd Michigan, with their Colt's rifles, had to fire three volleys in one furious charge of the enemy before they would check their advance. The last fire fairly flashed in the faces of their horses before they turned. Finally, however, they gave up the pursuit. Our loss was considerable, as was that of the enemy; and though our cavalry was forced back, it did so steadily, and lost no honour in the fight. They did all that men could do, but the superior numbers of the rebels were too much for them.

A detachment of the 6th Illinois Cavalry, under Lieutenant Colonel Loomis, while encamped near Somerville, Tennessee, on the 29th of March, were surprised by a body of rebel troops, when, after a most sanguinary fight, they were driven off, but not until they had killed and wounded over forty of the Illinoisans.

On the 1st of April, Captain Mosby, of the rebel cavalry, made his appearance near Broad Ran, Virginia. His band was immediately attacked by a portion of the 1st Vermont Cavalry Regiment. After a short fight, the guerrillas fled, and sought safety behind a high fence, whence it was found impossible to dislodge them. In this fight, Captain Flint, a lieutenant, and several men of the Vermonters were wounded.

General Stanley made a successful scout against the rebels located near Snow Hill, Tennessee, on the 2nd of April. Here the 7th Pennsylvania Cavalry and the 2nd and 4th Ohio Cavalry charged upon their line in rear, breaking it, and scattering the rebels in all directions. Colonel Minty, with his cavalry, at the same time attacked them in front. Forty were killed and wounded, and sixty taken prisoners; besides which, three hundred horses were also taken and carried into Murfreesborough. The Union loss was very light.

Two companies of the 1st Arkansas Union Cavalry, under Captain Worthington, made a scout in Carroll County, Arkansas, in April, in which they had four fights with the guerrillas and rebels, killing twenty-four and taking seven prisoners. Captains Smith and McFarland were killed, and Captain Walker was taken prisoner.

A detachment of the 11th Pennsylvania Cavalry was attacked in the vicinity of Suffolk, Virginia, by a strong body of rebels, on the 13th of April, and were forced to take refuge behind some works; but, being re-enforced, they sallied out in the afternoon, and easily put the rebels to flight.

General Van Born attacked the town of Franklin, Tennessee, on the 11th of April, and, after a severe fight, was driven off. The main feature of the battle was a magnificent charge made by the 4th United States Regular Cavalry, under command of Captain James B. McIntyre, upon the enemy's lines, in which he captured six pieces of artillery and two hundred prisoners! It was pronounced one of the finest charges ever made by United States troops. Second Lieutenant Thomas Healy, of that regiment, was mortally wounded, and died at Franklin on the 23rd of April.

GRIERSON'S RAID

On the 17th of April, 1863, Colonel Benjamin H. Grierson, of the 6th Illinois Cavalry, left La Grange, Tennessee, with his own regiment, and the 7th Illinois and 2nd Iowa, commanded respectively by Colonels Edward Prince and Edward Hatch, on a raid through the State of Mississippi, for the purpose of destroying the enemy's railroad and ascertaining their resources. On the 18th—the 7th Illinois moving in advance—they left camp at eight o'clock, passing through Kipley, and moved south toward New Albany.

One battalion, under Captain Graham, was sent on the direct road, to save the bridge across the Tallahatchie and to drive away a party of soldiers who were attempting to destroy it. The rest of the command crossed three miles east of New Albany, and arrived in that town at half past five p.m., whence the command, 6th and 7th Illinois, moved south five miles and encamped on Mr. Sloan's plantation.

Colonel Hatch, with the 2nd Iowa Cavalry, was detached at Ripley, Mississippi, with orders to move eastwardly and then southwardly, to cross the Tallahatchie some five miles above New Albany, with a view of rejoining the command five or six miles below that place, which Hatch accomplished the following day with good success. On this day the 7th Illinois captured four prisoners belonging to rebel commands.

On the morning of the 19th two companies were sent, under command of Captain Trafton, back to the Tallahatchie, driving a body of rebels out of New Albany, and rejoined the command at ten a.m. Colonel Prince also sent two companies to the right to look after a company of rebels, but they had retired during the night. This detachment captured three men of Chalmers's command, and destroyed some camp and garrison equipage. Two companies were also sent to the left to find some horses which were secreted in the woods, and they returned at ten o'clock, having met with good success.

The command left camp shortly after ten o'clock a.m., and reached Pontotoc at four p.m., and encamped on a plantation eight miles south of that place. At Pontotoc a rebel named Reno was killed who persistently continued to fire upon the advance of the command. The distance travelled on the 18th and 19th was about sixty miles.

On the 20th the command left camp at four o'clock a.m. Before leaving, about one hundred and twelve men, with a number of led horses, were sent back to La Grange, under command of Major Love, of the 2nd Iowa. In the evening Grierson's men encamped at Clear Springs, Mississippi, having travelled about forty miles and passed around Houston.

On the 21st the command left camp at daylight. Here Colonel Hatch, with the 2nd Iowa Cavalry, was detached and sent eastward, with orders to proceed toward Columbus and destroy as much of the Mobile and Ohio Railroad as he could. He took no farther part in the raid. The two Illinois regiments travelled along all day in a pelting rain, making about forty-five miles, and encamped eight miles south of Starkville.

At daylight on the 22nd the command was again in motion, and, after traveling about two miles, Captain Forbes, of company C, 7th Illinois, was detached, and ordered to proceed to Macon and break up the Mobile and Ohio Railroad, to destroy the telegraph wires, and do as much damage as possible to the enemy's transportation. It became a matter of vital importance to the expedition that the railroad com-

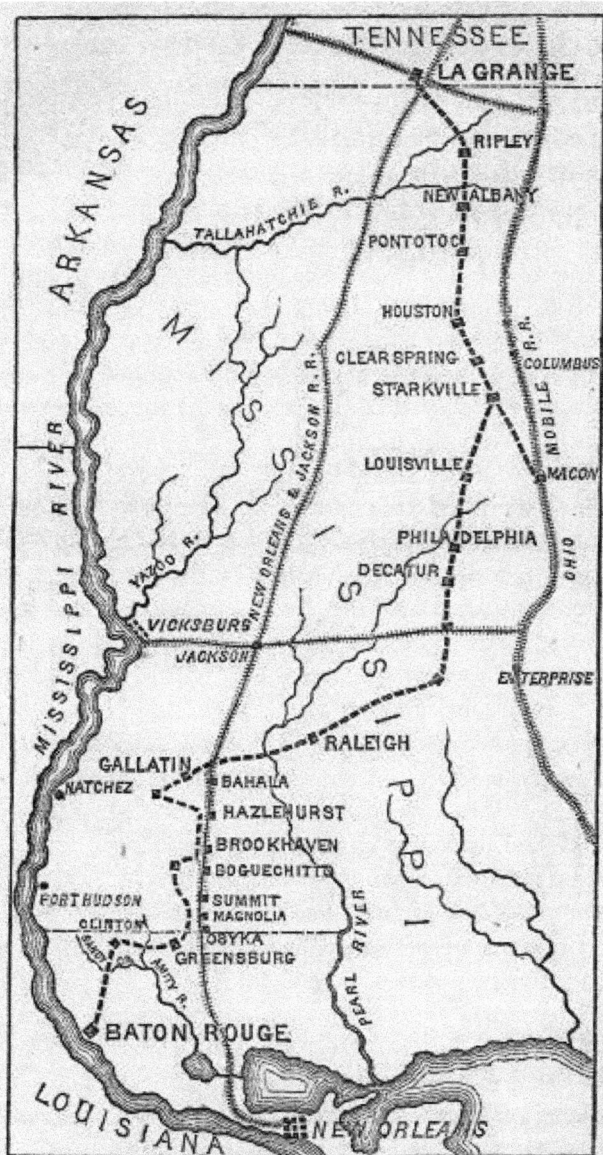

MAP OF GRIERSON'S RAID.

munication, or, at least, telegraphic communication, should be cut off between Macon and Okolona as near Macon as possible, and Captain Forbes was sent on this perilous errand.

He and his men took leave of their comrades, not knowing but this was the last time they would see them on earth. Before marching on the 22nd, Captain Graham, with a battalion, had destroyed a Confederate factory containing a large quantity of boots, shoes, and hats, belonging to the rebel army, and capturing a quartermaster who was getting supplies for his regiment. The march of the 22nd was terrible, as the swamps of the Okanoxubee River were overflowed, and the water on the road was from three to four feet deep, with mire-holes in which both horse and man would occasionally be lost to sight.

To those near the rear of the column the march was truly painful, and about twenty noble horses were abandoned and drowned, as they could not extricate themselves from the mud. The saddles were transferred to other animals, and thus the march continued until one o'clock on the morning of the 23rd. This dreary night-march was made along dark roads, rendered doubly black by the overhanging branches of the great trees which loomed up on each side of the way in the swamp. The distance travelled was fifty-seven miles.

After resting three hours the men were again in the saddles, and, knowing Pearl River to be very high on account of recent rains, Colonel prince pushed, forward with great energy, and arrived at the bridge over that river just in time to save it, as the rebels had commenced tearing it up; and had they succeeded, the expedition would have been a failure. At ten o'clock p.m., Lieutenant Colonel Blackburn, of the 7th Illinois, was sent forward with two hundred men to Decatur, which place he reached at four o'clock on the morning of the 24th, and captured two trains of cars and two locomotives at Newton Station at seven o'clock. The rest of the command arrived at nine.

The bridges and trestles were burned six miles each side of the station, seventy-five prisoners captured and paroled, two warehouses full of commissary stores utterly destroyed by fire, and also four car loads of ammunition, mostly for heavy artillery. The bridges on the east side of the station were burned by Major Starr, with a battalion of the 6th Illinois. On the night of the 24th the command encamped twelve miles below Newton, having travelled eighty miles on the 23rd and 24th without scarcely halting.

On the 25th the command marched about twenty miles. On the 26th they left camp at daylight, passed through Raleigh, crossed Strong

River near Westville, and halted near Strong River Bridge, having marched forty-one miles. Colonel Prince was sent forward with two hundred men on the morning of the 27th at one o'clock, and reached the bank of the Pearl River before daylight, when, contrary to his expectation, he found the ferry boat on the opposite side.

A short time afterward, an old man, who kept the ferry, came down to the bank of the river, and, seeing the cavalrymen, supposed they were Alabamians, and asked if they wished to cross. Being answered affirmatively, he poled his boat over, which was seized by our men, and thenceforth became Yankee property. All of our people crossed safely, and were soon followed by Captain Forbes, who had been detached, as before mentioned, on the 22nd. Having been unable to take Macon, he returned, and followed the trail of Grierson's men to Newton, where he was informed that our cavalry had gone to Enterprise, on the Mobile and Ohio Railroad. He followed on to that place with his company, where he found about two thousand rebel troops just getting off the cars.

He promptly raised a flag of truce, and boldly rode forward, demanding the surrender of the place to Colonel Grierson, as he saw this was the only way to extricate himself. The rebel officer, Colonel Goodwin, asked one hour to consider the proposition, and he would then let Colonel Grierson know his determination. This was all Captain Forbes wanted; and, moving leisurely out of town and out of sight of the rebels, he put spurs to his jaded horses, and left as much ground between himself and Colonel Goodwin as he could possibly do. It is not known to this day what conclusion Colonel Goodwin came to with regard to the surrender of the town of Enterprise. This was really a capital ruse on the part of Captain Forbes.

Grierson's command being once more together, he moved to Hazlehurst, and thence to Gallatin, and encamped. A thirty-two-pounder rifled Parrott gun, with one thousand four hundred pounds of powder, was here captured, *en route* to Grand Gulf. The distance travelled this day was thirty-seven miles.

The command left camp at seven o'clock on the morning of the 28th, Captain Trafton's battalion, which had been sent out the day before to proceed to Bahalia and destroy the railroad and transportation, having returned at four o'clock in the morning, having had some skirmishing, and captured about thirty prisoners. In the afternoon, the 6th Illinois had a skirmish with the enemy near Union Church, in which two of the rebels were wounded and several captured.

On the 29th the men were in the saddle by sunrise, directing their course toward the New Orleans and Jackson Railroad. At Brookhaven they burned the depot, some cars, and bridges; captured and paroled two hundred and one prisoners. They encamped six miles south west of the town, having marched twenty-five miles.

The last day of April the sun found our men again on the march, and, visiting Bogue Chitto, burned depot, cars, and bridges. Left that place at ten a.m., burning all bridges and trestles between there and Summit, where they arrived at five o'clock p.m., and again burned several cars and a large amount of rebel government property. They went into camp southwest of Summit, having marched over twenty-eight miles.

May 1st Grierson's men left camp by daylight, and proceeded in a south-westerly direction without regard to roads, until they came into the Clinton and Osyka Road, near a bridge four miles northeast of Wall's Post-office. About eighty rebels were lying in ambush near the bridge, and as the brave Lieutenant-Colonel Blackburn, of the 7th Illinois, was crossing at the head of his men, he was shot in two places, and expired in a short time afterward. Thus fell a brave and daring soldier. The men near the colonel, stung by this deed, rushed upon the rebels, and all who were not killed were speedily seeking safety in flight. They crossed the Amite River without opposition—the picket being asleep—about ten o'clock p.m., and continued to travel nearly all night. They had marched nearly forty miles this day.

The last day of this raid, May 2nd, the men started early, and surprised and burned a rebel camp at Sandy Creek Bridge. About nine o'clock a.m., as a crowning glory to this most extraordinary series of adventures, they captured Colonel Stewart and forty-two of his regiment of Mississippi Cavalry on Comite River.

About noon on the 2nd the command reached Baton Rouge, Louisiana, where their arrival sent a thrill of joy through every loyal heart which it is impossible to describe. During the last thirty hours the command had scarcely slept at all, except what they could do on their horses, and both men and animals were fatigued out.

This was a noble raid, and is without an equal in the annals of the cavalry service. The damage done to the enemy has been estimated at $6,000,000.

The Battle of Fayetteville, Arkansas, was fought on the 18th of April, 1863, by the Union troops, under Colonel M. La Rue Harrison, of the 1st Arkansas Union Cavalry, and a large body of rebels, under command of General Cabell. The 1st Arkansas Union Cavalry behaved very well during the fight, which lasted six hours, when the enemy was beaten off with considerable loss. Captain Harrison was wounded, and his conduct, as well as that of Lieutenant-Colonel Bishop and Majors Fitch and Hunt, is highly spoken of. All of these officers belonged to the 1st Arkansas Union Cavalry.

CHAPTER 15

Cavalry Battle at Beverly's Ford

A brisk fight occurred near Patterson, Missouri, on the 20th of April, between the 10th Missouri State Militia Cavalry, under Colonel Smart, and the rebels. In his dispatch Colonel Smart says:

> The attack began about twelve o'clock on the Reeves Station Road with a scout I had sent out in that direction. I then sent Major Wood on to re-enforce with a battalion. He held them in check, and skirmished them into town. This gave me time to load my trains and have them ready to move if I had to retreat. Before I left town, I destroyed what stores I could not bring away. The fight continued to Big Creek, eight miles this side of Patterson. The engagement was severe in the extreme. After fighting hand to hand at Big Creek, they got in my front, and at tempted to cut off my retreat, but I forced my way to the north side of the creek. The enemy did not renew the engagement. My loss in killed, wounded, and missing in the action was about fifty.

Major McConnell, of the Union troops, was wounded. The rebels were commanded by General Marmaduke, who was acting in concert with General Cabell, who attacked Fayetteville, Arkansas, as before mentioned.

General Marmaduke, with his forces, fell back, and, on the 26th of April, attacked the post of Cape Girardeau, Missouri, on the Mississippi River. The garrison consisted of the 1st Nebraska Regiment, under Lieutenant-Colonel Baumer, then serving as infantry, and the 1st Wisconsin Cavalry, under Colonel La Grange, with some artillery. After a fierce fight of some hours, Marmaduke withdrew his forces, and fled toward Arkansas. In the defence of the town, Colonel Dan. Huston, Jr., of the 7th Missouri Cavalry, rendered valuable assistance.

Brigadier-General McNeill had command of the Union forces, and started in pursuit, being joined by the troops under Brigadier-General Vendever, consisting of the 1st Iowa Cavalry, 3rd Missouri Cavalry, under Colonel Glover, a portion of the 2nd Missouri State Militia Cavalry, and some artillery. Several skirmishes occurred on the line of the retreat, in which Lieutenant-Colonel Carrick and Captain Mitchell, of the 3rd Missouri Cavalry, were wounded.

The 1st Iowa Cavalry surprised the advance regiment of the rebel forces on the 28th of April, and two small howitzers, loaded with musket-balls, were discharged simultaneously within thirty yards of them, killing and wounding a large number. At the same time the First Iowa Cavalry charged upon them, and not a man of the entire regiment escaped, all who were not killed or wounded being taken prisoners.

Major-General Samuel R. Curtis was at this time in command of the department of the Missouri, and his disposition of the cavalry of his command was most admirable. The writer of these pages was then serving on his staff as chief of cavalry, and had a good opportunity of judging. His cavalry was successful in almost every instance.

While these things were going on in Missouri, Colonel Louis D. Watkins, of the 6th Kentucky Cavalry, in command of a party of national cavalry, left Murfreesborough on the night of the 26th of April, and next morning at daybreak succeeded in capturing the Texan Legion of rebel troops, posted at a point eight miles from Franklin, Tennessee, between the Columbia and Carter's Creek Turnpikes. Several rebels were killed and wounded.

A detachment of the 5th New York Cavalry, commanded by Lieutenant-Colonel McVicar, numbering one hundred and ten men, while reconnoitring in the vicinity of Spottsylvania Court-house, Virginia, on the 30th of April, were surrounded by four regiments of rebel cavalry, under General Fitzhugh Lee, and fifty-two of their number killed, wounded, and captured. The rest, numbering fifty-eight, cut their way out. Lieutenant-Colonel McVicar was killed at the first rebel onset.

A skirmish took place near La Grange, Arkansas, on the 1st of May, between a detachment of the 3rd Iowa Cavalry, under Captain J. Q. A. De Huff, and an over whelming rebel force, which resulted in a retreat of the Union men, with a loss of forty-one in killed, wounded, and missing.

About three hundred rebels made an attack upon Warrenton Junction, Virginia, on the 3rd of May, between eight and nine o'clock in the morning. They dashed upon some eighty men of the 1st Virginia

Union Cavalry, who were dismounted, feeding their horses. These men, finding they could not have time to mount, prepared to fight on foot. As the rebels came up, they gave them a volley, which emptied a number of saddles and checked the onset. A desperate fight now occurred, and for a short time the national troops succeeded in keeping them at bay. But numbers told, and the rebels captured about half the force, the others, fighting gallantly.

Meanwhile a battalion of the 5th New York Cavalry, led by Major Hammond, had come up, and they gallantly charged the rebels with the sabre, completely routing them, and re capturing all our men. Major Hammond pursued them beyond Warrenton. The rebels fought desperately. Their loss was heavy, their dead being left on the field and scattered along the roadside. The Union loss was seventeen killed and wounded. Among the latter were, Major Steele, 1st Virginia Union Cavalry, mortally; Captain William A. McCoy, 1st Virginia, slightly; Captain Krom, 5th New York; and Lieutenants Frank Munson and Samuel McBride, 5th New York. Our officers and men behaved with great gallantry, particularly Major Hammond, Captains Krom, Penfield, and McMasters, of the 5th New York, Captain Harris, 1st Virginia, and Captain Bean, of the 1st Vermont Cavalry.

STONEMAN'S RAID

On the 29th of April, 1863, Major-General Stoneman started on his celebrated raid, having under his command the greater portion of the cavalry belonging to the Army of the Potomac. The object of the expedition was to break up railroad communication in rear of Lee's army, and to prevent supplies reaching him from Richmond and farther south. He entered the enemy's lines by way of Kelly's Ford; one division, however, under General Averill, forded the river near the Orange and Alexandria Railroad, and, soon after crossing, encountered a small body of the enemy's cavalry, and a fight, in which artillery was employed for a short time, ensued, the enemy retiring after a brief contest, the loss on either side being trifling.

Averill was ordered to proceed along the road toward Culpepper and Gordonsville, and, by a dashing flank movement, to keep the enemy's troops known to be located in that vicinity employed, while detachments from the main column were engaged in the most important duty of cutting off the Rebel Army of the Rappahannock from its base of operations. Unfortunately, General Averill's command did not protect the right of the main body, and, as a consequence, the

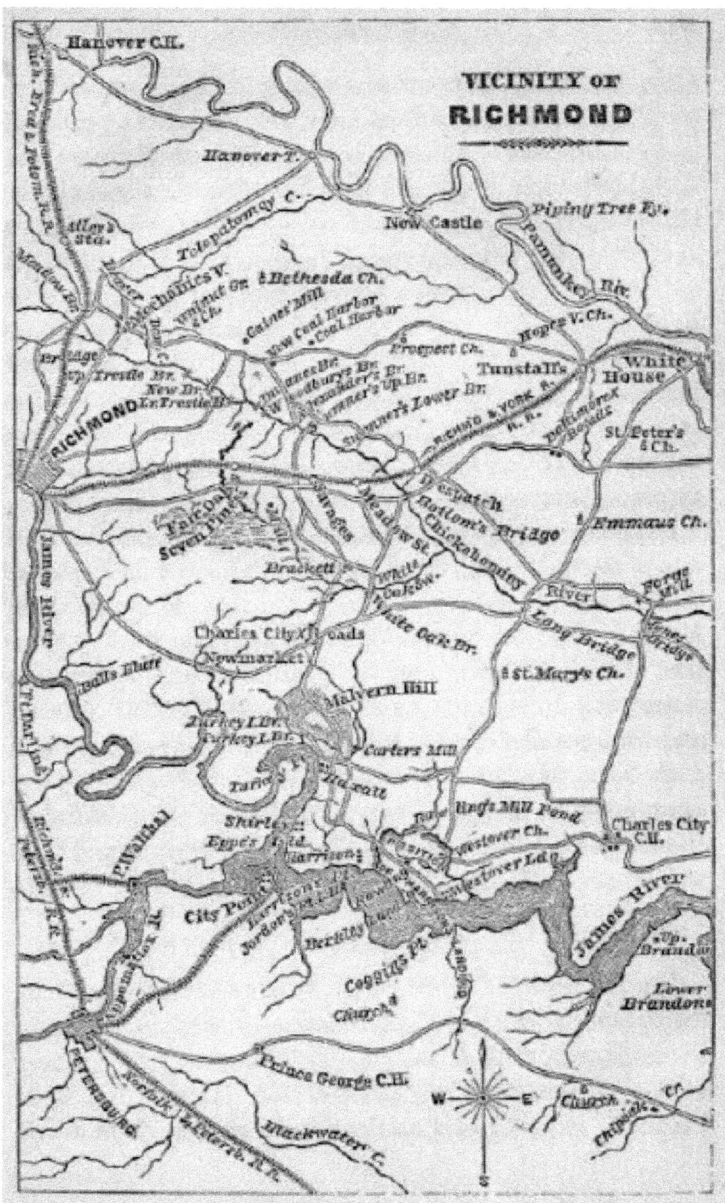

VICINITY OF
RICHMOND

Hanover C.H.

Hanover T.

Piping Tree Ey.

New Castle

Pamunkey Riv.

Alley's Sta.

Totopotomoy C.

Hope's V. Ch.

Nicholet's V.

Bethesda Ch.

Gaines' Mill

Walnut Gr.

New Cool Harbor
Cool Harbor

Prospect Ch.

Tunstalls

WHITE
HOUSE

Bridge

Trestle Br.

New Br.
Lr. Trestle Br.

Pamunella Br.
Woodbury's Br.
Alexander's Br.
Grapevine's Up. Br.

Sumner's Lower Br.

RICHMOND & YORK R.R.

Pamunkey Roads

St. Peter's
Ch.

RICHMOND

Despatch

Emmaus Ch.

Fair Oaks
Seven Pines

Meadow St.

Bottom's Bridge
Chickahominy

Forge Mill

Brackett

White
Oak Sw.

River

Long Bridge

Charles City Roads

Newmarket

White Oak Br.

St. Mary's Ch.

Malls Bluff

Malvern Hill

Turkey I. Br.
Turkey I. Br.

Carters Mill

Ft. Darling

James River

Shirley
Epp's Ford

Turout

Harrison's

Haxall

Ruffs Mill Pond

Westover Ch.

Charles City
C.H.

City Point

Harrison's
Jordon's P't. H.

Berkley

Westover Ldg.

James River

Up.
Brandon

Richmond & Petersbg. R.R.

Appomattox R.

Coggins Pt.
Church

Lower
Brandon

Petersburg

Prince George C.H.

W   E

S

Church

Church

Cr.

Chippoke

Norfolk & Petersb. R.R.

Blackwater C.

operations at different points were somewhat interfered with.

General John Buford went to the left, after crossing Kelly's Ford, and had a skirmish with the enemy, who were repulsed. Our cavalry chopped down some trees and obstructed the way, so that when they again charged, they were halted, and a volley from our troops sent them reeling back, and they gave us no more trouble.

General Stoneman, with the greater portion of the command, remained near Kelly's Ford until nightfall, when the order of march was given, and all hands crossed Fleshman's River, a small stream, now much swollen by rains, and bivouacked a short distance beyond. Here, in an open, ploughed field, the troops slept soundly, without other protection from a cold, driving rainstorm, that prevailed all night, than that afforded by their blankets and rubber cloths. The night was dreary in the extreme.

All bugle calls were dispensed with, and orders were given in a low voice from one officer to another, in order not to betray to the enemy, who were close about, the strength of the forces. The rebel scouts attacked our pickets during the night and early in the morning, but nothing happened worthy of any particular mention,

On the morning of the 30th of April, the command, which had been picked over before, was again culled, and all doubtful horses and sick and weak-kneed men were sent back across the river. The command was in light marching order, and was now within the enemy's lines, where the greatest caution was necessary. After proceeding through the woods in parallel lines a few miles, the command was halted, and the whole country patrolled for an enemy.

The advance of General Buford's column arrived near Minot's Ford, on the Rapidan, at one o'clock p.m., when a squadron of the 5th Cavalry was sent across, and falling in with a considerable body of the enemy put them to flight in great haste. At night the whole force encamped on a hill commanding Raccoon Ford, with orders to be in the saddle by two o'clock next morning.

Friday, May 1st, the men were "to horse" at the hour indicated, after having spent another cold and disagreeable night, but did not start until daylight, as a guide was needed. At last Major Falls came dashing along, with a "reliable contraband" on the saddle behind him, creating no small amusement to the soldiery, and, with this black guide in advance, the column started.

At Orange Springs our people came upon a party of secession cavalry, who sought safety in flight; but one lieutenant, named Mount, was overhauled and captured, and the rebels were forced to throw away several wagon-loads of provisions, and abandon some horses and accoutrements.

A few stragglers were picked up, including a rebel engineer, who was taken, with all his instruments. Colonel Wyndham was sent in pursuit of a party of rebels in the direction of Madison, but they, having great respect for personal liberty, put themselves beyond the reach of harm. Peach brandy was found in several of the farmhouses along the course pursued by Stoneman's men, and some of them, getting too much, straggled away. Far in the night the command continued to march, the only sounds which broke the stillness of the scene being the crunching of the horses' hoofs along the road, the jingling of the cavalry accoutrements, and the baying of the watch-dogs, as the column moved steadily along.

About three o'clock on the morning of May 2nd a halt was made at Greenwood, one mile west of Louisa Court-house. At this point the Central Virginia Railroad was reached, and parties were sent up and down the track for miles, to destroy it, burn the bridges and culverts, and to guard against a surprise of the main body. The work was thoroughly done, and just at daylight Colonel Kilpatrick, with his regiment, dashed into Louisa Court-house. His coming was unexpected, and was a complete surprise. Several rebel soldiers were captured, and the people of that place arose in the morning to find themselves in the power of the hated Yankees. They had fully expected to be murdered by our troops, and were much relieved when they found that their lives would be spared, and no property interfered with, except such as was actually necessary for the wants of our troops. After this assurance the people became more easy, and conversed freely with our officers and men.

While halting at Louisa, a squadron of the 1st Maine Regiment, on picket, was attacked and driven in by a greatly superior force, with a loss of two killed. The 1st Maine and 2nd New York Regiments were sent out to their support, when the rebel troops fled in all directions. The bridges over Greenwood and Hickory Creeks having been destroyed, and our troops well supplied with rations and forage, the command was moved about four o'clock on the afternoon of May 2nd to a hill to the east of the town, and there awaited the attack of the rebel troops, who were known to be approaching from Gordonsville.

However, when they came in sight of the two regiments of cavalry which had been left on the road to receive them, they thought better of it, and commenced a retrograde movement. At five o'clock the command started, and reached Thompson's Four Corners about half past eleven o'clock p.m. At midnight Stoneman called his principal officers about him, and explained what he expected them to do; and at half past two o'clock on Sunday morning, May 23rd, the different expeditions started out to cut the enemy's lines of communication.

It was a bright moonlight night, the roads were comparatively good, and everything seemed to work in harmony. Brigadier-General Gregg, with his command, was sent in one direction; Colonel Wyndham, with the 1st Maine and 1st New Jersey Regiments, in another; Colonel Kilpatrick, with his New York Regiment, in another; and Lieutenant-Colonel Hasbrouck Davis, with the 12th Illinois Regiment, in another.

Colonel Wyndham took a southerly direction, and reached Columbia, on the James River, about eight o'clock a.m. The approach of his force had been heralded, but no one believed it, until Major Beaumont, with the advance, came dashing into town. Several canal boats and bridges were burned, and a large quantity of rebel commissary, quartermaster, and medical stores burned or thrown into the canal. Our people vainly attempted to destroy the massive stone aqueduct which crosses James River. After doing all the damage he could, Colonel Wyndham returned to the main body under Stoneman.

Colonel Kilpatrick destroyed the depot at Hungary, broke the telegraph wires, and tore up the Fredericksburg Railroad for several miles, and, charging a body of rebel troops, *followed them within two miles of the city of Richmond, and captured Lieutenant Brown and eleven men inside the fortifications which surround that place!* His men destroyed several pieces of railroad, burned three wagon trains, destroyed several cars, and captured quite a number of prisoners. Lieutenant Estis and eleven men of Kilpatrick's regiment were captured by the rebels, but were recaptured by company F, of the 6th New York Cavalry. He passed entirely around Lee's army, and reached Gloucester Point, where the stars and stripes were waving.

Lieutenant-Colonel Davis struck the Fredericksburg Railroad at Ashland, where the telegraph wire was cut, and the trestle-work south of the town was consumed by fire. A railroad train was taken, full of sick and wounded soldiers, and these, with the train-guard, were paroled. After this his force moved across to the Central Railroad, which he reached about eight o'clock p.m. Here another long trestle-work, a train of cars, and the depot were burned, the telegraph wire cut, and the road torn up.

About thirty officers and men at the depot were paroled. After doing this he marched to within seven miles of Richmond, and bivouacked until eight o'clock the next morning, when he marched to Williamsburg.

At Tunstall's Station his advance was opposed by a body of rebel infantry and artillery. He charged upon them, but could not break them, as they were protected by rifle-pits, and he was obliged to turn off, after having lost two men killed and several wounded, among whom was Lieutenant Marsh, who received a severe wound in his right arm. He brought the remainder off, and reached Gloucester Point in safety.

Sunday, and nearly all day Monday, General Buford's command was stationed at Shannon Hill, and a detachment was sent out to destroy the canal and bridge near Cedar Point, which work was most successfully accomplished. Sunday night, May 3rd, it is believed that both Wade Hampton and Fitzhugh Lee's brigades of rebels were encamped within two miles of General Buford.

On the morning of the 4th, a picket, consisting of sixty men, commanded by Lieutenant Stoddard, of the 5th Cavalry, was attacked, and fifteen of our men were captured.

On Friday morning, May 8th, the whole of Stoneman's force reached Kelly's Ford in safety, Kilpatrick and Davis having passed out by Gloucester Point, as before mentioned.

The amount of damage done to the rebels by Stoneman can scarcely be estimated. For nine days he and his horsemen roamed at will between Lee's army on the Rappahannock and the rebel capital, and disabled every line of communication. This was done with a loss to our side of not over one hundred men. On the other hand, our people captured and paroled over five hundred rebel officers and soldiers.

During the expedition he destroyed twenty-two bridges, seven culverts, five ferries, three trains of railroad cars, and one hundred and twenty-two wagons; burned four supply trains, five canal-boats, two store-houses, four telegraph stations, and three depots; broke canals in three places, and railroads in seven; captured three hundred and fifty-six horses and one hundred and four mules, and cut the telegraph wire in five places. This was a fair offset for the raid of Stuart in Pennsylvania, and taught both the secessionists and our people at home to respect our cavalry.

The 2nd Indiana Cavalry, under Colonel Edward M. McCook,

made a scout near Stone River, Tennessee, on the 9th of May, visiting the hiding-places of several guerrilla bands, and capturing eight of them, who were properly dealt with.

Two days afterward a fight took place in the vicinity of Greasy Creek, Kentucky, between a force of national troops, under command of Colonel Richard T. Jacob, of the 9th Kentucky Cavalry, and a greatly superior force of rebel cavalry, commanded by John Morgan. After a desperate fight of several hours' duration, Colonel Jacob and his men were obliged to retire, after having killed and wounded nearly a hundred of them, with a loss to himself of twenty-five killed and wounded.

Lieutenant-Colonel Breckinridge, with a detachment of the 1st Tennessee Union Cavalry, numbering fifty-five men, were taken across the Tennessee River on the United States gunboats, and, after being landed, they dashed across the country to Linden, Tennessee, where he surprised a rebel force of more than twice his number, capturing Lieutenant-Colonel Frierson, one captain, one surgeon, four lieutenants, thirty rebel soldiers, ten conscripts, and fifty horses. The court-house, which had been used as a rebel depot, was burned. This occurred on the 12th of May.

On the 15th of May, a company of Union Cavalry was surprised and captured at Charlestown, Jefferson County, Virginia. Upon learning this, General Milroy sent out a strong detachment of Virginia Union and Pennsylvania cavalry, under Captain Vitt. On the afternoon of the 16th, they were recaptured at Piedmont Station, in Fauquier County; at the same time two rebels were killed, and forty rebel soldiers, with their horses, captured.

Captain Vitt, the leader of the Union Cavalry, was killed, and Major Adams, with a detachment of the 1st New York Cavalry, continued the pursuit of some, rebels who had escaped, but did not succeed in overtaking them.

Major Lippert, commanding a portion of the 13th Illinois Cavalry, had a desperate fight with a numerically superior body of rebels in the vicinity of Doniphan, Missouri, on the 28th of May, in which the Union troops were forced to retreat, but not until they had lost eighty men killed, wounded, and missing. The brave Major Lippert was mortally wounded.

Colonel Powell Clayton, of the 5th Kansas Cavalry, in command of the 1st Indiana, 5th Illinois, and 5th Kansas Cavalry Regiments, left Helena, Arkansas, on the 6th of May, 1863, on a scout against the enemy. He marched to Clarendon, and then moved toward Mount Vernon. When near that place, they charged upon a body of rebel cavalry, and at first forced them back; but they rallied, and in turn forced our troops to seek refuge in the timber behind some fallen trees.

The rebels being re-enforced, they came down upon our troops in column at a full gallop; but the fire becoming too hot, they fell back, reformed, and came on again, and again were driven back. A third time they attempted it, but their troops would not come up. Failing in their efforts to dislodge our troops, they sent for some artillery, and in a short time compelled our men to retreat, which they did in good order. Our loss was fifteen killed and wounded, while that of the rebels was somewhat greater. Captain McKee, of a Texas regiment, was taken prisoner.

On the night of the 21st of May, General Stanley, with two brigades of cavalry, attempted to surprise the enemy's camp near Middleton, Tennessee. The attack was unsuccessful, and our forces returned, having lost several men. Second Lieutenant Francis C. Wood, of the 4th United States Cavalry, was mortally wounded, and died on the 23rd of May.

Colonel Edward J. Davis, of the 1st Regiment of Texas Union Cavalry, left Levieck's Ferry, on the Amite River, Louisiana, May 12th, on an expedition along the Jackson Railroad. They struck the railroad at Hammond Station, where they cut the telegraph and burned the bridge. At Pontchatoula he encountered a party of rebel guerrillas and Choctaw Indians, whom, after a brief skirmish, he dispersed, taking seventeen Choctaws prisoners. He afterward destroyed the rebel camp. On the 15th of May, in the vicinity of Camp Moore, Louisiana, he fought a body of rebels, defeated them, and routed them with great slaughter. After the fight, Colonel Davis advanced on Camp Moore, which he burned, together with the rail road depot and bridge, and a great quantity of property.

Colonel Florence M. Cornyn, of the 10th Missouri Cavalry Volunteers, returned to Corinth, Alabama, on the 31st of May, from a successful raid into Alabama. He, with his command, was absent five days, during which time he had a fight with Colonel Roddy's cavalry, of the rebel army, and defeated them with considerable loss.

His men destroyed seven cotton-factories, with all their contents, valued at one million five hundred thousand dollars; a number of steam flour-mills, saw-mills, and blacksmiths shops; a quantity of arms, with some ammunition; burned the bridge at Florence, Alabama, and returned with six hundred head of horses, mules, and oxen, and one hundred prisoners.

Previous to this Colonel Cornyn had made two expeditions into the enemy's country, and had inflicted great damage. The first of these was in the neighbourhood of Tuscumbia, in February, and the next, in the early part of May, toward Tupelo, Mississippi. On the 6th of the month, while encamped near Tupelo, his force was attacked by a body of rebels, commanded by General Ruggles, and, after a fight of half an hour's duration, Ruggles retreated, leaving behind him a great many small-arms, and ninety of his men as prisoners. Cornyn's loss was severe.

In the meantime, several changes had taken place among the field-officers of the regular cavalry regiments. The bill retiring officers from active service who had served faithfully for forty years, or who had become unfit for service from incapacity resulting from long and faithful service, from wounds or injury received, from disease contracted, or from exposure in the line of duty, had passed Congress and become a law, and under its provisions several officers had retired.

Colonels Benjamin L. Beall, of the 1st Cavalry, and John S. Simonson, of the 3rd; Majors Llewellyn Jones, of the 1st, and Washington I. Newton and John W. T. Gardiner, of the 2nd Cavalry, went upon the retired list.

Several field-officers, as already mentioned, had resigned and joined the cause of the rebels, and our service now contained but few men who were not true to the Union. Captain Robert M. Morris, of the 3rd Cavalry, was promoted Major in the 6th Cavalry, March 11th, 1863, in place of Lawrence A. Williams, dismissed; and Captain Samuel H. Starr, of the 2nd Cavalry, was promoted Major in the 6th Cavalry, April 25th, 1863, in place of Edward H. Wright, resigned. Colonel P. St. George Cooke, of the 2nd Cavalry, was promoted Brigadier-General on the 12th of November, 1861; and Lieutenant-Colonel Delos B. Sacket, of the 5th Cavalry, was promoted Inspector General, October 1st, 1861.

During the rebellion there had been many changes in the organisation of cavalry regiments; and to such an extent had it been carried by the various Acts of Congress that it was to the officers themselves a matter of impossibility to say what really was the legal organisation of a horse regiment.

Finally, however, General Order No. 110, from the War Department, Adjutant General's Office, dated Washington, April 29, 1863, was published, and definitely settled the matter. It was as follows:

Regiment of Cavalry—Twelve Companies or Troops.

1 Colonel.	1 Regimental Commissary
1 Lieutenant Colonel.	(an extra Lieutenant).
3 Majors.	1 Chaplain.
1 Surgeon.	1 Veterinary Surgeon.
2 Assistant Surgeons.	1 Sergeant Major.
1 Regimental Adjutant (an	1 Quartermaster Sergeant.
extra Lieutenant).	1 Commissary Sergeant.
1 Regimental Quartermaster	2 Hospital Stewards.
(an extra Lieutenant).	1 Saddler Sergeant.

1 Chief Trumpeter.

A Company or Troop of Cavalry.

1 Captain.	5 Sergeants.
1 First Lieutenant.	8 Corporals.
1 Second Lieutenant.	2 Trumpeters.
1 First Sergeant.	2 Farriers or Blacksmiths.
1 Quartermaster Sergeant.	1 Saddler.
1 Commissary Sergeant.	1 Wagoner.

And { 60 Privates—Minimum.
{ 78 Privates—Maximum.

CAVALRY BUREAU.

On the 28th of July, 1863, the Cavalry Bureau of the War Department was established. I can give no better idea of its purposes than by presenting General Orders Nos. 236 and 237, from the War Department, Adjutant General's Office, dated as above. General Order No. 236 says:

A bureau will be attached to the War Department, to be designated the Cavalry Bureau. This bureau will have charge of the organisation and equipment of the cavalry forces of the army, and of the provision for the mounts and remounts of the same. The purchases of all horses for the cavalry service will be made by officers of the Quartermaster's Department, under the direction of the Chief of the Cavalry Bureau. Inspections of horses offered for the cavalry service will be made by cavalry officers. Depots will be established for the reception, organisation, and discipline of cavalry recruits and new regiments, and for the collection, care, and training of cavalry horses. The depots will be under the general charge of the Cavalry Bureau.

Copies of inspection reports of cavalry troops, and such returns

223

as may be at any time called for, will be sent to the bureau established by this order.

The enormous expense attending the maintenance of the cavalry arm, points to the necessity of greater care and more judicious management on the part of cavalry officers, that their horses may be constantly kept up to the standard of efficiency for service. Great neglects of duty in this connection are to be attributed to officers in command of cavalry troops. It is the design of the War Department to correct such neglects by dismissing from service officers whose inefficiency and inattention result in the deterioration and loss of the public animals under their charge.

General Order No. 237 says:

The following instructions, intended to promote the efficiency of the cavalry service, are promulgated for the guidance of all concerned. Inspections will be made of all cavalry troops at the end of every month, reports of which inspection will be forwarded without delay through the army or department commander to the head of the Cavalry Bureau at Washington. These reports will exhibit the condition of the cavalry service in general, and especially the condition of the mounts.

The reports shall state what service the troops inspected have done since last inspected; how many miles their horses have travelled within the month; what character of service has been required of them, and under what circumstances it has been rendered; what appears to have been the care taken of them as regards treatment, shoeing, etc., etc.; what has been the quantity and character of the rations of forage issued to them; if there have been any deficiency of forage, and who is responsible therefor, etc., etc.; and shall convey any other information pertaining to the objects of the inspection which it may be advisable should come to the notice of the bureau.

Inspection reports shall divide cavalry horses into four classes:

First, those which are to be condemned as unfit for any use whatever in any branch of the service. With regard to this class proceedings are to be had as required by existing regulations.

Second, those now unfit for cavalry service, and not likely to be efficient again for such service, which may be used for team or draught horses, or for herding purposes. Horses of this class are to be turned into the Quartermaster's Department.

Third, those which are now unfit for service, or nearly so, but which, by timely care and treatment in depots, will regain condition. Such horses are to be sent to such depots as may be established for the army, to be replaced by an equal number of good animals from the depots. As soon as serviceable, the horses turned in will be eligible for reissue.

Fourth, serviceable horses.

The number of each class of horses will be given in every report of inspection for each troop in the service.

A suitable number of officers of the Quartermaster's Department will be directed to report at once to the Chief of the Cavalry Bureau, to be charged with disbursements for the objects of his bureau under his direction.

Purchases will be forthwith made of a sufficient number of horses to meet the present and prospective wants of the service up to September, 1863, and the horses placed in depots for issue from time to time.

Requisitions for remounts will be made through the intermediate commanders on the Chief of the Cavalry Bureau, who will give orders on the depots for the horses needed to fill them.

Officers of the Quartermaster's Department assigned to duty under orders of the Chief of the Cavalry Bureau will make their reports and returns of money and property, as required by existing laws and regulations, to the accounting officers of the Treasury and to the Quartermaster General, and will also make to the Chief of the Cavalry Bureau such reports and returns as he may require for his information.

Estimates for funds will be submitted to the Chief of the Cavalry Bureau for his approval before being finally acted upon by the Quartermaster General.

Under the foregoing regulations the Cavalry Bureau was organised, and Major-General George Stoneman (Major in the 4th Regiment United States Cavalry) was selected as the chief, and continued to act as such for some time. It is fair to say that this bureau has done much good to the service.

GREAT CAVALRY BATTLE AT BEVERLY'S FORD.

The great cavalry battle at Beverly's Ford, Virginia, was fought on the 9th day of June, 1863, and here, for the first time on the American continent, occurred a real cavalry action, where the sides were nearly equal, and the men equally determined. The Union troops were commanded by Brigadier-General Pleasanton, seconded by Brigadier-Generals Buford and Gregg. It is doubtful whether there ever was a cavalry fight to excel it on earth. The United States horsemen numbered something over ten thousand, while those of the rebels numbered about the same.

Our forces, with a brigade of infantry, crossed the Rappahannock between Beverly's Ford and Culpepper, and attacked Stuart's rebel cavalry, under the immediate command of Generals Fitzhugh Lee and Wade Hampton, about five o'clock in the morning. After getting in line, our people pushed the rebels back some three miles, they carrying with them their sixteen field-pieces, and disputing every inch of ground as our line advanced. The battle lasted until three o'clock in the afternoon, and was fought almost entirely with the sabre. Among the Union officers killed and wounded were the following, *viz.*:

Killed.—Colonel Benjamin F. Davis, 8th Regiment New York Cavalry, and Captain in the 1st regiment United States Cavalry; Lieutenant-Colonel Irvin, 10th New York Cavalry; Captain Charles W. Canfield, 2nd United States Cavalry; Lieutenant-Colonel Broderick, mortally wounded; Major Stillwire, 1st New Jersey Cavalry, mortally wounded.

Wounded.—Colonel Wyndham, 1st New Jersey Cavalry.

Missing.—Major Morris, 6th Pennsylvania Cavalry.

The United States loss was about five hundred killed, wounded, and missing. The Confederate loss was fully as great. This was the greatest cavalry achievement of the war, and for a time checked the advance of the rebels into Maryland and Pennsylvania.

I only notice this battle in this place, as it is not my object to bring my history down to a later period than June 1st, 1863.

In regard to the Battle of Beverly's Ford, Virginia, Major-General Hooker says:

The attack was made, and the enemy were driven two miles before Pleasanton, at Beverly's Ford, and many prisoners were taken. But for the appearance of a corps of infantry, of which I had no knowledge, General Pleasanton would have succeeded in routing their entire cavalry force. From the prisoners taken, I learned that the whole of the enemy's cavalry had been assembled there. The cavalry from North Carolina and from the

Shenandoah Valley had been brought in, and had been reviewed by General Lee, whose headquarters were then at Culpepper, preparatory to making the movement which followed. This satisfied me that it was more than a raid; that an invasion was contemplated. As a full account of the fight, I submit the following from General Pleasanton, and my reply to him:

(Cipher.)

Headquarters Cavalry, Rappahannock Station,
June 9, 1863, 10 45 p.m.;

Major-General Hooker:

A short time after my last dispatch to you, General Gregg, with his infantry and cavalry, joined me about two miles from the river, to which point I had driven the enemy. He reported that he had encountered a much superior number of the enemy's cavalry, and had a severe fight; also, that a train of cars had been run up to Brandy Station filled with infantry, who opened on his men. I also received information from letters and official reports captured in the enemy's camp, as well as from prisoners, that the enemy had upward of twelve thousand (12,000) cavalry, which was double our own force of cavalry, and twenty-five (25) pieces of artillery.

I also learned from contrabands and prisoners that a large force of infantry had been sent for from Culpepper, as well as Longstreet's command at Ellis's Ford. Having crippled the enemy by desperate fighting, so that he could not follow me, I returned with my command to the north side of the Rappahannock. Gregg's command crossed at Rappahannock Bridge. Tomorrow morning Stuart was to have started on a raid into Maryland—so captured papers state. You may rest satisfied he will not attempt it. Buford's cavalry had a long and desperate encounter, hand to hand, with the enemy, in which he drove back before him, handsomely, very superior forces. Over two hundred prisoners were captured, and one battle-flag. The troops are in splendid spirits, and are entitled to the highest praise for distinguished conduct.

A. Pleasanton, Brig. Gen. Commanding.

June 10, 1863.

Commanding Officer, Cavalry Corps:

I am not so certain as you appear to be that the enemy will

abandon his contemplated raid. With this impression I have felt a little hesitation in withdrawing the infantry.

Will you be able to keep him from crossing the river with the cavalry and batteries with you? If not, and you consider that the infantry will be of service in preventing a passage, please have it retained until farther orders. I desire that you will send me your opinion on this subject.

We shall be able to send up to you one thousand more cavalry tomorrow. There has been great delay in the transmission of dispatches.

Joseph Hooker, Maj. Gen. Commanding.

First Lieutenant Isaac M. Ward, of the 6th Cavalry, was killed in this battle, and First Lieutenant Caesar R Fisher, of the 1st Cavalry, died on the 21st of June, 1863, of wounds received in action at Ashby's Gap, Virginia.

During the two years which had elapsed since the breaking out of the rebellion, several officers had been killed and wounded whose names have not been given in the foregoing pages. On the 24th of May, 1862, at Middletown, Virginia, Major Jonathan P. Cilley, Captain Black Hawk Putnam, and Lieutenant Llewellyn G. Estes, all of the 1st Maine Cavalry, were wounded.

First Lieutenant Alton E. Phillips, of the 1st Massachusetts Cavalry, was killed at Rapidan Station, Virginia, May 1st, 1863, and Lieutenant Daniel H. L. Gleason, of the same regiment, was wounded at Sulphur Springs, Virginia, on the 3rd of June.

Colonel Warren Stewart, of the 15th Illinois Cavalry, was killed in a skirmish opposite Vicksburg, Mississippi, early in the year 1863. First Lieutenant Richard Burns, of the 11th Illinois Cavalry, was killed at the Battle of Shiloh, and First Lieutenant Calvin Terry, of the 2nd Illinois Cavalry, was killed at Union City, Tennessee, in August, 1862.

Captain Albert G. Bacon, of the 3rd Kentucky Cavalry, was killed at Sacramento, McLean County, Kentucky, December 28th, 1861; Major Charles Milward, of the 7th Kentucky Cavalry, was killed at the Battle of Richmond, Kentucky, August 23rd, 1862; and Lieutenant-Colonel Gabriel Netter, of the 15th Kentucky Cavalry, was killed at Owensboro', Kentucky, September 19th. 1862.

In the Missouri Cavalry Regiments there were many killed, and I give the names of such officers as have been reported. First Regiment, Lieutenant Charles B. Golden, mortally wounded at Springfield,

Missouri, February 16th, and died April 4th, 1862. Second Regiment, Major George C. Marshall, killed October, 1861; Captain J. W. Baird, killed in action, September 6th, 1862; First Lieutenant Joseph V. Myers, killed. Fourth Regiment, Second Lieutenant Edward G. Clowes, killed in action at Sugar Creek, Missouri, March 7th, 1862. Seventh Regiment, Major Eliphalet Bredett, killed at the Battle of Prairie Grove, Arkansas, December 7th, 1862; Second Lieutenant Alfred M. Baltzall, killed at Lone Jack; and Second Lieutenant S. M. Baker, mortally wounded at the same place, August 16th, 1862 (mentioned earlier). Tenth Regiment, Captain Henry G. Bruns, killed in Cornyn's fight near Iuka, July 10th, 1863. Captain Gideon T. Potter, of Phelps's Missouri Cavalry Regiment, killed at the Battle of Pea Ridge.

Second Lieutenant William J. Phillips, of the 1st Wisconsin Cavalry, was killed at Chalk Bluff, Arkansas, May 15th, 1862.

First Lieutenant Terence P. McEntee, of the 3rd Michigan Cavalry, was killed in action, December 18th, 1862, and Second Lieutenant Oscar H. Bingham, of the same regiment, was killed by guerrillas at Jackson, Tennessee, April 29th, 1863.

In the Iowa Cavalry the following officers were killed and wounded, *viz.*: First Regiment, Lieutenant Samuel C. Dickinson, killed by guerrillas in Arkansas, October 28th, 1862; Captain Herman H. Heath, wounded in Missouri, August 1st, 1862. Second Regiment, Captains Henry Egbert and William Lundy, and Lieutenant Benjamin Owen, were wounded in the charge made at Farmington, Mississippi, an account of which has been mentioned earlier. Third Regiment, Captain Emanuel Mayne, killed, and Captain Jesse Hughes and Mitchell I. Burch, wounded, near Kirkville, Calloway County, Missouri, July 28th, 1862; Second Lieutenant Alvin H. Griswold, killed at Stewart's Plantation, Arkansas, June 27th, 1862, as mentioned earlier. Fourth Regiment, Second Lieutenant William A. Heacock, killed at Talbot's Ferry, Arkansas, April 19th, 1862. Fifth Regiment, Major Carl S. De Bernstein, killed at Lockridge's Mills, Tennessee, May 5th, 1862, and First Lieutenant Michael Gallagher, killed at Garrettsburg, Kentucky, November 6th, 1862.

CHAPTER 16

A List of Cavalry Regiments

(Which have been in the service of the United States during the Great Rebellion, with the names of the colonels or commanding officers.)

REGULAR ARMY OF THE UNITED STATES.

1. 1st Regiment Cavalry, Colonel George A. H. Blake.
2. 2d Regiment Cavalry, Colonel Thomas J. Wood.
3. 3d Regiment Cavalry, Colonel Marshal S. Howe.
4. 4th Regiment Cavalry, Colonel John Sedgwick.
5. 5th Regiment Cavalry, Colonel George H. Thomas.
6. 6th Regiment Cavalry, Colonel David Hunter.

VOLUNTEERS.
Maine.

7. 1st Cavalry, Colonel Charles H. Smith.
8. 2d Cavalry, Colonel E. W. Woodman.

New Hampshire.
9. 1st Cavalry, Colonel John L. Thompson.

Vermont.
10. 1st Cavalry, Colonel Lemuel B. Platt.

Massachusetts.
11. 1st Cavalry, Colonel Horace B. Sargent.
12. 2d Cavalry, Colonel Charles R. Lowell, Jr.
13. 3d Cavalry, Colonel Thomas E. Chickering.

Rhode Island.

14. 1st Cavalry, Colonel Robert B. Lawton.
15. 2d Cavalry, Major Augustus W. Corliss.

Connecticut.

16. 1st Cavalry, Colonel Brayton Ives.

New York.

17. 1st Cavalry, Colonel Andrew T. McReynolds
18. 2d Cavalry, Colonel Henry E. Davis.
19. 3d Cavalry, Colonel Simon H. Mix.
20. 4th Cavalry, Colonel Louis P. di Cesnola.
21. 5th Cavalry, Colonel Othniel De Forest.
22. 6th Cavalry, Colonel Thomas C. Devin.
23. 7th Cavalry, Colonel J. Mansfield Davies.
24. 8th Cavalry, Colonel Benjamin F. Davis.
25. 9th Cavalry, Colonel John Beardsley.
26. 10th Cavalry, Colonel John C. Lemmon.
27. 11th Cavalry, Colonel James B. Swain.
28. 12th Cavalry, Colonel James W. Savage.
29. 13th Cavalry, Lieutenant Colonel Henry S. Gansevoort.
30. 14th Cavalry, Colonel Thaddeus P. Mott.
31. 15th Cavalry, Colonel Robert M. Richardson.
32. 16th Cavalry, Colonel Henry M. Lazelle.
33. 18th Cavalry, Colonel Joseph J. Byrne.
34. 19th Cavalry, Colonel Alfred Gibbs.
35. 20th Cavalry, Colonel Newton B. Lord.
36. 21st Cavalry, Colonel William B. Tibbetts.
37. 22d Cavalry, Colonel George C. Cram.
38. 24th Cavalry, Colonel William C. Raulston.
39. 25th Cavalry, Colonel Gurden Chapin.
40. 1st N. Y. Mounted Rifles, Colonel Edwin V. Sumner.
41. 2d N. Y. Mounted Rifles, Colonel John Fisk.

New Jersey.

42. 1st Cavalry, Colonel Percy Wyndham.
43. 2d Cavalry, Colonel Joseph Karge.

Pennsylvania.

44. 1st Cavalry, Colonel John P. Taylor.
45. 2d Cavalry, Colonel R. Butler Price.
46. 3d Cavalry, Colonel John B. McIntosh.
47. 4th Cavalry, Colonel James K. Kerr.
48. 5th Cavalry, Lieutenant Colonel William Lewis.
49. 6th Cavalry, Lieutenant Colonel James McArthur.
50. 7th Cavalry, Colonel William B. Sipes.
51. 8th Cavalry, Colonel Pennock Huey.
52. 9th Cavalry, Colonel Thomas J. Jordan.
53. 11th Cavalry, Colonel Samuel P. Spear.
54. 12th Cavalry, Colonel L. B. Pierce.
55. 13th Cavalry, Colonel Garuck Mallery.
56. 14th Cavalry, Colonel J. M. Schoonmaker.
57. 15th Cavalry, Colonel William J. Palmer.
58. 16th Cavalry, Colonel J. Irvine Gregg.
59. 17th Cavalry, Colonel J. H. Kellogg.
60. 18th Cavalry, Colonel T. M. Bryan, Jr.
61. 19th Cavalry, Colonel Alexander Cummings.
62. 20th Cavalry, Colonel John E. Wynkoop.
63. 21st Cavalry, Colonel William H. Boyd.
64. 22d Cavalry, Colonel Jacob Higgins.

Delaware.

65. 1st Battalion Cavalry, Major N. B. Knight.

Maryland.

66. 1st Cavalry, Colonel Andrew W. Evans.
67. 2d Cavalry, Captain W. F. Bragg.
68. 3d Cavalry, Lieutenant Colonel C. Carroll Trevis.
69. Battalion Potomac Home Brigade Cavalry, Major Henry A. Cole.
70. Battalion Purnell Cavalry, Captain Robert E. Duvall.
71. Independent Cavalry Company, Captain G. W. P. Smith.

West Virginia.

72. 1st Cavalry, Colonel H. Anisansel.
73. 2d Cavalry, Colonel William H. Powell.
74. 3d Cavalry, Colonel David H. Strother.
75. 4th Cavalry, Colonel Joseph Snider.

Alabama.

76. 1st Cavalry, Colonel George E. Spencer.

Texas.

77. 1st Cavalry, Colonel Edward J. Davis.

Arkansas.

78. 1st Cavalry, Colonel M. La Rue Harrison.
79. 2d Cavalry, Colonel John E. Phelps.

Tennessee.

80. 1st Cavalry, Colonel James P. Brownlow.
81. 2d Cavalry, Lieutenant Colonel Prosser.
82. 3d Cavalry, Lieutenant Colonel Thornberg.
83. 4th Cavalry, Lieutenant Colonel J. Thornberg.
84. 5th Cavalry, Colonel Stokes.
85. 6th Cavalry, Colonel Hurst.
86. 7th Cavalry, Colonel Hawkins.
87. 8th Cavalry, Colonel Patton.
88. 9th Cavalry, Colonel Parsons.
89. 10th Cavalry, Lieutenant Colonel Bridges.
90. 11th Cavalry, Colonel Young.
91. 12th Cavalry, Colonel Spaulding.
92. 13th Cavalry, Colonel Miller.

Kentucky.

93. 1st Cavalry, Colonel Frank Wolford.
94. 2d Cavalry, Colonel Thomas P. Nicholas.
95. 3d Cavalry, Colonel Eli H. Murray.
96. 4th Cavalry, Colonel Wickliffe Cooper.
97. 5th Cavalry, Colonel O. L. Baldwin.
98. 6th Cavalry, Colonel Louis D. Watkins.
99. 7th Cavalry, Colonel John K. Faulkner.
100. 8th Cavalry, Colonel Ben. H. Bristow.
101. 9th Cavalry, Colonel Richard T. Jacob.
102. 10th Cavalry, Colonel Charles J. Walker.
103. 11th Cavalry, Colonel A. W. Holman.
104. 12th Cavalry, Colonel Eugene W. Crittenden.
105. 13th Cavalry, Colonel James W. Weatherford.
106. 14th Cavalry, Colonel H. C. Lilly.
107. 15th Cavalry, Lieutenant Colonel A. P. Henry.
108. 17th Cavalry, Colonel S. F. Johnson.

Ohio.

109. 1st Cavalry, Colonel B. B. Eggleston.
110. 2d Cavalry, Colonel August V. Kautz.
111. 3d Cavalry, Colonel Charles B. Seidell.
112. 4th Cavalry, Colonel Eli Long.
113. 5th Cavalry, Colonel Thomas T. Heath.
114. 6th Cavalry, Lieutenant Colonel William Steadman.
115. 7th Cavalry, Colonel Israel Garrard.
116. 8th Cavalry, Colonel Wesley Owens.
117. 9th Cavalry, Colonel William D. Hamilton.
118. 10th Cavalry, Colonel Charles C. Smith.
119. 11th Cavalry, Lieutenant Colonel William O. Collins.
120. 12th Cavalry, Colonel Robert W. Ratliff.
121. Independent Battalion Cavalry, Major Joseph T. Wheeler.
122. Independent Battalion Cavalry, Major John F. Ijams.

Michigan.

123. 1st Cavalry, Colonel Peter Stagg.
124. 2d Cavalry, Colonel Thomas W. Johnson.
125. 3d Cavalry, Colonel John K. Mizner.
126. 4th Cavalry, Colonel Robert H. G. Minty.
127. 5th Cavalry, Colonel Smith H. Hastings.
128. 6th Cavalry, Colonel James H. Kidd.
129. 7th Cavalry, Lieutenant Colonel George G. Briggs.
130. 8th Cavalry, Colonel Elisha Mix.
131. 9th Cavalry, Colonel George S. Acker.
132. 10th Cavalry, Colonel Luther S. Trowbridge.
133. 11th Cavalry, Colonel Simeon B. Brown.

Indiana.

134. 1st Cavalry, Colonel Conrad Baker.
135. 2d Cavalry, Colonel Edward M. McCook.
136. 3d Cavalry, Colonel Scott Carter.
137. 4th Cavalry, Colonel Isaac P. Gray.
138. 5th Cavalry, Colonel Felix W. Graham.
139. 6th Cavalry, Colonel James Biddle.
140. 7th Cavalry, Colonel John P. C. Shanks.
141. 8th Cavalry, Colonel Thomas J. Harrison.
142. 9th Cavalry, Colonel George W. Jackson.
143. 10th Cavalry, Colonel Thomas N. Pace.
144. 11th Cavalry, Colonel Robert R. Stewart.
145. 12th Cavalry, Colonel Edward Anderson.
146. 13th Cavalry, Colonel Gilbert M. L. Johnson.

Illinois.

147. 1st Cavalry, Colonel Thomas A. Marshall.
148. 2d Cavalry, Colonel Silas Noble.
149. 3d Cavalry, Colonel Lafayette McCrillis.
150. 4th Cavalry, Colonel T. Lyle Dickey.
151. 5th Cavalry, Colonel J. Hall Wilson.
152. 6th Cavalry, Colonel Benjamin H. Grierson.
153. 7th Cavalry, Colonel Edward Prince.
154. 8th Cavalry, Colonel D. R. Clendenin.
155. 9th Cavalry, Colonel Albert G. Brackett.
156. 10th Cavalry, Colonel Dudley Wickersham.
157. 11th Cavalry, Colonel Robert G. Ingersoll.
158. 12th Cavalry, Colonel Hasbrouck Davis.
159. 13th Cavalry, Colonel Joseph W. Bell.
160. 14th Cavalry, Colonel Horace Capron.
161. 15th Cavalry, Colonel Warren Stewart.
162. 16th Cavalry, Colonel Robert W. Smith.
163. 17th Cavalry, Colonel John L. Beveridge.

164. 1st Cavalry, Colonel John F. Ritter.
165. 2d Cavalry, Colonel Lewis Merrill.
166. 3d Cavalry, Colonel John M. Glover.
167. 4th Cavalry, Colonel George E. Waring, Jr.
168. 5th Cavalry, Colonel Joseph Nemitt.
169. 6th Cavalry, Major Bacon Montgomery.
170. 7th Cavalry, Colonel Daniel Huston, Jr.
171. 8th Cavalry, Colonel W. F. Geiger.
172. 10th Cavalry, Colonel Florence M. Cornyn.
173. 11th Cavalry, Colonel William D. Wood.
174. 12th Cavalry, Colonel Oliver Wells.
175. 1st Missouri State Militia Cavalry, Colonel James B. McFarren.
176. 2d Missouri State Militia Cavalry, Colonel John McNeill.
177. 3d Missouri State Militia Cavalry, Colonel Walter King.
178. 4th Missouri State Militia Cavalry, Colonel George H. Hall.
179. 5th Missouri State Militia Cavalry, Colonel William R. Pennick.
180. 6th Missouri State Militia Cavalry, Colonel E. C. Catherwood.
181. 7th Missouri State Militia Cavalry, Colonel John F. Phillips.
182. 8th Missouri State Militia Cavalry, Colonel J. W. McClurg.
183. 9th Missouri State Militia Cavalry, Colonel Odon Guitar.
184. 10th Missouri State Militia Cavalry, Colonel Edwin Smart.
185. 12th Missouri State Militia Cavalry, Lieutenant Colonel B. F. Lazear.
186. 13th Missouri State Militia Cavalry, Colonel Albert Sigel.
187. 14th Missouri State Militia Cavalry, Colonel John M. Richardson.

Iowa.

188. 1st Cavalry, Colonel D. Anderson.
189. 2d Cavalry, Colonel Edward Hatch.
190. 3d Cavalry, Colonel Cyrus Bussey.
191. 4th Cavalry, Colonel E. Winslow.
192. 5th Cavalry, Colonel William W. Lowe.
193. 6th Cavalry, Colonel David S. Wilson.
194. 7th Cavalry, Colonel Samuel W. Summers.
195. 8th Cavalry, Colonel Joseph B. Dorr.
196. 9th Cavalry, Colonel Matthew M. Trumbull.

Wisconsin.

197. 1st Cavalry, Colonel O. H. La Grange.
198. 2d Cavalry, Colonel Thomas Stevens.
199. 3d Cavalry, Colonel William A. Barstow.
200. 4th Cavalry, Colonel Joseph Bailey.

Minnesota.

201. 1st Battalion Cavalry, Major Alfred B. Brackett.
202. 1st Regiment Cavalry, Colonel Samuel McPhail.

Kansas.

203. 2d Cavalry, Lieutenant Colonel O. A. Bassett.
204. 5th Cavalry, Colonel Powell Clayton.
205. 6th Cavalry, Colonel William R. Judson.
206. 7th Cavalry, Colonel T. P. Herrick.
207. 9th Cavalry, Colonel Ed. Lynde.
208. 11th Cavalry, Major P. B. Plumb.
209. 14th Cavalry, Major Thomas Moonlight.
210. 15th Cavalry, Colonel C. R. Jennison.

California.

211. 1st Cavalry, Colonel Oscar M. Brown.
212. 2d Cavalry, Colonel William Jones.
213. 1st Battalion Native California Cavalry, Major Salvador Vallejo.

Oregon.

214. 1st Cavalry, Colonel Reuben F. Maury.

Colorado.

215. 1st Cavalry, Colonel John M. Chivington.

Nebraska.

216. 1st Cavalry, Colonel R. R. Livingston.

Nevada.

217. 1st Battalion Cavalry, Captain Elias B. Zabriskie.

New Mexico.

218. 1st Cavalry, Colonel Christopher Carson.
219. 2d Cavalry, Colonel Miguel Valdez.
220. 3d Cavalry, Colonel José G. Gallegos.

District of Columbia.

221. 1st Cavalry, Colonel Baker.

222. 1st United States Colored Cavalry, Colonel ———— .

223. 2d United States Colored Cavalry, Colonel James H. Ford.

224. 3d United States Colored Cavalry, Colonel E. D. Osband.

225. 4th United States Colored Cavalry, Colonel ———— .

226. 5th United States Colored Cavalry, Colonel James S. Brisbin.

227. 6th United States Colored Cavalry, Colonel James F. Wade.

In addition to these cavalry regiments, there were a number of mounted infantry regiments, which did excellent service in the rebellion, and were, to all intents and purposes, cavalry.

Captain May's Charge at Resaca de la Palma

By J. Frost

General Taylor had left Point Isabel on the evening of the 7th of May, and moved with the main body of the army towards the Rio Grande. After marching seven miles, they bivouacked on their arms, and resumed the march on the following morning. At noon they discovered the enemy, prepared to oppose their progress, stretched out on the flat prairie more than a mile.

We give here the clear and concise account of this battle, given by General Taylor in his official despatches, reserving for another portion of the work more minute details and personal anecdotes:—

"About noon, when our advance of cavalry had reached the water hole of 'Palo Alto,' the Mexican troops were reported in our front, and were soon discovered occupying the road in force. I ordered a halt upon reaching the water, with the view to rest and refresh the men, and to form deliberately our line of battle. The Mexican line was now plainly visible across the prairie, and about three-quarters of a mile distant. Their left, which was composed of a heavy force of cavalry, occupied the road, resting upon a thicket of *chaparral*, while masses of infantry were discovered in succession on the right, greatly outnumbering our own force.

"Our line of battle was now formed in the following order, commencing on the extreme right:—5th Infantry, commanded by Lieutenant-Colonel McIntosh; Major Ringgold's artillery; 3rd Infantry, commanded by Captain L. N. Morris; two eighteen-pounders, commanded by Lieutenant Churchill, 3rd Artillery; 4th Infantry, commanded by Major G. W. Allen; the 3rd and 4th Regiments composed the Third Brigade, under command of Lieutenant-Colonel Garland; and all the above corps, together with two squadrons of dragoons un-

CAPTAIN C. A. MAY, 2ND DRAGOONS

der Captains Ker and May, composed the right wing under the orders of Colonel Twiggs. The left was formed by the battalion of artillery commanded by Lieutenant-Colonel Childs. Captain Duncan's light artillery, and the 8th Infantry, under Captain Montgomery—all forming the first brigade, under command of Lieutenant-Colonel Belknap. The train was packed near the water, under direction of Captains Crossman and Myers, and protected by Captain Ker's squadron.

"At two o'clock we took up the march by heads of columns, in the direction of the enemy—the eighteen-pounder battery following the road. While the columns were advancing, Lieutenant Blake, topographical engineer, volunteered a reconnaissance of the enemy's line, which was handsomely performed, and resulted in the discovery of at least two batteries of artillery in the intervals of their cavalry and infantry. These batteries were soon opened upon us, when I ordered the columns halted and deployed into line, and the fire to be returned by all our artillery. The 8th Infantry on our extreme left, was thrown back to secure that flank. The first fires of the enemy did little execution, while our eighteen-pounders and Major Ringgold's artillery soon dispersed the cavalry which formed his left.—Captain Duncan's battery, thrown forward in advance of the line, was doing good execution at this time. Captain May's squadron was now detached to support that battery, and the left of our position.

"The Mexican cavalry, with two pieces of artillery, were now reported to be moving through the *chaparral* to our right, to threaten that flank, or make a demonstration against the train. The 5th Infantry was immediately detached to check this movement, and supported by Lieutenant Ridgely, with a section of Major Ringgold's battery and Captain Walker's company of volunteers, effectually repulsed the enemy—the 5th Infantry repelling a charge of lancers, and the artillery doing great execution in their ranks. The 3rd Infantry was now detached to the right as a still farther security to that flank yet threatened by the enemy. Major Ringgold, with the remaining section, kept up his fire from an advanced position, and was supported by the 4th Infantry.

"The grass of the prairie had been accidentally fired by our artillery, and the volumes of smoke now partially concealed the armies from each other. As the enemy's left had evidently been driven back and left the road free, as the cannonade had been suspended, I ordered forward the eighteen-pounders on the road nearly to the position first occupied by the Mexican cavalry, and caused the first brigade to take up a new position still on the left of the eighteen-pounder battery. The 5th was advanced from its former position and occupied a point on the extreme right of the new line. The enemy made a change of position corresponding to our own, and after the suspension of nearly an hour the action was resumed.

"The fire of artillery was now most destructive—openings were constantly made through the enemy's ranks by our fire, and the constancy with which the Mexican infantry sustained the severe cannonade was a theme of universal remark and admiration. Captain May's squadron was detached to make a demonstration on the left of the enemy's position, and suffered severely from the fire of artillery to which it was for some time exposed. The 4th Infantry, which had been ordered to support the eighteen-pounder battery, was exposed to a most galling fire of artillery, by which several men were killed, and Captain Page dangerously wounded. The enemy's fire was directed against our eighteen-pounder battery, and the guns under Major Ringgold, in its vicinity. The major himself, while coolly directing the fire of his pieces, was struck by a cannon ball and mortally wounded.

★★★★★★★★★★

The death of Major Ringgold was universally lamented. He was a native of Washington county, Maryland, born in 1800. He was educated at the Military Academy, West Point; graduated in 1818; entered the army as Lieutenant; promoted to the rank of First Lieutenant in 1822, and to that of Captain in 1834. His brevet rank of Major was the reward of severe service in the Florida war. To his exertions in perfecting the discipline of the light artillery, the country is chiefly indebted for the efficiency of that important arm of the national defence.

Major Ringgold's connections were of the first respectability. His father was General Samuel Ringgold, and his mother was a daughter of General John Cadwalader, who was greatly distinguished in the war of the Revolution. His conduct and character as an officer and a gentleman were in every respect worthy of so highly honourable a descent.

★★★★★★★★★★

"In the meantime, the battalion of artillery under Lieutenant-Colonel Childs, had been brought up to support the artillery on our right. A strong demonstration of cavalry was now made by the enemy against this part of our line, and the column continued to advance under a severe fire from the eighteen-pounders. The battalion was instantly formed in square, and held ready to receive the charge of cavalry; but when the advancing squadrons were within close range a deadly fire of canister from the eighteen-pounders dispersed them. A brisk fire of small arms was now opened upon the square, by which one officer, Lieutenant Luther, 2nd Artillery, was slightly wounded; but a well-directed volley from the front of the square silenced all farther firing from the enemy in this quarter. It was now nearly dark, and the action was closed on the right of our line, the enemy having been completely driven back from his position, and foiled in every attempt against our line.

"While the above was going forward on our right, and under my own eye, the enemy had made a serious attempt against the left of our line. Captain Duncan instantly perceived the movement, and by the bold and brilliant manoeuvring of this battery, completely repulsed several successive efforts of the enemy to advance in force upon our left flank. Supported in succession by the 8th Infantry and Captain Ker's squadron of dragoons, he gallantly held the enemy at bay, and finally drove him, with immense loss, from the field. The action here and along the whole line, continued until dark, when the enemy retired into the *chaparral* in rear of his position.

"Our loss this day was nine killed, forty-four wounded, and two missing. Among the wounded were Major Ringgold, who has since died, and Captain Page dangerously wounded, and Lieutenant Luther slightly so. I annex a tabular statement of the casualties of the day.

"Our own force engaged is shown by the field report, herewith transmitted, to have been one hundred and seventy-seven officers and two thousand one hundred and eleven men; aggregate, two thousand two hundred and eighty-eight. The Mexican force, according to the statement of their own officers, taken prisoners in the affair of the 9th, was not less than six thousand regular troops, with ten pieces of artillery, and probably exceeded that number—the irregular force not known. Their loss was not less than two hundred killed, and four hundred wounded—probably greater. This estimate is very moderate, and founded upon the number actually counted on the field, and upon the reports of their own officers.

"As already reported in my first brief despatch, the conduct of our officers and men was everything that could be desired. Exposed for hours to the severest trials—a cannonade of artillery—our troops displayed a coolness and constancy which gave me throughout the assurance of victory. I purposely defer the mention of individuals until my report of the action of the 9th, when I will endeavour to do justice to the many instances of distinguished conduct on both days."

The Mexicans evinced great determination in this first day's battle, and remained almost within sight of the American Army during the night. General Arista employed the night in writing a despatch to the minister of war and marine, giving an eloquent account of what he claimed as his victory, and at daybreak on the 9th, slowly moved into the *chaparral*, leaving General Taylor in possession of the battlefield. Fearing that the enemy might dispute his progress towards Fort Brown, as the fortification opposite Matamoras was now named, he ordered the train to be strongly parked. An intrenchment was thrown up, and the artillery battalion, with two eighteen-pounders and two twelve-pounders were assigned to its defence.

The army then moved over the plain in line of battle with lively music, marking everywhere around them the evidences of the terrible destruction produced by the American artillery on the previous day. Wounded soldiers, dying of thirst and hunger, received relief from their generous enemies. The ground was covered with torn clothing, military caps, gun-stocks, and large quantities of cartridges for muskets and artillery. On the edge of the *chaparral*, the army halted at a place convenient to water.

A detachment under Captain McCall was sent forward into the *chaparral* to ascertain the position of the enemy. General Taylor then rode back to the train, accompanied by Lieutenant J. E. Blake of the topographical corps, who had displayed the utmost gallantry on the previous day. At the train, Lieutenant Blake dismounted from his horse to procure some refreshment, and expressed gratification at the prospect of a little rest, his labours during the previous twenty-four hours having been very arduous. He unbuckled his holsters and threw them on the ground, when one of the pistols unaccountably exploded, throwing the ball upwards into his body. He was mortally wounded, and expired shortly after, expressing his regret that he had not died on the battlefield on the preceding day.

Captain McCall with the advance guard found the enemy intrenched at La Resaca de la Palma, the Dry River of Palms, a strong position entirely commanding the approach to Fort Brown. At this place the road crosses a ravine sixty yards wide and nearly breast high, the bottom being wet, forming long and serpentine ponds through the prairie. Along the banks of this dry river, and more particularly on the side then occupied by the Mexicans, the *chaparral* grows most densely, and at this time, save where it was broken in by the passage of the road, formed almost a solid wall. The enemy occupied this ravine in double line; one behind and under the front bank, and the other intrenched behind the wall of the *chaparral* on the top of the rear ridge.

A battery was placed in the centre of each line on the right and left of the road, and a third battery was on the right of the first line. Six or seven thousand troops were thus strongly fortified in a form resembling a crescent, between the horns of which the army had to pass, while the Mexican batteries were enfilading and cross firing, the narrow road which formed the only unobstructed approach to their position. Lieutenant Ridgely, the successor of Ringgold, was ordered forward on the road, while the 3rd, 4th, and 5th Regiments of Infantry were ordered forward as skirmishers to cover the battery and engage the infantry of the enemy. General Taylor and his staff came up with Captain McCall and his party at four o'clock. He immediately deployed Captain McCall to the left of the road, and Captain C. F. Smith to the right, with orders to bring on the action.

Having received orders to advance, Lieutenant Ridgely moved cautiously forward with Captain Walker, who was charged with assisting him to find the enemy's batteries. At the instant they discovered them, they received a fire from them, which Ridgely, moving about a hundred yards to the front, returned with spirit. This contest was maintained for some time, their balls filling the air, and passing through Ridgely's battery in every direction. His men worked at their guns with invincible determination, and he himself sighted them with all the coolness and certainty of ordinary target practice. These well-directed charges were necessary to keep off the enemy who were constantly charging upon him, and whom he had sometimes to beat back with his own sword.

The rapid firing of the artillery on both sides produced an unintermitted roar. Colonel Duncan's battery was at the edge of the ravine, but he could not use it; Lieutenant Ridgely holding the only position from which the enemy could be assailed without galling our troops. These had come into the action in the most extraordinary manner, the firing of their musketry being heard at almost the same instant that Ridgely opened his fire in the centre.

★★★★★★★★★

It is to be observed that the artillery, during the whole course of the present war, has proved the most efficient arm of the service in determining the fate of battles, with, perhaps, the exception of the rifle corps in the recent battles near the city of Mexico. Nothing can exceed the efficiency and bravery of the rifle corps. General Scott's pointed eulogy of their conduct was richly deserved.

The efficiency of this arm of the national defence, as we have had occasion to remark in another place, is greatly owing to the indefatigable exertions of Major Ringgold. In this important service the major was aided by Captain Duncan, whose battery rendered most efficient service in the battles of the 8th and 9th of May, as well as in the other most important engagements of the war. The batteries of Sherman, Bragg, and Washington have also become famous, especially by their efficient service at Buena Vista.

The services of the artillery in the Battle of Buena Vista were so essential, that it is considered by all military men, that the absence of a small portion of it would undoubtedly have occasioned the loss of the battle.

★★★★★★★★★★

The 6th Regiment under Lieutenant-Colonel Mcintosh supported Ridgely's battery. The 3rd Regiment with a part of the 4th came up on the enemy's right, and the other portion of the 4th joined with the 5th on the left. The 3rd and 4th were separated by the *chaparral*, through which the soldiers literally pushed each other into squads of five or six, and they were obliged to form in the ravine. The 8th, under Captain Montgomery, with Smith's light and other corps, faced to the right. The best troops of Mexico were now contending with the greatest bravery for victory. The contest with artillery and musketry, the sword and the bayonet, at the end of two hours, resulted in the Americans gaining possession of the ravine in which the enemy were posted at the beginning of the action.

Yet the batteries in the centre still stood firm, pouring a perfect shower of grape and shells into the American front, and prevented General Taylor from reaping the advantages which the bravery of his troops would otherwise have secured. Captain May rode back to the general, and asked if he should charge the battery on the other side of the ravine. "Charge, captain, *nolens volens*," was the reply, and away dashed the gallant fellow. (Henry's Campaign Sketches.)

He rode to the head of his command; every rein and sabre was tightly grasped. Raising himself in the saddle, he shouted to his command, "We are ordered to take that battery—follow!" In columns of fours, they dashed along the narrow road, until they came to where Lieutenant Ridgely obstructed their advance. "I am ordered to charge those batteries," said May, coming to a halt. Ridgely knowing the perilous nature of the duty, said, "Wait, Charley, till I draw their fire!" All begrimed with powder and labouring with his own hands, he fired his pieces slowly and with the usual deadly effect. A storm of copper balls came whizzing and crushing among the artillerists in reply, while Ridgely and his men limbered up, jumped on their pieces, and cheered as May dashed forward.

An overwhelming discharge of grape and bullets from the other battery destroyed his first and second platoons, but he was unhurt, and with those who lived swept to the left of the road leaped over the battery and drove the Mexicans from their guns. But they seemed determined to retain their pieces or die: they rushed back to them with the bayonet, and commenced to load them again with grape. May then charged back upon our own lines, and the enemy shrunk in terror from the stroke of his sword. One man, General La Vega, alone maintained his ground, and tried to rally his men; but was made a prisoner by Captain May, and carried under a galling fire from his own countrymen to our lines.

The infantry now gathered round the batteries in masses, crossing bayonets for their possession, over the very muzzles of the guns. In a short time, Captain Belknap, with the 8th infantry, and Captain Martin Scott, with the 5th, were engaged in a hand-to-hand conflict with the far-famed Tampico veterans, who had been in twenty battles and were never defeated. The battery was carried, and the 8th and the 5th charged up the ravine amidst a terrible fire from the enemy's right and front. The battery of Colonel Duncan now came into the front, and the retreat of the enemy was hastened by his deadly fire. While the centre battery of the enemy was being carried, Lieutenants Ruggles and Crittenden, with a small command of the 5th and the 8th Infantry, all under Captain Montgomery, routed the right wing and carried the right battery.

Between this and the centre battery, the Tampico Regiment had been posted, all of whom, except seventeen, are said to have fallen at their posts. Their tri-colour was the last Mexican flag waving on the field, and the gallant fellow who bore it, when all hope was lost, tore it from the staff, and concealed it about his person while he attempted to fly. He was ridden down by the dragoons, however, and made a prisoner, and his flag was a trophy of the victory.

The hurry of the Mexicans to escape was so great, that many of them were drowned in the river. Immense quantities of baggage, military stores, and camp equipage fell into the hands of the Americans; the personal, public, and private property of Arista, and all his despatches being among the spoils. The American Army passed the night on the battlefield, in the enjoyment of the festival which had been prepared by the followers of the Mexican camp to regale their friends after the anticipated victory. In his despatch after this brilliant victory General Taylor says:—

> The loss of the enemy in killed has been most severe. Our own has been very heavy, and I deeply regret to report that Lieutenant Inge, 2nd Dragoons, Lieutenant Cochrane, 4th Infantry, and Lieutenant Chadbourne, 8th Infantry, were killed on the field. Lieutenant-Colonel Payne, 4th Artillery, Lieutenant-Colonel Mcintosh, Lieutenant Dobbins, 3rd Infantry, Captain Hooe and Lieutenant Fowler, 5th Infantry; and Captain Montgomery, Lieutenants Gates, Selden, McClay, Burbank, and Jordan, 8th Infantry were wounded. The extent of our loss in killed and wounded is not yet ascertained, and is reserved for a more detailed report.